D0210792

Simon and Garfunkel

Old Friends

SIMON AND GARFUNKEL

OLD FRIENDS

A Dual Biography

by Joseph Morella
and Patricia Barey

A Birch Lane Press Book
Published by Carol Publishing Group

A Birch Lane Press Book
Published by Carol Publishing Group
Birch Lane Press is a registered trademark of Carol Communications, Inc.

Editorial Offices: 600 Madison Avenue, New York, N.Y. 10022
Sales & Distribution Offices: 120 Enterprise Avenue, Secaucus, N.J. 07094
In Canada: Musson Book Company, a division of General Publishing Company, Ltd.,
    Don Mills, Ontario M3B 2T6

Queries regarding rights and permissions should be addressed to Carol
Publishing Group, 600 Madison Avenue, New York, N.Y. 10022

Carol Publishing Group books are available at special discounts for bulk
purchases, for sales promotions, fund raising, or educational purposes.
Special editions can be created to specifications. For details contact:
Special Sales Department, Carol Publishing Group, 120 Enterprise Avenue,
Secaucus, N.J. 07094

Manufactured in the United States of America

10   9   8   7   6   5   4   3   2   1

Library of Congress Cataloging-in-Publication Data

Morella, Joe.
    Simon and Garfunkel : old friends / by Joseph Morella and Patricia
Barey.
        p.   cm.
    "A Birch Lane Press book."
    ISBN 1–55972–089–1
    1. Simon, Paul, 1941–   . 2. Garfunkel, Art.   I. Barey,
Patricia. II. Title.
ML420.S563M7   1991
782.42164'092'2—dc20
    [B]   91–26563
                                                                    CIP
                                                                    MN

TO OUR PARENTS

Acknowledgments

Grateful thanks to Roy Dropps, John Madden, Jim Bliss, and all the people who granted interviews for this unauthorized biography.

Simon and Garfunkel

Old Friends

On a cool autumnal evening a half million expectant people streamed into New York's Central Park to celebrate a reunion —of two old friends and of a whole generation. To these world-weary veterans of the sixties, the coming together represented a last chance to recapture the spirit of their youth. Paul Simon, as always, had said it best: "A time of innocence / A time of confidences."

Although the musical team of Simon and Garfunkel had lasted a mere five years and had produced only six albums, they had become the voice of an era. Everyone in America knew who Mrs. Robinson was and that the sounds of silence were painful, inescapable, and universal. Within soaring, seamless harmony, Simon and Garfunkel had asked vital questions and had seemed to bring some order into a chaotic world wracked by war, drugs, alienation, and the passing of youth.

In the process, Paul Simon and Art Garfunkel had become rich and famous. But celebrity had taken its toll. Each had been divorced, and, like most of their generation, their youthful hopes and dreams had been tempered by pain and disappointment. They were approaching their fortieth birthdays and were depressed a great deal of the time. Paul Simon was in the middle of a tumultuous love affair with Carrie Fisher, at that time a troubled young woman deeply involved with drugs. Art was still feeling guilty and bewildered after his lover's suicide.

1

Like a lot of men their age, they had sacrificed their personal lives for careers which now seemed to be slipping. They had abandoned Simon and Garfunkel at the height of its phenomenal success, and each had spent more than a decade trying to shape a separate identity as a solo star. Recently, both had been battered by the critics. The film project in which Paul had invested his energy and over a year of his life had been dismissed as a vanity production, and, worse, was a box-office disaster. Art's singing and acting careers had stalled.

Since their split eleven years before, they had kept a wary distance from each other both professionally and personally. But now the outside world had become too harsh —just as it often had earlier for two teenage boys from Queens—and they were drawn together again by their love for making music. Perhaps their vocal harmony could dispel some of their pain and disappointment. It was always the harmony that made them special. As a team they made a sound far superior to any either of them could make alone. Their personalities as well as their musical talents seemed to be inseparable halves of the same whole.

Ironically, it was when they were in the process of recording the album *Bridge Over Troubled Water*, their masterpiece on the theme of reconciliation and the healing power of selfless love, that the partnership finally unraveled. Beneath the tightly knit surface of sweet musical harmony lay a ragged personal history marked by jealousy and betrayal and a struggle for domination.

Critics had sniped that tonight's reunion was a callous attempt to breathe new commercial life into two flagging careers. But the fans didn't care. To the vast crowd the motive was pure and simple—to recapture, if only for an evening, the spirit of a better time. If Paul and Art could recreate their harmony, there was hope for all.

Coming back together wasn't simple. People who had witnessed the tension in recent rehearsals knew old, unresolved conflicts were still simmering just beneath the surface and could erupt at any moment. Paul and Art still had a lifetime of unfinished business between them.

1

heir dream of making it big in the music business had taken
root in the quiet, suburban streets of Queens, a borough of New
York City. Just after the birth of Paul Simon on October 13, 1941,
in Newark, New Jersey, his family moved to Kew Gardens, a
section of Queens near Forest Hills. Paul's father, Louis, was a
professional bass player and his mother, Belle, a schoolteacher.

Three weeks after Paul's birth, on November 5, 1941, Arthur
Garfunkel was born, the second son of a housewife and a traveling
salesman in the garment and container industries. The Simon and
Garfunkel families lived in identical row houses just three blocks
apart.

As they grew up, Art and Paul frequently saw each other on the
playground of their grade school, PS 164. When they were in the
fourth grade, the boys began to notice each other: how alike they
seemed, and, at the same time, how different from everyone else.
Each boy had a passion for music which bound them together and
made them special.

When young Artie Garfunkel discovered the startling effect his
sweet tenor voice had on people, especially girls, he quickly
became a neighborhood phenomenon. In the Garfunkel house,

Art's parents sang and encouraged their children to sing and to study music. Art loved the sounds his parents made when they harmonized on popular songs like "The Red, Red Robin," and often sang along with them, in three-part harmony. Blessed with perfect pitch, at the age of eight Art would sing aloud each day as he walked to school, amusing himself by experimenting with his voice. He would trill "You'll Never Walk Alone," a recent hit tune from the Broadway musical *Carousel*, in one key, then in another, and another.

This habit of singing adult, popular songs by himself while other kids spent their time yelling and playing in groups set him apart. And so did his left-handedness. A loner both physically and psychologically, Art sensed early on that he approached the world differently from most other children. As he later noted, "Left-handed people are off the mainstream. They're the minority group, and they do things around the side. Lefties throw more curve balls, righties throw fast balls. I identify with all those lefty images."

Artie may have felt like a stranger among his playmates, but he soon learned he could find acceptance and praise by simply opening his mouth to sing. He said he sang "to justify my 'weirdness' in the neighborhood."

When Artie sang, Paulie Simon's first reaction was envy. Paul heard him sing "(They Tried to Tell Us We're) Too Young" at a school assembly and later recalled, "When he sang…all the girls were talking about him. After that, I decided to try singing, too. I said, 'Hey, I want to cut in on some of this myself.'"

Artie knew about Paulie Simon, too—he had a reputation for rough-and-tumble leadership at school and on the playground. Artie was delighted to discover the little, dark-haired tough guy also was interested in music. And so the angelic voice which set Art apart brought him his first real friend.

As the adult Garfunkel reflected on their early attraction: "By the time we reached fifth grade, we were probably the only two males in school who thought of ourselves as singers."

Teachers also noticed the two talented boys and cast them in a sixth-grade production of *Alice in Wonderland* — Paul as the White Rabbit and Art as the Cheshire Cat. During daily after-school rehearsals the boys had a chance to get to know each other better, and their friendship grew. They talked about sports, especially baseball, school, girls, and most of all, music. Art thought Paul the funniest boy he had ever met, and Paul's initial envy of Art's vocal gift subsided.

Artie was a shy boy, ambivalent about singing in front of a crowd. Paul had no such inhibitions—he was fascinated by the magical power of performing.

Music literally poured out of the Simon household. Louis Simon played bass in dance bands on the ballroom circuit around New York, and his son loved to visit him on the job. The small, wide-eyed boy often would stand near the throbbing bandstand at Roseland, tapping his foot to the beat of his father's music. While he waited for his father to pack up his bass and take him home, Paul also got a taste of the more exotic rumba and samba rhythms played by Latin bands on the bill.

In the fifties Louis also worked with the house orchestras of various television shows that were broadcast live from Manhattan. He sometimes would be "jobbed" into the bands that played for Arthur Godfrey, Garry Moore, or Jackie Gleason. Often Paul, his younger brother Eddie, and their mother, Belle, would sit in front of their television set in Queens, eager to catch a glimpse of Louis playing bass when the TV cameras panned across the band. Paul adored his father and the exciting world of music he represented. Years later, Paul paid homage to Louis Simon in his 1970 song "Baby Driver," referring to him as the "family bassman."

Paul took piano lessons from his father, but when the boy lost interest, Louis didn't force him to continue, believing he would find his own musical direction in time.

Paul's favorite instrument was his own singing voice. A very special moment occurred when Paul was still enthralled by his acting debut in *Alice in Wonderland*. His parents had bought him a set of *Alice* records, and Paul played them repeatedly. One evening, as Paul sang along, his father, dressed in a tuxedo for that night's ballroom engagement, passed by his bedroom. Impressed by what he heard, Louis Simon leaned into the doorway and offered, "That's nice, Paul. You have a nice voice." This simple moment of praise was pivotal in the young Paul Simon's life, and the mature musician has never forgotten it. Basking in the warm glow of his father's approval, Paul's interest in music blossomed.

With single-minded adolescent fervor, Paul explored his vocal abilities, spending hours in the family's small, neatly tiled bathroom, fascinated with the sound of his voice as it bounced from wall to wall. These echoes still reverberated years later when the moment came to use them in his songwriting. At this same time Art Garfunkel was trying out his voice in the tiled stairwell at school, experimenting with the echoes there.

Paul and Art were achievers in school. When they finished sixth grade, both moved on to Parsons Junior High to enter a special accelerated academic program designed to save a school year. Each day began with a twenty-minute walk to Parsons through neighborhoods much rougher than their own, and the two boys were often bullied by local toughs. Their walk frequently ended in a shakedown for lunch money or with a bloody nose. Both boys found the harrowing experience bearable only because they had each other for protection. Their bond of friendship strengthened.

They now spent nearly all their time together, and when they tired of talking music or singing, they turned to baseball.

Always a New York Yankee fan, Paul listened to games on the radio throughout childhood and adolescence, and his allegiance grew stronger with every season. Wearing his team cap, he fiddled with the radio dials to locate the station well before the game's starting time. Scanning the stations on either side of powerful WNEW, he would often hear snatches of soulful black gospel beamed live from church services in the South. As game time approached, however, he fixed the dial on the Yankee network and patiently waited for Joe DiMaggio and his other heroes to take the field.

In the spring of 1954, Paul got his first taste of rock 'n' roll as he waited for the broadcast of a Yankee game to begin. Martin Block, a popular New York deejay, had been playing "Y'all Come," by Bing Crosby, "Young at Heart," by Frank Sinatra, and "Secret Love," by Doris Day. One Saturday he offered "Gee!," a new song by a group with a peculiar name—the Crows. Block's disdainful introduction caught Paul's attention: "This record is so bad that if it's a hit, I'll eat it." But the Crows' song was a hit, and Paul searched the radio dial for more new sounds like it.

The Crows were in the vanguard of a musical revolution which would soon give Block and the traditional popular music business a permanent case of indigestion. A host of new groups appealed to kids like Paul Simon and Art Garfunkel who were becoming bored with the conformity of suburban life and who suspected there was something missing from the predictable emotional range they heard in the songs of Patti Page and Perry Como. These kids were waiting for something exciting to happen.

The year 1954 also saw the debut of the Cadillacs and their hit "Gloria," the Midnighters, whose "Work With Me Annie" would sell enough records to attain gold status, as well as the Platters and the Crew Cuts. In August, Elvis Presley had his first hit record, "That's All Right."

It wasn't long before "Earth Angel," "Sh-Boom," and "Shake, Rattle, and Roll" were battling with Kitty Kallen's "In the Chapel in the Moonlight" for position on the hit parade. But most adult record buyers still preferred lush romantic ballads like Don Cornell's "Hold My Hand," a song from one of the year's hit movies, *Susan Slept Here,* which starred America's teenage sweetheart, Debbie Reynolds. Also firmly entrenched in the top forty were Doris Day, Rosemary Clooney, and a small Jewish boy from Philadelphia with a very big voice, Eddie Fisher.

In the public mind, fans of the new "rock" were quickly associated with "juvenile delinquents" and dangerously unstable personalities like singer Johnny Ace who, backstage at a Houston concert, had recently killed himself playing Russian roulette. Supporters and enemies of the new music rapidly divided along generational lines.

Art favored the Crew Cuts' "Crazy 'Bout Ya, Baby" and "Sh-Boom." He later recalled that he and Paul, like so many other white middle-class kids, were primed for the excitement of rock 'n' roll to happen and when it did, "We both jumped on singing and listening to rock 'n' roll."

Their new musical passion even made inroads on the time Paul and Art devoted to baseball. Art already was bored with playing ball, but he remained a fan of the Philadelphia Phillies, a team he chose for the sheer contrariness of wearing a Phillies' cap in the Yankee stronghold of Queens: "I liked their pin-striped uniforms, and they were underdogs. And there were no other Phillies fans."

Paul's reasons for being a Yankee fan reveal streaks of loyalty and pragmatism in his personality: "I'm a Yankee fan because my father was," and "I choose not to reveal my neuroses through the

Yankees....They gave me a sense of superiority...I felt there was enough suffering in real life, why suffer with your team? What did the suffering do for Dodger fans?"

Paul loved baseball's blend of team and individual achievement and the intense competition of the diamond. He harbored dreams of playing alongside his heroes and tried out for the school team every year. When summer came to an end, he remembers, "I oiled my glove and wrapped it around a baseball in the winter and slept with it under my bed."

In autumn 1954, at the age of thirteen, both Paul and Art had their Bar Mitzvahs, the Jewish ceremony marking a boy's passage into manhood. Art later revealed, "I hated it....I was acutely uncomfortable being the center of attention. But I did like the singing part. I was even the cantor at my own service. In fact, I used to sing in a High Holiday choir. I didn't stop until I was fifteen."

Religion played an important part in both the Simon and Garfunkel households, but Paul subsequently told friends that the High Holidays at his house were full of tension because his father was less observant of the traditional customs than his mother was and always resisted the annual rituals. Nevertheless, both boys were well grounded in their religious heritage.

Although the synagogue was a place where Art Garfunkel could hone his singing talent in public, like Paul, he preferred to find other opportunities to sing. At school dances there were impressionable young girls in the audience.

The rock 'n' roll virus had spread rapidly throughout Simon and Garfunkel's junior high school. Alan Freed, a deejay from Cleveland, was now at New York radio station WINS, where his unorthodox record selection and promotion of rock 'n' roll music made him a hero to rock-starved teenagers all over the city. One day in the ninth grade Art intercepted a note which read: "Listen to Alan Freed's rock 'n' roll show tonight. I have a dedication for you." Art was curious: "I listened and was hooked in right away, and so was Paul. I started listening every night. So, I think from the earliest time we listened, I think we sort of saw ourselves competitively. I did, anyway. I listened and I said, 'I can do all that stuff, too.'" Paul and Art were confident that, with enough practice, they could replicate the sounds they heard or even produce better ones.

As soon as portable tape recorders became widely available, Art's parents bought him one. He was enthralled and soon convinced his parents to buy a second machine so he could harmonize with himself and with his friend, Paulie. Together they experimented with making rudimentary sound tracks in Art's basement.

In late spring of 1955, just before graduation from Parsons Junior High, the boys made their first official public appearance together. At a high school yard dance, a crowd of teenagers made a semicircle around the nervous team. The chattering stopped as Paulie and Artie broke into a letter-perfect a cappella imitation of the Crew Cuts' hit, "Sh-Boom." As the boys sang, the kids began to sway to the polished harmonies, and when the song ended, applause rang out. Their classmates loved their musical debut—all their hard work had paid off. At last, they were popular and accepted. Paul should have been happy, but he wasn't.

Around this time Paul's family noticed a startling change in his personality. In a 1987 discussion of his childhood, Paul revealed: "In retrospect, it was very happy and exciting. But I know that in this period of time my personality changed to this personality that's always been described as 'melancholy, moody.' Until that time, I was always a very happy kid. I remember my mother saying, 'What's happening? You always used to be smiling and happy, and now you're very sullen....'" He had begun to experience some of life's cruel ironies.

Paul had been playing in the city softball league for boys under five feet tall. His parents were short—Belle was a shade under five feet, and Louis only five feet, four inches. Brother Eddie, four years younger, had already grown to nearly his size, and Paul was beginning to be painfully self-conscious about his height.

The Queens "Under Five Foot League" had made it to the city championship match against Staten Island. Since it was a critical game, just before the start officials measured each player to make sure he was under five feet. Paul was as shocked as league officials to find he had grown since the last measurement. Now an inch over the limit, he couldn't play in his biggest game—a crushing blow. More frustrating, after spurting to five feet, one inch his growth seemed to stop.

He has said, "For a while I stopped growing, but I think it was some deeper thing. But I don't know what it is. It can only be some covered-up injury of childhood."

Changes in his relationship with his father may also have been part of Paul's problem. Simon has called his mother "extremely supportive," and through the years he has credited his father with encouraging his interest in music. But in a 1991 interview on "60 Minutes" with Ed Bradley, Paul revealed that his father actually scorned the rock 'n' roll music Paul loved.

Paul vividly remembered the moments of alienation from his father. Like every other teenager in America, he was wild about "Earth Angel," a hit tune so popular that versions of it by the Crew Cuts, Gloria Mann, and the Penguins all made it to the charts. Paul rushed out to buy the Penguins' "Earth Angel" which he played for Louis, wanting to share with his father the most exciting thing he had ever heard. He turned the volume up and exclaimed: "Dad, you gotta hear this!" His father coldly replied: "That's awful. What about the words? They're stupid." Paul tried to explain that the words were the whole point. "Earth Angel" was a revelation to Paul because, for the first time, he understood the power of a musical metaphor and how profoundly it could move him. He pointed at the ground and said, "Dad, listen— earth, earth," and then he pointed to the sky and said, "angel, Dad, don't you see how great those two ideas are together?" His father only repeated his scathing assessment, deflating Paul's enthusiasm.

Louis Simon thought Paul was wasting his time listening to rock 'n' roll, but he was even more intolerant when Paul sang it. Once they were riding in the family car when the radio played another of Paul's favorites, "I Went to Your Wedding," and Paul sang along. His father said, "God! That's awful." Wounded, Paul said to himself, "Okay, I guess I won't sing for you anymore." A chasm which would not close for decades opened between father and son.

Paul still had his music and his friend Artie. However, his constant companion was beginning to tower over him. At the time, Paul's failure to grow taller was even more distressing than his father's disapproval. He later admitted that being short "had the most significant single effect on my existence, aside from my brain. In fact, it's part of an inferior-superior syndrome. I think I have a superior brain and an inferior stature, if you really want to get brutal about it."

Whatever the reason for the personality change, Paul's unsmiling face and often "sullen" mood became permanent—he was turning inward, developing lifelong habits of introspection.

Art's teenage years were proving to be rocky as well, but he handled his problems in a very different way. A good student, he distracted himself from his inner turmoil by excelling academically. He later recalled, "When I was in high school, I withdrew a lot. My friends were reduced to one or two. I read a lot, and I played the game of 'doing well in school'—maybe by default. My parents never pushed me, or were overly proud, though. I could never accept myself as 'one of the gang.' Everything I did was cast in the image and perspective of the outsider. I had become a sociologist in spirit, an incessant observer."

In the fall of 1955, the two teenagers entered tenth grade at Forest Hills High School. Both appeared relieved to be back in a familiar, safe neighborhood near home.

In October, convinced of his seriousness about music, Paul's parents bought him a twenty-five-dollar guitar. Paul's brother Eddie has said, "Nobody thought that Paul would be very good on guitar...but he fooled us and got good quickly."

Fourteen-year-old Paul began practicing night and day, obsessed by the adolescent fantasy that a nice Jewish boy from Queens could actually become Elvis Presley if he practiced hard enough.

Simon gravitated to the distinctly black sounds of rhythm and blues groups like the Cadillacs, the Monotones, and the El Dorados, with their strong emphasis on vocal harmony. But his most significant influence was Elvis, the southern white performer steeped in the tradition of black music which he adapted and made acceptable to record-buying, white, middle-class America. In the mid-fifties, Elvis transformed the music scene—and Paul's life— forever.

Art, too, had singled out his models—the Crew Cuts, the Four Aces, and other groups that favored close vocal harmonies. "It was always the groups," Art later recalled. But he also liked Little Richard and Fats Domino, who "made records that cooked."

Another strong influence on Art and Paul was doo-wop, an a cappella vocal form that flowed from the street corners of New

York. Paul and Art were fascinated by the close harmonies and intricate rhythms of doo-wop groups like the Penguins, the Orioles, the Moonglows, and the Five Satins.

Paul Simon no longer would sing for his father, but he and Art were determined to sing for anyone else who would listen. Hour after hour Paul and Art would record their voices, lay down tracks, dub and overdub, and explore an endless combination of harmonic possibilities. The tedious work in their primitive recording studio strongly appealed to Garfunkel's growing interest in mathematics. He loved the challenge provided by the precise verbal and melodic repetition. Garfunkel later explained, "We'd be sitting nose to nose, looking right at each other's mouths to copy diction. I'd want to know exactly where his tongue would hit the top of his palate when he'd say a 't' to know exactly how to get that 't' right. And I could see that you could be almost right, or even better than almost right, and that all of that really was the difference between whether or not it sounded professional. Then once you had it very precise, you cooled it out and made it seem effortless."

For their part, both boys loved to hear their voices blend, peel away, and match up once again. Their voices seemed perfectly and naturally aligned from the start. Playing with their voices created a wonderfully pleasurable sensation—two friends learning to play a unique musical instrument simultaneously. Becoming serious scholars of the mechanics of harmony, they also studied and analyzed other groups' vocal arrangements. They began to realize that the sound they made together packed considerably more wallop than anything they could do alone. They were committed to working together to achieve success in the musical world. Slowly the bright dream of a shared future took shape.

And before long, the obsessive practice sessions did indeed make the razor-sharp harmonies seem effortless. The two voices would produce mirror-image sounds more commonly found in siblings like the Andrews Sisters or the Ames Brothers—singing groups that developed their harmonies as they grew up together. The boys' professional sound astonished their friends and family.

While 1955 ended with traditional crooner hits like Dean Martin's "Memories Are Made of This" and the Four Aces' "Love Is a Many-Splendored Thing," more and more hits in the top twenty were by unfamiliar names like Ray Charles, Joe Turner, and the Heartbeats. By far the group that caused the most excitement that year was Bill Haley and His Comets.

When the spit-curled, barrel-chested Haley screamed "We're gonna rock around the clock tonight," he spoke the code words millions of teenagers were waiting to hear, words which would liberate them from the stultifying norms of traditional American social values: "One, two, three o'clock, / four o'clock, rock / We're gonna rock around the clock tonight." Embedded in the apparent nonsense syllables, kids heard a declaration of independence: "We don't care what you think, we're gonna do it anyway." "Rock Around the Clock" was a call to rebellion—and it came with strong sexual overtones. It frightened parents. It terrified the music business.

Haley had a string of hits with "Crazy Man Crazy," "Shake, Rattle and Roll," "Dim Dim the Lights," "Razzle Dazzle," and "Burn That Candle." But his most memorable hit, the first anthem of the rock generation, "Rock Around the Clock" packed a double punch. The new sensation was featured over the opening and closing credits of the movie *Blackboard Jungle,* confirming parents' fears that rock 'n' roll was, indeed, the music of juvenile delinquents.

Other "rock" movies followed. Theater marquees across America proclaimed the musical revolution: *Shake, Rattle and Rock,* with songs by Joe Turner and other rockers, and *The Girl Can't Help It,* with music by Fats Domino, Little Richard, and Gene Vincent.

Each week more new groups appeared on the radio and on the pop-music charts. Paul and Art drank them in: the Diamonds, Frankie Lymon and the Teenagers, the Coasters, the Cliftones, the Channels, the Four Preps, and the Five Satins. In his meticulous way, Art devised a system to chart the progress of hit singles from week to week. He remembered, "I used to dig the idea of lists. I'd keep charts of the top-forty songs on big sheets of graph paper. Each record was a colored dot on a vertical line. The records became very personal to me; I'd watch a song fall from number two to number seven and then strain to get back up to number four."

Art and Paul often noticed that a new group might score a hit then vanish from the charts in a few weeks, never to be heard from again. The Magnificents, the Galahads, the Cadets, the Teen

Queens, the Four Voices, and the Three Friends all lacked staying power. But at least they got their big chance and made it to the top once or twice before they fell. Rock 'n' roll opened up a world of possibility.

The teenage demand for rock 'n' roll seemed insatiable and its effect on the music business was profound. Until this time, slow-moving giants like Columbia, RCA, Decca, Capitol, and Mercury Records had dominated traditional pop music. Sensing the shift in taste, small independent labels sprang up to take advantage of the reluctance of the big companies to embrace the new music. The newcomers rushed to produce records for teenagers with money to spend. Labels like VeeJay, Atlantic, RPM, King, Sun, ABC Para-mount, and dozens of others flooded record retailers and radio stations. The profit potential was enormous, especially with "one-hit wonders," since new groups with no track record could be signed to do a record for very little money. Production costs were also minimal, and the record company reaped a huge profit even if the group slipped rapidly into oblivion.

Alan Freed branched out from radio to spread the gospel of rock 'n' roll with live stage shows at the St. Nicholas Arena in New York City. CBS radio broadcast Freed's "Rock and Roll Dance Party" live, and the deejay himself became a star, appearing in three rock 'n' roll movies including the seminal *Rock Around the Clock* with Bill Haley and His Comets.

By far the most eagerly awaited rock-music film was Elvis Presley's *Love Me Tender*. Across the country, teenage girls hungered to see his winsome spit curl, defiant sneer, and raw sexual energy bigger than life on the silver screen.

In the history of rock 'n' roll, 1956 was the "Year of Elvis." He owned five number-one hits, and eleven times this messenger of black music—the very embodiment of the generation gap—wriggled into American living rooms by way of the television screen. On their programs, Jackie Gleason, Milton Berle, Steve Allen, and Ed Sullivan introduced the most subversive force in American pop culture as parents gasped and teenagers held their breath. Many rock 'n' rollers had hit singles during 1956, but only Elvis made the year's top-ten singles charts. Elvis would soon be king.

Like millions of his peers, Paul was infatuated with Presley, but Art Garfunkel's interest still lay in duplicating the harmonies of the popular doo-wop groups. At fourteen, Paul and Art began writing songs together and quickly copyrighted their first effort, "The Girl for Me." According to Art, they recorded their first song "in one of those booths at Coney Island for twenty-five cents. It was early Alan Freed. We laughed a lot."

The giggles subsided when the duo discovered songwriting skill and soaring harmonies weren't enough to make the shimmering dream come true. What was needed was a relentless engine to push it forward. Aggressiveness wasn't in Artie's nature, but Paul possessed enough raw nerviness and ambition for two.

From his father's work in show business, Paul knew where to begin—home plate was the Brill Building at 1619 Broadway in Manhattan—a rabbit warren of tiny, smoke-filled offices where dozens of music publishers and producers ground out a majority of the nation's hit music. The two determined teenagers developed a disciplined work ethic. They regularly rode the dingy, noisy, and sometimes dangerous subway from Queens into Manhattan to knock on music publishers' doors. It was an arduous and humbling process. At first very selective, they worked through careful lists of the record companies whose names were on the labels of their favorite songs. In a triumph of circular logic, the boys reasoned that their own songs would be well received by these companies, since these labels clearly possessed the good taste and judgment to record music they liked.

Paul and Art would corner hapless secretaries, hoping to charm them into getting their bosses to give the boys' songs a hearing. They soon learned to accept rejection as an integral part of the process and, fueled by youthful optimism, moved on after each failure to repeat their act in the next office down the hall.

Artie hated every encounter: "You'd go up and knock on the door, and there would be this weird freaked-out black guy or this very fat, cigar-smoking Jewish businessman, and they'd be gruff and you knew it was really a hard thing to get into." More than once, they both talked about giving it up, but Paul would usually deliver an impassioned pep talk to bolster Art's (and his own) sagging spirits, and the two would push on, riding the slim hope that their big break really did lie waiting within the blue cigar haze next door.

Finally, success. They were elated to land a contract with a small promoter. It seemed as if all their hard work had finally paid off, but the months slipped by. They were anxious to record, but the contract expired without the boys having set foot in a recording studio. Later Art remembered the dogged, frustrating effort as "Three years of that kind of shit." But it only seemed like forever. In reality, the two had been at the dismal routine only a year and a half.

It was 1957. The sounds of Elvis, Fats Domino, Johnny Ace, Little Richard, and the doo-wop groups now dominated the airwaves. One day Paul heard "Bye Bye Love." Before the record was finished, he was on the phone to Artie saying, "just heard this great record. Let's go out and buy it." They played it again and again. Art and Paul listened to the electrifying new sound—intertwining voices that sounded so much like their own it was astonishing. They had discovered the Everly Brothers.

It seemed almost too good to be true. The Everlys were a southern, more polished version of Art and Paul, singing razor-sharp harmony to a rock beat. Within a few weeks, the boys could do a letter-perfect imitation of their new idols.

The new inspiration provided by the Everly Brothers refueled the boys' flagging career drive. They decided to give the promoters one last try.

They risked twenty-five dollars to make a real studio demo of a new song they wrote together, "Hey, Schoolgirl." They made an appointment at Sanders Recording Studio on Seventh Avenue in Manhattan and brought along another song for the flip side. True to their dream scenario, this was to be their lucky day. One of the faceless businessmen who peopled the music world of the Brill Building happened to be outside the studio and overhead the recording session. When the excited duo took its first break between songs, the man asked Paul and Art to wait around while he recorded his own act's demo. He told them he was impressed by their harmonies and called them "the greatest thing since the Everly Brothers." Just like in the movies, he said he would make them stars.

Despite the long-awaited magic words, Paul and Art had seen enough of the music business by now to be wary of the promises and wily ways of record promoters. But this man turned out to be different. He was record producer Sid Prosen, the man who had written Teresa Brewer's hit "Till I Waltz Again With You," and he was constantly trolling for new talent. Still, Paul and Art's experience with their first go-nowhere contract had taught them to read the fine print in recording contracts. They knew it was important to record quickly and to steer clear of long-term commitments, so they brazenly demanded that Prosen release "Hey, Schoolgirl" within sixty days. Amazingly, Prosen agreed. He promptly recorded several tracks and prepared to release the single on his new label, Big Records.

Art and Paul decided to continue using the stage names Tom and Jerry that they had been using for some time around their neighborhood. But this was no high-school sock hop. They needed last names, too. Paul borrowed the name *Landis* from current girlfriend Sue Landis. Art chose *Graph* because he strongly identified with the orderly precision of graph paper.

Prosen made good on his promise. In late 1957 he released "Hey, Schoolgirl" with "Dancing Wild" on the flip side, both cowritten by Paul and Artie.

Prosen discovered a promotional advantage in Tom and Jerry. By now they had made countless personal appearances at school and neighborhood social functions. At fifteen, they were seasoned veterans with an act ready to go if the record took off. Personal appearances could really boost record sales. The two gladly grinned at the camera for publicity photos. This was the big time.

For his part, Prosen pushed the record hard. Since payola was the custom of the day, he spent two hundred dollars to buy air time on the Alan Freed radio show to spur record sales. The record sold well enough to enable Prosen to book Tom and Jerry on the wildly popular new teenage TV dance program "American Bandstand," broadcast live on ABC from Philadelphia.

Dick Clark, a young deejay, had taken over as host only a few months earlier, and by November 1957, the program was a solid hit. The show's studio audience was made up of local high school teenagers, and the format was simple: Clark introduced the latest hits, and the kids danced to them. It wasn't long before the studio kids became celebrities themselves.

The popularity of "American Bandstand" with teenagers is easy to understand. On the show's most popular segment, Clark asked teenagers, who had been raised to be seen and not heard, to be arbiters of taste. Every afternoon, millions of teenagers rushed home from school to watch their peers pass judgment on the beat and danceability of the latest rock 'n' roll tunes. And each program featured two or three of the hottest new recording stars lip-synching their current hits. On Friday, November 22, 1957, the show featured the explosive Jerry Lee Lewis doing "Great Balls of Fire." Perhaps as an antidote, Tom and Jerry, a clean-cut pair from Queens in conservative suits and ties, then sang about schoolboy passions.

Understandably, to the boys it was all a blur. Paul later recalled, "One month Artie and I were watching 'American Bandstand' on television, and the next month we were on the show. It was an incredible thing to have happen to you in your adolescence. I had picked up the guitar because I wanted to be like Elvis Presley, and there I was!"

They returned home as conquering neighborhood heroes. On their bedroom radios, they heard themselves sandwiched in among the Everly Brothers' "Wake Up, Little Suzie," Sam Cooke's first big hit, "You Send Me," Paul Anka's "Diana," and Rick Nelson's "I'm Walkin'." They were even reviewed in *Billboard,* the record industry's bible, which called them "a cross between the Everly Brothers and the DeJohn Sisters." Fame had touched them, and they were deliriously happy.

And they were in demand. After the "Bandstand" appearance, they went to Cincinnati for four days of record hops, then to Hartford's State Theater, Connecticut's equivalent to New York's Apollo. There were nine acts on the bill including Laverne Baker and Little Joe and the Thrillers. Art said, "We were the white group. Sort of comic relief."

Even the cautious, passive Art enjoyed the heady rush of stardom: "I never thought I was seriously going to make my living this way. I thought sooner or later I would do something more...reputable. But I sure did always want to be famous."

Like Art, Paul dreamed of fame, but being part of the "new" Everly Brothers wasn't enough. Even at this early stage, Paul Simon had second thoughts about sharing the spotlight, and he continued to fantasize about becoming the next Elvis.

Even while Tom and Jerry were still on the pop charts, Paul and Prosen were working on other recording projects without Art.

2

In January 1958, Big Records released the single "True or False" with the flip side "Teen Age Fool." Paul Simon had recorded them as a solo act under a fanciful new stage name, True Taylor.

The record's title would hold special meaning for Art. He was devastated by what seemed to be Paul's casual betrayal. He felt rejected and angry about Paul's defection from their partnership.

Art also was surprised to learn Paul's father had written "True or False." In spite of his earlier disapproval of his son's passion for rock 'n' roll, Louis Simon was enough of a pragmatist to see that Paul and his friend had had a modest, but genuine, hit single with "Hey, Schoolgirl." He knew a career in the pop recording field could be lucrative, even if rock 'n' roll didn't measure up to his own musical standards.

In writing Paul's first solo effort, Louis Simon proved he grasped the letter, if not the spirit, of Elvis Presley's style. "True or False" is an accurate, though bloodless, imitation of Elvis, down to Paul's muttered diction and soft slurring of the lyrics. But no one mistook True Taylor for Elvis, and the record didn't cause a ripple.

Paul had also recorded two instrumental solos for Prosen: "Tijuana Blues" and "Simon Says." They were credited to Simon and Prosen as composers. "Simon Says" was never released as a single, but "Tijuana Blues" would later surface when Prosen sold the tracks to another record company.

"Hey, Schoolgirl" turned out to be a modest hit, eventually selling roughly 120,000–150,000 copies, but it stayed on *Billboard*'s "Top 100" for nine weeks. It got as high as number forty-nine before falling from the charts. True Taylor never even made it to the charts.

Art could take some comfort in Paul's solo flop, but the hurt Paul had caused him would never fully heal. This was the first conflict to seriously threaten their relationship, but they were unwilling to confront the painful problem. It was easier to ignore Paul's betrayal than to give up their shared dream of rock 'n' roll stardom. By now, they were experienced show-business veterans who knew their best chance for sustained success lay in teamwork "Tom and Jerry" was still a moderate success, so they set aside their personal differences and ambitions for the good of the act. Their music was unaffected, but their personal harmony had been shattered. Art would nurse the wound for more than thirty years.

This first estrangement established a pattern that would repeat itself throughout their careers—no matter how severe the test, the bond between them would bend but never break.

Paul and Art recorded other tracks for Prosen; in quick succession, Big Records released "Don't Say Goodbye," with flip side "That's My Story," and "Our Song," backed by "Two Teenagers," all of which quickly failed. Even payola didn't boost sales. Now that the music business was awash in fifty to a hundred new groups a year and twice as many singles, hit records had become as much a matter of luck and persistence as talent. Prosen was tenacious. In the spring Big Records released Tom and Jerry's new song "Baby Talk," again using "Two Teenagers" as the flip side. Anything could happen, and there seemed no reason why another Tom and Jerry song couldn't hit it big. In all, Tom and Jerry recorded seven of Art and Paul's songs for Prosen.

Throughout 1958 and into 1959, hope still remained that their mutual career could be resuscitated. In those freewheeling days of New York's pop-record business, aspiring artists' tracks frequently were bought and sold. Small-time operators often closed down one record label to open another a few weeks later, creating a big demand for new and used tracks. Prosen sold Tom and Jerry's old tracks to various companies: Hunt Records released "That's My Story," and the Bell label rereleased "Baby Talk" as the flip side of the Ronnie Lawrence single "I'm Going to Get Married." For several years Tom and Jerry tracks would occasionally float to the surface on a series of new labels.

In those early days, artists were paid up-front lump-sum fees since royalties seldom materialized later, but Tom and Jerry's modest hit did manage to generate some residual income. Paul and Artie's earnings from "Hey, Schoolgirl" amounted to about two thousand dollars each. Paul saved his money and, two years later, indulged a weakness for fast cars by buying a bright-red Impala convertible souped up with three carburetors. He loved to cruise the neighborhood, sporting the rewards of his recent success, but he didn't have the car long before it caught fire just around the corner from the Garfunkel house and burned to a total loss. The car and, it seemed, the dream of musical stardom were reduced to ashes.

When their parents urged them both to enter college, it was an easy choice for the practical Art. Not as driven by the music dream as Paul, he was more sobered by the demands of the music business as well as by a deep disappointment in Paul's lack of fidelity. Art saw a college education as preparation for the day when there would be no music.

They both registered for college and went their separate ways. Paul Simon lived at home and majored in English at neighboring Queens College, while Art eventually moved to Manhattan and enrolled in the liberal arts program at Columbia University. With other goals on the horizon, the adolescent intensity of the relationship cooled. There was, however, always the possibility the team would click again, since yet another record label, King Records, had reissued "Hey, Schoolgirl," while ABC Paramount tried to resurrect the team with two more previously unreleased tracks, "Surrender, Please Surrender" and "Fighting Mad." Nothing happened. Tom and Jerry's moment in the spotlight was over.

But Paul couldn't stop thinking about a musical career. In every spare moment, he listened to rock music, strummed his guitar, and scribbled song lyrics. His teenage music was still derivative. He had an excellent ear for mimicry, and all his early songs were patterned on whatever style was at the top of the charts. Like so much early rock 'n' roll, his songs often were an exercise in gimmickry because he knew that in the pop-music world, lightning often struck in the same place twice. He felt his songs could catch teenagers' fancies and propel him to the top at any moment.

Paul and Art separately continued to work part-time in the music business. Paul was producing demos of new songs for record producers and artists, earning a healthy income while learning more about how hits were made. For twenty-five or thirty dollars a session, Paul sang the lead vocal, overdubbed harmony, played drums, bass, piano, and sang the backup doo-wahs. He learned to be a one-man band. Of his record-demo period he has said, "That's how I learned to be a recording artist: how to stand in front of a microphone, sing background parts, learn about a control room, mike technique, how musicians treated one another." He used his demo experience to produce a steady stream of his own songs, but although he sold a few, he was unable to establish a solid music career.

Paul briefly collaborated with fellow Queens College classmate Carole Klein, who later became famous as Carole King. As he remembered, "Carole would play piano and drums and sing. I would sing and play guitar and bass. The game was to make a demo at demo prices and then try to sell it to a record company. Maybe you'd wind up investing three hundred dollars for musicians and studio time, but if you did something really good, you could get as much as a thousand for it. I never wanted to be in groups. I was only after that seven-hundred-dollar profit. I always tried to get my money up-front, because you were never sure of getting your royalties if they put the record out. You were dealing with a lot of thieves in those days."

Carole proved even more adept than Paul at creating pop formula hits. In her sophomore year, she dropped out of college and, with classmate Gerry Goffin (who later became her husband), wrote one rock 'n' roll hit after another for Don Kirshner's record publishing factory, whose office was in Paul's old haunt, the Brill Building.

Paul had tried to convince Carole to finish her degree even though he, too, considered dropping out of school to churn out pop music full time. But Paul soberly assessed his chances and saw that, in spite of his experience, talent, and ambition, the likelihood of his becoming a big success was very slim. Like Art, he needed a college degree as an option once the music stopped. Even his father, a professional musician, was thinking about returning for a graduate degree so he could become a teacher.

When Paul occasionally did sell his own tunes, his phantom recording career would again take substantial form—but the spasms of mild success only increased his frustration. He tried everything he could think of to make it work, including recording under a string of disposable names.

As "Jerry Landis," the name he had used when teamed with Art, Paul broke into the top one hundred with "The Lonely Teen Ranger," a novelty number in the style of the Coasters' "Searchin'." Landis sang about a boy whose girlfriend is so in love with her horse, she hasn't time for the "Teen Ranger." Again as Landis, he recorded "Lisa," "I'm Lonely," "I Wish I Weren't in Love," and "Just a Boy." In the last song, he almost whispers that he is "unwise and full of fears" but his love will give him "the wisdom of many years." The soft, delicate vocal is a precursor of the Simon and Garfunkel sound. Also as Landis, Paul sang the slightly suggestive "I Want to Be the Lipstick on Your Collar," as well as "Anna Belle" and "Loneliness." Paul's themes typically revolved around the agonies of teenage love, but a nascent preoccupation with the topic of alienation also began to appear in these late-adolescent songs.

When Paul recorded "Motorcycle," he called himself the faintly exotic "Tico and the Triumphs," a name that conjured up black leather rather than white bread. Using a studio backup group, Tico/Paul had a minor hit with "Motorcycle" in 1962 when it reached number ninety-nine on the top one hundred. As Tico, he also recorded "Wild Flower," "Express Train," and "Cry, Little Boy." Simon also wrote and produced for other performers. Dottie Daniels on the Amy label recorded "Play Me a Song," which Paul wrote with his brother Eddie. In the wake of successful novelty dance numbers such as "Mashed Potato Time" and "The Stroll," Paul tried his hand with "Get Up and Do the Wobble." Wobbling, however, did not sweep the nation.

The lack of a magical name was not the most serious hindrance to Simon's dream of rock 'n' roll stardom. Paul hated the way he looked—more like an elf than an Elvis—and there wasn't much hope of changing that. His height had topped out at five feet, three inches. (Through the years it would be reported anywhere from five feet, one inch to five feet, four inches.) Like many short teenage boys, Paul had hoped for a growth spurt in his late teens, but it never came. He brooded over his appearance and spent more time alone with his guitar, writing lyrics that eased his disappointment. The aura of melancholy and alienation settled in as permanent aspects of his adult personality. His "inferior stature" drove him to experiment with folk songs and ballads, musical forms more suitable to his moods.

Meanwhile, although Art Garfunkel had never been as single-minded about music as Simon, their brush with stardom had left some hopes alive. Like Simon, he now knew how the process worked—go to Manhattan, sell a song, make a record, hope for a hit. While Paul occasionally called himself Jerry Landis, Art had changed his professional name from Tom Graph to Artie Garr, an anglicized version of his own name. Art sold a song he'd written to Jack Gold at Octavia Records, which released "Private World" with a melody strongly reminiscent of the classic English folk ballad, "Greensleeves," and an arrangement clearly influenced by a new group, the Kingston Trio. The single's other side was "Forgive Me," by a writer with the mysterious single name Raphael. This song tells the story of someone who's "lived a big lie," will soon commit suicide, and then be taken away by "a man with a smiling face. The song ends with an admonition not to live a life like his, to be happy and carefree and to love and be loved. Art also recorded "Beat Love" for the Warwick label, but Garr's single records sank faster than the worst flops of Tom and Jerry.

Lacking a genuine passion for the business, Art retreated into his college work. Like many of his generation, he was restless, rebellious, and impressionable. In his sophomore year he had read Ayn Rand's *The Fountainhead*, a novel about an idealistic architect, and promptly decided to major in architecture. He later revealed, "I was attracted to architecture for the sound of the word 'architect.' I think I like the 'a' and the 'r,' you know…I like the crispness of 'tect' at the end. It sounded respectable. 'Architect.' You could smoke a pipe, wear corduroy pants, gum-bottomed shoes." Later, Paul Simon would use this detail, like so many others from their personal lives, in a song lyric. In "A Simple, Desultory Phillipic," Paul wrote "I been Ayn Rand'd, nearly branded Communist, 'cause I'm left-handed."

The new course of study did little to calm Art's restlessness, so he did what a lot of sons and daughters of the middle class were doing in the early sixties—he dropped out of school and headed for a vagabond tour of Europe to "find himself." He left New York with little more than a backpack and the clothes he was wearing and headed for the Continent, where he rented a motor scooter, stayed in cheap youth hostels, and camped out under the stars.

On his return to the States, still clinging to his ambition to become an architect, Art worked as a draftsman in New York City. His practical experience in the field led to disenchantment with the profession. A decade later he explained: "I had an unpleasant experience with architecture. I'm angry at that whole field. It's a deception. People who go into architecture feel they're going to be artists, and they don't know that they're going to be businessmen." After a while boredom set in again, and he made his way to San Francisco, where he occasionally toiled as a carpenter's assistant.

But Art hadn't abandoned his youthful monitoring of the music business. In San Francisco he noticed a new, exciting trend. Conservative music executives were eager to find another fad, one they fervently hoped would overtake and eventually eliminate rock 'n' roll from the airwaves. Their prayers had been answered when the Kingston Trio strummed "Tom Dooley" all the way to gold-record status in 1958. The clean-cut, buttoned-down trio, who started out singing for beer as Stanford underclassmen, eschewed rock 'n' roll as the province of teenagers. They decided college students needed something more intellectually challenging in their music. The Kingston Trio found that something in the long-dormant American folk-music tradition and, working within that framework, offered their own sophisticated and witty commentary on American social life. Their melodies and subject matter strongly resonated with student sensibilities, and their music ushered in the folk revival which would, in turn, give birth to the protest songs of the sixties.

The times were changing, and the tide was running strongly in favor of youth. In 1961, a vigorous young President, his beautiful wife, and their adorable children symbolized the country's generational shift. The dreams, fears, hopes, and emotions of youth became the dominant threads of the country's social fabric.

The country was also rapidly moving toward unprecedented

domestic turbulence. In 1963, Martin Luther King, Jr., still in his thirties, was leading a small idealistic army of volunteers in a nonviolent but nonetheless dangerous fight for human rights in the South. America was beginning to slide into the quagmire of Vietnam. Violence came into nearly every American's living room on television when John Kennedy became the first victim of what would be a ghastly series of assassinations of public figures during the sixties. A scruffy, skinny folksinger rasped the apocalyptic news: "The times they are a-changin'" and prophesied that "A hard rain's a-gonna fall."

Bob Dylan's music, as sung by Dylan, was then only marginally popular. His songs found their largest audience when performed by the less-threatening heirs to the folk legacy of the Kingston Trio. Joan Baez sang Dylan's rebellious lyrics in a pure soprano voice and made a habit of introducing the composer at her packed concerts. Peter, Paul, and Mary's sweet harmonies made Dylan's "Blowin' in the Wind" and "Don't Think Twice" accessible to millions of young people who were searching for some direction in those troubling times.

Throughout Art's restless wandering in the early sixties, his interest in folk music had grown stronger. Partly because of folk music's connection with social and political currents, California was fast succeeding New York as the cradle of musical innovation. And Art Garfunkel was there to observe and absorb it all. He spent a lot of time hanging around the music scene in San Francisco and began to sing frequently at small folk clubs in the Bay area and in the student union at the University of California at Berkeley. He discovered a natural affinity for the folk tradition with its mature themes and emotions. He continued to sing under name of Artie Garr, even though he had definitely switched from rock 'n' roll to folk ballads.

Back in New York, Paul, too, had changed his focus from rock to folk.

3

By the early 1960s, Art Garfunkel was back in New York to reregister at Columbia. His wanderings had given him some badly needed perspective, and now he was determined to finish his undergraduate degree and, not incidentally, maintain his student draft deferment. He had given up his apartment in Manhattan and was back at home, living with his parents in Kew Gardens. Meanwhile, Paul, who had been classified 4F because of a heart murmur, was completing his degree at Queens College. Just three blocks apart, it was inevitable that the two would meet again.

One afternoon as Garfunkel was walking across a bridge near his home, he bumped into his old partner. They filled each other in on their years apart and on their latest performances. They discovered their mutual interest in the folk scene and joked about their solo record flops. Older now and more mature, Art seemed to have gotten over his feeling of betrayal, but time would prove he had only buried it. Paul later summed up their reunion: "I hadn't seen him for years. We renewed our friendship—the one that had split up over my making the solo record at fifteen. I'd been writing, and we started to sing those songs, became fast friends, smoked our joints together."

Art found that Paul's own lyrics and melodies had changed dramatically. Simon had been reading the major poets in his literature studies and had new standards for his artistic aspirations. He began questioning what he called the "dumb teenage lyrics" he had been writing, even though they were still in demand. Teenager Leslie Gore was singing "It's my party," while the Crystals were hitting it big with "Da Doo Ron Ron" and the Angels with "My Boyfriend's Back." But Paul later candidly noted, "I had just about finally decided that if I was going to be a failure as a songwriter, I would be a proud failure."

Paul and Art fell back into the boyhood habit of singing together. Paul was often invited to sing and play at student activities on the Queens College campus, and one night he invited Art to join him in a performance at a fraternity party. Paul was known as a solo act, but he called Art up on stage to harmonize on a couple of numbers, and the duo drew a strong reaction from the crowd. Art recalled, "The first night that we got back together we started singing these songs. We did it in the Alpha Epsilon fraternity house in Queens, and the echo was right. The rooms were bare plaster walls with no furniture, and the sound was a lot of fun."

Rehearsing and singing together again gave them both a comfortable, reassuring feeling. They were excited about the intellectual and emotional range folk tunes added to their repertoire.

Throughout that school year Art and Paul continued to sing together. Still not totally convinced of the financial wisdom of a music career, Paul had enrolled at law school in Brooklyn. Although Belle Simon was always supportive of her son's musical ambitions (after all, her husband was a professional bass player), she was still, at heart, a Jewish Mother who wanted her son to enter a more stable profession, like medicine or law.

Paul was ambivalent about becoming a lawyer, but decided to give it a try. He had managed to finish college and pass the law school entrance exams while pursuing a musical career, so there seemed to be no reason why he couldn't also attend law school and work in the business simultaneously.

But this time it wasn't so easy, and before long Paul was flunking out. He simply couldn't take his mind off music to concentrate on his studies. It seemed silly to continue pretending he was going to do anything other than music for a living anyway.

He dropped out of law school, arguing with his mother that he could always return in a year or two if his music career failed. Freed from other demands, Simon devoted himself entirely to his music.

He got a part-time job as a song plugger for the E. B. Marks Publishing Company. It was familiar territory—he peddled songs to artists' agents and, in the process, gained access to the industry's most influential people.

As Art and Paul explored contemporary folk music more carefully, they recognized the superior talent of Bob Dylan, whose rough poetry and driving rhythms offered a unique vision of America.

Art remembered Dylan's early influence on Paul: "When I met up again with Paul...he was starting to get into this new style. When Dylan came along, it really got interesting. We could really connect with that. So Dylan got Paul into this singer-songwriter-poet kind of thing, and I was fascinated by Dylan."

Dylan's music, above all, expressed revolutionary attitudes about war, hypocrisy, conformity, peace, and love that swept college campuses all over America. At last, popular music was beginning to deal with important ideas.

Paul began to formulate his own artistic vision and wrote lyrics that told more complex, personal stories. Like Dylan, Paul was especially interested in relevant social issues. Newspapers and television were full of stories about the valiant civil-rights freedom fighters in the South who were being beaten and killed for their beliefs. Moved by their bravery and the importance of the struggle, he wrote his first protest song, "He Was My Brother," and showed it to Art, who remembers hearing it in June 1963, "a week after Paul wrote it." Art described the song as "cast in the Bob Dylan mold...I was happy to feel the way the song made me feel."

This new direction in Paul's music, with its combination of thoughtful lyrics, appealing melodies, and close harmonies, impressed Art. He recognized Paul's considerable talent and felt truly comfortable, perhaps for the first time, with the direction in which Paul's new music was taking the team.

The two had drifted back together without any formal partnership, as the casual pattern of singing together at fraternity parties and other small gatherings continued. Soon Art and Paul performed exclusively as a duo. They had always respected each other's talents, and their voices still blended in an extraordinary way. They were having fun again.

The two began to spend a great deal of time in Greenwich Village. The folk scene was in full swing at such clubs as Gerde's Folk City, the Café Wha, and the Gaslight. Like many other young performers of the time, Paul and Art used to sing at impromptu concerts under the arch in Washington Square. Art, who still wasn't totally comfortable with public performance, didn't like street singing, but open-air concerts offered a chance to practice their songs on a live audience. These free street concerts taught both performers a lot about what their audience wanted to hear and helped them build a following.

At this point, Paul and Art were buddies more than partners. Their mutual career had not progressed far enough to warrant a detailed discussion of formal conditions of reteaming. Art decided to go back to Berkeley to spend the summer of 1963, a last fling before buckling down to finish his degree. Over the summer, Paul finished a second folk song and began work on a third.

When Art returned from his summer in California, Paul was eager to play his newest effort, "Sparrow," which told the story of a quest for comfort and communication in a world dominated by selfishness and rejection. Art admired its themes and began to work with Paul on harmonies for "Sparrow" and "He Was My Brother." They finally landed a booking at Gerde's, where they planned to sing folk standards and introduce the new material.

But even more thrilling was the news that Paul had interested Tom Wilson, an important producer at Columbia Records, in "He Was My Brother." At first, Art didn't understand why Paul was so excited until he, too, realized their good luck: "He's Dylan's producer!"

On a warm September night, billed as "Kane and Garr," Paul and Art sang the two new songs at Gerde's and got a warm reception. It wasn't until that night, according to Art Garfunkel, that "we formed the partnership." Past differences were buried for the moment as once again Paul and Art looked forward to a bright future together as recording artists.

This time, Paul, as songwriter, got top billing even though they were not yet comfortable enough with their real names to use them in public. There was another significant difference in the relationship since their teenage days: They were partners again, but now each harbored his own personal ambition. While the partnership lasted, they tacitly agreed to hold their individual career goals in check for the good of the act, a separate entity they each came to refer to as "Simon and Garfunkel." In time, the act would grow to legendary proportions, and each would struggle against its powerful bond.

For now, however, they busied themselves with the hard work of building the act. Gradually, they clarified their roles within the partnership.

Art no longer participated directly in writing the music or lyrics as he had as a teenager. Of course, his emotions and experiences and the life he shared with Paul would still have a powerful influence on Paul's writing. Art articulated the terms of their new collaboration: "We wrote rock 'n' roll songs together, but suddenly one of us could write poetic folk songs. I really connected with that...so the rejoining, after several years, was on the basis of the two of us as singers and Paul as the songwriter."

The arrangement sounds simple and straightforward. However, as with all artistic collaborations, no clear-cut lines could really be drawn. Paul may have written the lyrics and melody, but as the two began to develop the music, creative contributions became blurred. Since childhood, Paul and Art had refined their working relationship to an almost seamless blend. Paul would play a melody and sing a lyric while Art listened. Art would then suggest a harmonic arrangement which might require a subtle change in the rhythm or tempo. Paul would think about the suggestion and then, if he felt it was useful, make an alteration in the song. There was constant dialogue between the two. Over the years, they had developed a kind of creative shorthand to give—and take— advice, criticism, and praise. The process seemed remarkably free of ego or animosity. After all, they had been doing this since they were boys, and had learned to focus all of their energies on shaping the music.

Tom Wilson, the Columbia Records producer, saw potential in "He Was My Brother." Wilson, who was black, was very moved by the song's message of sympathy for the civil-rights cause. But there was a catch. Wilson was interested in the song for the Pilgrims, a folk group which Columbia was promoting. Paul was disappointed because he didn't want to sell the song for someone else to sing. He and Art had teamed up again, and he wanted to be loyal to their goal, which was for them to record his songs. Simon argued to Wilson that he and his singing partner could do more justice to the material than any other group. Persuaded by the young writer's passion and conviction, Wilson relented and set up a session for Paul and Art to record an audition tape. In what would turn out to be another remarkable stroke of luck, he teamed the boys with recording engineer Roy Halee.

The demo didn't wow the decision-makers at Columbia, but it was good enough for the executives to request a second audition tape. When Simon and Garfunkel returned to the studio the following week, they asked specifically for the engineer in the yellow, oxford-cloth, buttoned-down shirt. They couldn't remember his name, but they had recognized Halee's skill and sensed his enthusiasm for their work. Roy Halee became one of their early champions, and his good opinion helped Wilson convince Columbia to sign the team for an album.

Although it was Paul's song that gained them entry to Columbia, Paul and Art were signed as recording artists, not as songwriters. Columbia was trying to cash in on the folk craze and needed new performers to compete with its rival, Capitol Records. Simon and Garfunkel's album would contain some folk standards, folk songs by other contemporary writers, and a few of Paul's originals.

That was fine with Paul. This was the big time—not a contract for a single on an off-beat label, but a contract for an album to be released by a prestigious and powerful company. Of course, it was also a contract with standard options, and they could be dropped at any time. But for the moment, Paul and Art were euphoric. They would have months to work with top professionals in laying down tracks. Better still, in Paul's view, the album would contain at least four or five original Simon songs.

Paul had recently finished "Bleecker Street," a dark rumination on the hopelessness of skid row, and he showed it to Art. Art found the song's bleak imagery and message "too much," but Paul finally convinced him the song belonged on the album. Together with Wilson, they chose the others, including folk classics like "Peggy-O," "Go Tell It on the Mountain," and "Last Night I Had the Strangest Dream," by Ed McCurdy. Not surprisingly, the trio also chose Bob Dylan's "The Times They Are A-Changin'." Not only were Paul and Art big fans, but Wilson produced Dylan's albums, and Columbia liked to cross-promote its artists and music.

Still, Paul wanted more originals. In November he began struggling with a haunting melody which would become "The Sounds of Silence." Paul had toyed with the idea for this song for years. As a boy, he had played his guitar in the bathroom of his parent's house because he liked the echo effect the tiled room produced. He'd strummed and sung "Hello darkness, my old friend / I've come to talk with you again" a thousand times since then, but that was as far as the song had developed. Simon now focused on that slender thread, and, according to Garfunkel's description, on February 19, 1964, after months of anguish, the rest of the lyric "burst forth." The song "practically wrote itself."

The team needed more original songs for the album, and Paul, always a painfully slow writer, thought a change of scene might accelerate the process. So, in the spring of 1964, he left for Europe, where he was sure he would find inspiration to complete the songs for the album. He knew folk music was popular there, and he planned to support himself singing in clubs, living the life of an itinerant troubadour. In Paris, he met David McLausland who ran a folk club near London. McLausland offered "Paul Kane" a performance date, and he eagerly accepted it.

On the first night he performed at the Brentwood Folk Club, he met a dark-haired girl named Kathy, a secretary from a little town near Essex and a part-time ticket-taker at the club that night. Their attraction for each other was instant. Kathy became his friend, lover, and, some say, muse for the next two years.

While Paul was seeking inspiration in England, a British group had invaded America and taken it over amid a storm of ear-piercing teenage squeals. The Beatles had arrived. A few months before, showman Ed Sullivan had noticed screaming crowds of fans around the mop-haired group at an airport in England. Sullivan had never heard the group, but he recognized that they generated the same excitement Elvis did, and he booked them for his television program.

If 1956 could be dubbed "The Year of Elvis," 1964 was surely "The Year of the Beatles." The group registered six number-one hits, including "I Want to Hold Your Hand," "Can't Buy Me Love," and "Do You Want to Know a Secret?" On the year-end lists, they had three of the top ten singles and four of the top ten albums. They would win the Grammy for Best New Artists of the Year and would star in their own film, *A Hard Day's Night*.

Throughout the year, other British groups, including the nastier sounding Rolling Stones and Animals, would saturate the airwaves, but there was still plenty of room for diversity in the pop-music arena. Topping the charts were the Temptations' "The Way You Do the Things You Do," Roger Miller's "Dang Me," the Four Tops' "Baby I Need Your Loving," Roy Orbison's "It's Over," Al Hirt's "Java," and Bobby Vinton's "There, I've Said It Again." In addition, the Beach Boys, the Supremes, the New Christy Minstrels, and, of course, Elvis were still fixtures on the hit parade.

Shortly after Paul met Kathy, Tom Wilson summoned him back to New York, where pressure was mounting to produce the songs necessary to complete the album. Six months had passed since they'd signed the contract. The change of scene had freed Paul's mental logjam, and he brought back another original song, "Wednesday Morning, 3 A.M." Art contributed "Benedictus," an arrangement of a centuries-old Gregorian chant that he'd researched at libraries in New York. Simon also suggested "The Sun Is Burning," which he'd heard British composer Ian Campbell perform in England, and that gave them the twelve cuts they needed. They laid down the final tracks.

The music complete, they now had to make several other important decisions. For the album title, all quickly agreed on *Wednesday Morning, 3 A.M.* For the cover, they chose a photo of Art and Paul on a gritty New York City subway platform, staring somberly at the camera.

But both Simon and Garfunkel still had reservations about using their real names as performers. They knew enough about the business to realize that being Jewish wouldn't stop them from being recorded, but getting air time, especially in Middle America, might be another matter. Folk music was almost exclusively the domain of all-American types with WASP-sounding names like Woody Guthrie, Pete Seeger, the Kingston Trio, and the New Christy Minstrels. Even Bob Dylan, born Robert Zimmerman, had masked his Jewish heritage by adopting the name of the Welsh poet Dylan Thomas.

Producer Tom Wilson approached the issue from a different perspective. He said, "Why don't we just use Simon and Garfunkel?" Paul reacted strongly. "Hey, man, people might think we're comedians or something!" According to Wilson, Art and Paul feared anti-Semitism would hurt their chances for success. This self-protective attitude outraged the black producer: "What the hell is your music about anyway? You want to be the black man's brother, but you don't want to take any heat." He pointed out that Paul and Art were trying to capitalize on the social and political movements of the day. They wanted to deal with injustice and prejudice—but only in their songs. He was adamant. However, Paul and Art were just as strong-willed. They repeated their concern that people would not buy folk songs sung by two middle-class Jewish men from Queens. The argument raged. "Finally," according to Wilson, "Norman Adler, who was the executive vice president at Columbia Records, slammed his hand down on the table and said, 'Gentlemen, this is 1964. Simon and Garfunkel. Next case.'"

Paul and Art remained uncomfortable about the name change. "He Was My Brother" had been copyrighted under the name of Paul Kane and would be credited to Kane on the album, although all of Paul's other songs were listed as written by P. Simon. The "Benedictus" cut on the album carries the credit: "Arrangement by Simon and Garr."

At the height of Simon and Garfunkel's popularity in the late sixties, Paul commented on the touchy issue: "Our name is honest. I think if we ever lie, they [the fans] are going to catch us. I always thought it was a big shock to people when Bob Dylan's name turned out to be Bob Zimmerman. It was so important to people that he should be true." Coming from a man who employed a series of pseudonyms and would use his own name only because of an executive order by a record company, the criticism seems rather disingenuous.

Ironically, Columbia's decision to be honest about the duo's ethnicity put Simon and Garfunkel in the forefront of making "Jewishness" not only acceptable but desirable in the popular culture of the late sixties. The subsequent success of Dustin Hoffman, Richard Benjamin, Barbra Streisand, and George Segal confirmed this trend.

With the name Simon and Garfunkel finally official, the "new" recording pair was officially launched. All the tracks for their album were completed, and master recording would take place that summer. Meanwhile, "Simon and Garfunkel," the act, was

booked into Gerde's to gain some exposure for the songs scheduled to be released later that year. Louis Bass, a doorman at the
club, remembers the 1964 premiere performance of "The Sounds
of Silence." "It was the first time they tested it publicly. At that
time, I never thought they would make it. They didn't sound as
good as some of the other acts. But that night at the club was some
sort of college reunion, so they went over well because it was their
friends."

On the nights audiences were not made up of their friends,
Paul's new songs weren't always well received. It wasn't the ethnic
sound of their names, but rather their suburban, clean-cut image
that was jarring to folk-club audiences. The rather cerebral
content of their lyrics, combined with their collegiate appearance,
set them apart from traditional folk artists of the mid-sixties.

"Simon and Artie were uptown guys, Queens guys...I was
struck by a kind of Mickey Mouse, timid, contrived side," noted
Robert Shelton, who covered the folk scene for the *New York
Times*. "And of course through Dylan, [Dave] Van Ronk, all those
guys, what was really being venerated was...a rough, natural,
dirty sound." Shelton knew Simon and Garfunkel from their
earliest days as folk performers. According to him, "They sounded
very suburban. Simon always struck me as a suburban type of
Dylan."

Shelton wasn't the only critic to compare Simon with Dylan and
to fault him as a bland imitation of the real thing. Paul was stung
by the criticism. He respected Dylan's lyric genius, but in later
years he thought critics unfairly ignored his own superior musi-
cianship in the comparisons.

With Art busy at school and no major bookings until the
album's release, Paul headed back to England. Kathy was waiting
there, and he wouldn't have to cope with as many annoying
references to Bob Dylan. He took a flat in Hampstead, a London
suburb, and continued his solo career as Paul Kane. It was almost
summer, and Art had promised to join Paul and Kathy as soon as
his semester was over. However, due to his heavy class schedule, he
could only manage a brief vacation that summer. Art wrote to
Paul about possible bookings but cautioned, "no singing in
streets."

While Paul and Art anticipated a summer of fun in Europe,
civil-rights workers in America regarded the coming months as a

pivotal time in the struggle for human rights. The Student Nonviolent Coordinating Committee (SNCC), an organization made up of black college students, narrowly voted to actively recruit and enlist white, northern college students to aid in their battle against racism. They and the Congress on Racial Equality (CORE) trained thousands of idealistic middle-class students in the techniques of nonviolence and bused them south to begin an intensive voter registration drive.

The movement focused its efforts in Mississippi, a state that epitomized the worst of the nation's racial sins. If SNCC could topple the racist political monopoly in Mississippi by registering black voters, its leaders reasoned the rest of the South would follow suit.

Tensions escalated, and the issue would soon inflame the country. Up to this time Paul and Art were too busy with their careers to take much notice of the ominous developments, but the situation would soon gain Simon's full attention.

In June 1964, Simon's former college classmate Andrew Goodman was one of three men slain near Philadelphia, Mississippi, during a voter registration drive. Paul later described his reaction: "I was in the American Express office in Paris. I had to walk outside. I was going to throw up. I felt dizzy. I was so panicked, so frightened, I couldn't actually believe that anybody I knew was dead."

Paul Simon has led people to believe he wrote "He Was My Brother" after Goodman's death. Regarding Goodman's murder, he has been directly quoted, "It hit me really hard. And that's when I wrote, I guess, my first serious song, "He Was My Brother."

In fact, Paul had already released the song in England on the Oriole label under the name Paul Kane, and it had become a staple of his folk-club repertoire. "He Was My Brother" was also the song which first caught the attention of producer Tom Wilson in the fall of 1963. Paul may have rewritten the lyric later for Goodman. The Columbia album cut, which would not be released until the fall in the States, says, "This town's gonna be your buryin' place," but in later versions of the song the line reads "Mississippi's gonna be your buryin' place."

Paul kept up a busy pace playing folk clubs and appearing at the Edinburgh and Cambridge folk festivals. Between classes, Garfunkel, too, was working as a solo act in New York clubs, singing Paul's songs and other folk ballads. He finally finished the year at Columbia University, and since he was available in New York, he oversaw the album's master recording. He battled with record executives to keep a harmonica accompaniment to "He Was My Brother," but lost the fight. The song was released with a simple guitar background in the classic folk mode.

As soon as school was over, Art met Paul in Paris, and for a while they rented motor scooters and became carefree tourists. It was the fulfillment of every middle-class collegian's dream: to have the time and money to explore Europe with a best friend. They shared expectations for a future brimming with creative endeavors, public recognition, and financial reward. And their personal friendship continued to deepen.

When Paul returned to England, Art tagged along. One night Simon got a call from the manager of London's Flamingo Club. He said his headline act hadn't shown up, and he asked Paul to go on instead. Paul seized the opportunity to try out their new material, including "The Sounds of Silence." He went on as a solo, and when the audience responded enthusiastically, he called Art up to the stage. The two sang "Benedictus," introducing it as another cut on their upcoming album. The audience was spellbound by the unique Simon and Garfunkel harmony.

As September approached, Art prepared to return to classes in New York. Paul told friends that he, too, would return to the States for the album's debut. To new friend Judith Piepe, he promised: "I'll be back in London for a few weeks in January." Judith had seen Simon perform at the Flamingo Club and wanted to further his career in England. She started to beg producers at BBC Radio to listen to Paul Simon's songs.

Paul brought Kathy with him back to the States for a long, cross-country car trip that fall. To earn some traveling money, he hoped to perform in folk clubs along the way where he would sing his own compositions but, to satisfy his audiences, also include songs associated with Bob Dylan, Tom Paxton, the Everly Brothers, and Woody Guthrie. This tour became the inspiration for his hit song "America."

Meanwhile, the album *Wednesday Morning, 3 A.M.* was released that October. It was a slick package that Columbia promoted as "exciting new sounds in the folk tradition." With a major record company release, Art and Paul braced for what they expected would be an onslaught of major club bookings and worried about squeezing time for appearances from Garfunkel's busy schedule at Columbia. He had again changed majors, this time from architecture to art history, and had scheduled a heavy class load.

Unfortunately, Simon and Garfunkel, the new Columbia recording artists, created no major stir among folk-music fans either in person or on record. In fact, the response to the album was less than enthusiastic. Critics and radio station programmers alike were lukewarm, and response from the record-buying public was almost nonexistent.

This second breakthrough into "the big time," years after their success with "Hey, Schoolgirl," seemed to be fizzling fast. Instead of increasing, club bookings fell off. Paul and Art consoled themselves with the usual rationalizations: It would take awhile for the songs to be heard, and even longer for word-of-mouth praise to affect album sales. But nothing happened.

Disappointed, Paul Simon returned to England where there was still some faint hope for his solo career. Judith Piepe had made good on her promise to sell him to the BBC. In January, Simon went to a recording studio there and taped twelve of his own songs for replay on the radio.

Then Paul, still billing himself as Paul Kane, booked himself into clubs all over England, while Judith tried to persuade the BBC to broadcast the new recordings. While Piepe worked on his behalf in London, Paul traveled, usually by train, to many of Britain's large cities. He was waiting in the Widnes railway station near Liverpool, anxious to get back to Kathy, when the idea for "Homeward Bound" first struck him. As always, he began with a simple, yet powerful, emotional moment—and played with the concept in his mind. Once the idea was firmly set, he spent months developing the song's story and shaping the melody. Paul continued to polish the song as he followed the English folk-club circuit.

While Simon was making some headway in Britain, the career of Simon and Garfunkel appeared to be going nowhere in the States. The album had sold only three thousand copies, a dismal showing. By now, there was no doubt Paul Simon again thought of himself as a solo act. The lyrics to "Homeward Bound" clearly defined his current self-image: "A poet and a one-man band."

Simon's lyrics from this period have a distinctive poetic quality and usually include a string of clear, evocative images. Since audiences around the world were, by now, already familiar with the rough poetry of Dylan, comparisons continued to follow him. Paul has always been uncomfortable with the description of himself as a poet and with comparisons to Dylan on any level: "The job of a folksinger in those days was to be Bob Dylan. You had to be a poet. That's what they wanted. And I thought that was a drag." But Simon was always very savvy about meeting the demands of the public, and he tried to fulfill their expectations.

Finally Judith Piepe's persistence paid off at the BBC. She squeezed Paul's songs into a brief slot in the religious programming schedule and over a two-week time span began to get some response. A small controversy over one of Simon's songs, "A Church Is Burning," a cautionary tale about the evils of the Ku Klux Klan, garnered some valuable publicity. The head of religious broadcasting didn't understand the symbolism of the lyrics and seemed horrified at the image of a burning church. The flap sparked enough interest in Simon's lyrics to warrant a British book, *The Religious Content of Simon's Songs*.

The BBC soon began to get letters from listeners regarding many of Paul's songs. People wanted to know where they could find recordings of his music. Fortunately for Simon, Columbia Records had just opened a branch in London and was looking for local performers to fill out their list. In May 1965, since Paul was still technically a Columbia-label artist, they somewhat grudgingly took up an option. Paul recorded his first solo album, *The Paul Simon Songbook*.

The album included "He Was My Brother" and "The Sounds of Silence." (Curiously, the title is "The Sounds of Silence," but the lyric is always sung as "the sound of silence.") On this album Paul introduced "I Am a Rock," "April Come She Will," "A Most Peculiar Man," and "Kathy's Song," written for his friend and lover. Kathy would also appear on the album cover, and Simon loved it: "This was a kick. For a twenty-four-year-old to have his own album with his girlfriend on the cover."

The album was completed in about an hour with only one microphone; each song was done in one take. The production cost amounted to approximately three hundred dollars. The low-budget *Songbook* renewed Paul's hopes for a recording career, this time as a solo performer.

Paul not only worked as a performer, he also earned money as a record producer and songwriter. He produced an album for Jackson Frank and collaborated with performer-composer Bruce Woodley, a member of the Australian group, the Seekers.

Such artistic collaboration has characterized Paul Simon's approach to music throughout his career. He learned through his working relationship with Art that a happy amalgam of taste and talent can often produce stronger, more interesting music than a single vision.

Around this time, Paul again indulged himself in his penchant for flashy cars when he bought a new Sunbeam convertible. Seeing him in this fancy sports car rankled some of his English folk-music associates. His ascetic attitudes were well known: "All I need is somewhere to eat and sleep and enough money to buy guitar strings. I haven't any real need for money."

Right or wrong, his reputation for arrogance, as well as feistiness, grew when he appeared on British television's popular variety program "Ready, Set, Go" in July of 1965. Because of time restraints, Simon had agreed to a shortened version of "I Am a Rock" so that another, more popular performer, P. J. Proby, could sing his current hit. Then Paul, convinced that his song was better, sang the full version of "I Am a Rock." Since the show was live, the angry producers were then forced to cut Proby's performance in mid-lyric.

Many British club owners and fans had already witnessed Simon's displays of artistic temperament. One British folk-club manager, Tony Molyneux, remembers, "I wasn't very impressed with his songs, his patter, or his seeming arrogance. I thought he was rather a conceited man, which came over in his songs. We had a chance to book him, and we turned him down."

But Paul found plenty of work in Britain. Years later he summed up this period of his life: "I felt perfectly in sync with myself. I was being paid what I deserved—about twenty pounds [then approximately sixty dollars U.S.]—and that was good for a kid. I had lots of friends. I was consciously aware that I was ecstatically happy. I'm sure that those will be the purest, happiest days of my life."

Art visited England again in the summer of 1965 and stayed with Paul at the apartment of his pal Judith Piepe, in the East End. Art studied the guitar while he and Paul worked on some new songs, including an arrangement of a classic English folk ballad, "Scarborough Fair." Their album, a total dud in America, hadn't even been issued in England, so there was little interest in Simon and Garfunkel in the folk clubs. Piepe finally managed to book a concert for the team. It was an unlikely audience for the delicate, sensitive sounds of two suburbanite American folksingers—Brixton Prison.

The career of Simon and Garfunkel seemed to be dead in the water. Art had decided to stay in school. His new academic interest was mathematics, and he had enrolled in a Ph.D. program at Columbia. The team of Simon and Garfunkel was disbanded, according to Clive Davis, then a Columbia Records executive. Paul was booked on a solo European tour.

However, the recording career of Simon and Garfunkel was not quite over. That spring in Boston, something odd had happened with one of their songs. A deejay on WBZ Radio found a cut he liked on the almost-forgotten *Wednesday Morning, 3 A.M.* album. He scheduled it often. The more he played "The Sounds of Silence," the more his listeners asked to hear it. His station was within range of tens of thousands of college students from Harvard, Tufts, MIT, Boston College, Wellesley, Emerson College, Boston University, Northeastern, and a dozen smaller schools. "The Sounds of Silence," with its painfully self-aware evocation of loneliness and alienation, struck a sympathetic chord with this audience. Until Simon and Garfunkel came along, no one had voiced these emotions or concerns quite so eloquently.

The unusual flurry of interest prompted the local Columbia promotions man to call Tom Wilson. Other reports indicated the song was getting airplay on a station in Cocoa Beach, Florida, a favorite vacation destination for many college students. The producer sensed that with some tinkering he might have a hit on his hands.

On June 15, 1965, Tom Wilson sat in on a Columbia studio session with Bob Dylan, who was working on "Like a Rolling Stone" with an electronic backup band. After Dylan had finished, using that same band, Wilson overdubbed bass, electric guitar, and drums onto the original track of "The Sounds of Silence," beefing it up with a rock beat.

Still in Europe, Paul and Art were unaware of the revision or the release of the single. Art later confirmed that Wilson never tried to contact them in Europe to ask for permission or advice. Wilson said, "You could do pretty much what you wanted with Paul and Artie in those days." Only after Art had returned to New York for the fall semester did Wilson call him into the studio to listen to the altered version. Art remembered, "I thought it was fair."

Columbia released the single of "The Sounds of Silence" for a new audience. It wasn't a folk song. It wasn't rock 'n' roll. It was folk-rock and appealed to both camps. With an extra push from the promotion department, "The Sounds of Silence" soon began to generate excitement around the country. Garfunkel later credited Wilson with changing the direction of Simon and Garfunkel from folk to folk-rock/pop.

While working in Denmark, Paul casually picked up a copy of *Cash Box*, a record industry trade paper, and found to his astonishment that "The Sounds of Silence" was among the top one hundred singles.

Al Stewart, a London pal of Paul's, recalled, "Tom Wilson mailed a copy of the new 'Sounds of Silence' to Simon, who was horrified when he first heard it. In fact, when you listen to that version, you can hear the rhythm section slow down at one point so that Paul and Artie's voices can catch up. The single went in at something like eighty-six, climbed to the thirties in the second week, and then Columbia rang Paul to say 'It's going to be number one.'"

Simon may have been horrified at what Wilson had done to the song, but he certainly was gratified when the single made it to the top of the charts. After nine years of struggle, it had all happened so fast neither Art nor Paul was prepared for success.

Paul has confirmed: "It was weird. I had come back to New York, and I was staying in my old room at my parents' house. Artie was living at his parents' house, too. I remember Artie and I were sitting there in my car, parked on a street in Queens, and the announcer said, 'Number one, Simon and Garfunkel.' And Artie said to me, 'That Simon and Garfunkel, they must be having a great time.' Because there we were on a street corner in Queens, smoking a joint. We didn't know what to do with ourselves."

4

Paul Simon and Art Garfunkel may not have known what to do with success, but by December 1965, Columbia Records was already in high gear to promote its new folk stars.

As with many show-business breakthroughs, popular success had been more a matter of luck than talent. Clive Davis summed it up: "If that disc jockey hadn't experimented with a song from an unknown year-old album, 'Simon and Garfunkel' probably would not exist today in music."

At the beginning of 1965 Paul Simon and Art Garfunkel had abandoned their dual career, but by the time the year drew to a close, they found themselves together once again, a step away from stardom. In January 1966 "The Sounds of Silence" zoomed to number one—for one week. It was overtaken the next week by the Beatles' new single, "We Can Work It Out," and the two singles locked into a seesaw battle for the top spot over the next several weeks.

The success of "The Sounds of Silence" signaled the existence of a vast, virtually untapped, record-buying audience. Huge numbers of affluent, white, middle-class college students, the leading edge of the baby boom, began to come of age, and national demographics skewed dramatically toward a "youth movement" that would soon dominate American society.

The electrified version of "The Sounds of Silence"— a fusion of rock and folk styles which expressed thoughts and emotions— represented the key to popular success that Simon and Garfunkel had been searching for since their boyhood days in Queens. The song described the nature of alienation and loneliness—important themes to a generation of self-absorbed young college students. Twenty-five years after it was written, its lyrics may seem precious, but the song still retains the mystery and emotional truth listeners have always found so appealing.

Simon's treatment of alienation and his subsequent analyses of loneliness, youthful rebellion, hypocrisy, materialism, and social injustice were the result of years of wrestling with these issues. In an incredible stroke of timing and luck, Paul Simon found a huge audience eager to share his own postadolescent concerns. As Paul later remembered, "It just happened that my pretensions became very popular and people bought them."

Simon and Garfunkel packaged elliptical—and sometimes subversive—emotional messages in sweet harmonies, and wrapped them in a squeaky-clean suburban image even parents could relate to. It promised to be a potent formula for commercial success.

The team was rushed into the studio to record its second album, which was called in a slight variant *Sounds of Silence*. Columbia wanted the album out as soon as possible to capitalize on the success of the title song. For the first time, Paul and Art would have to work under the extreme pressure of deadlines and contend with more interference from executives at Columbia.

No longer would they have the easy-going Tom Wilson as their producer. Wilson had fallen into disfavor, perhaps because the label knew he was being wooed by MGM Records. His top performers, including Bob Dylan, had been given to another producer, Bob Johnston. Columbia also assigned Simon and Garfunkel to Johnston, and the teaming did not sit well from the start. Egos clashed, but there was no time to argue, since the team had only three weeks to complete the album.

Luckily, Paul had the material ready. The songs not only were written, but Simon had thoroughly tested them in his days as a solo performer in England, an important advantage since there was no time to debate song selection. Paul was also trying to deal with the pressure of adjusting to being part of a team again. He had gotten used to answering to no one for his artistic decisions. But things were different now. He recognized that compromises had to be made. He didn't like it, but found it hard to argue because his solo album, *The Paul Simon Songbook*, had been a complete failure in England (in fact, it would soon be withdrawn from the market). Simon and Garfunkel's versions of the same material would give his songs a second chance. The team's harmonies and folk-rock rhythms had made his music a hit, and he realized once again that, without Art Garfunkel and the intervention of Tom Wilson, Paul Simon wouldn't have gotten this far. In addition, his songs now had a powerful company behind them to guarantee proper promotion of the new album. Both Art and Paul were willing to make the artistic trade-offs.

During those few hectic weeks, the team tried frantically to lay down tracks wherever a studio could be booked on short notice. They recorded in New York, Los Angeles, and Nashville, and the strain of working in different studios with unfamiliar equipment and engineers began to show. Art explained, "It was a case of business trying to make the music conform to the situation." Engineer Roy Halee couldn't make the session in Nashville, and the tracks they made without him for "I Am a Rock" didn't satisfy Paul. In spite of the pressure, they decided to rerecord the song with Halee. Although they knew they should look to their producer, Johnston, for direction, they realized that only Halee could produce precisely the sounds they wanted.

From Paul's English solo album, they took "I Am a Rock," "A Most Peculiar Man," "April Come She Will," and "Leaves That Are Green," giving them the full studio treatment. The two got their first real taste of working with the finest studio musicians in the business. Bob Johnston's old friend Joe South came from Atlanta to play backup on "Homeward Bound," and Paul Griffin played piano. Glen Campbell played guitar on "Blessed."

Only "Kathy's Song" was kept as Paul had originally conceived it—a solo with a simple guitar accompaniment. Four new Simon songs, previously unrecorded, were used as well. For the final selection on the album, Paul insisted on the guitar instrumental "Anji" by Davy Graham. Paul had heard the melody in England and had become obsessed with it. Some contended he chose the song because he wanted to help British composer-guitarist Graham, who was in desperate need of royalties.

As if the pressure of recording the album weren't enough, Columbia insisted on another song for a single release, since it was critical to follow up one hit single with another as fast as possible. As both Paul and Art knew from their experience as Tom and Jerry, it was impossible to establish a career with "one-shots"—only a series of hit records could ensure lasting success.

Paul and Art had been working on the close harmonies for "Homeward Bound," so the song was nearly ready to record. Harmony, which became the team's trademark, was much harder to come by in their other working relationships. Columbia insisted Bob Johnston work closely with Paul and Art on "Homeward Bound." While Johnston is often credited with solidifying Simon and Garfunkel's success, Paul did not get along with his producer, and he seldom hesitated to show his disdain: "Johnston? As a producer? He was only there to find out who wanted a chicken sandwich."

In late January 1966, the new single "Homeward Bound" was released. Paul's longing for home and Kathy in an English railway station touched a universal nerve in America. Two months later, it peaked at number five on the charts. In February, *Sounds of Silence* was released and quickly gathered steam. *Wednesday Morning, 3 A.M.* was reissued and promoted anew. By March it had hit number thirty on the album charts, while *Sounds of Silence* rose to number twenty-one.

In a few short months, Simon and Garfunkel became the voice of a generation. Music critic Ralph Gelason described an early Simon and Garfunkel concert this way: "It was starkly simple, almost painfully direct, and removed from all show-business clichés, with the songs themselves driving deeply and poetically into the very basis of contemporary problems." In spite of a tendency toward adolescent angst, Simon and Garfunkel's vision of the world seemed truthful and relevant. The audience was hungry for more.

With the songs on *Sounds of Silence*, Paul had begun what would become his lifelong meditation on alienation. Critics quickly tagged him a master of the theme. When interviewers noticed he wrote a lot about alienation, his commercial savvy allowed him to exploit his own youthful interest in the subject.

Paul remembered, "They said, 'Alienation seems to be your big theme.' And I proceeded to write more about alienation. And it was a self-fulfilling prophecy, so I wrote alienation songs."

Simon took the themes of isolation and despair to the limit on the second album when he twice dealt with suicide, in "Richard Cory," and again in the somber "A Most Peculiar Man." The last song on side two is "I Am a Rock," a fierce declaration of survival which tempers the two previous morose meditations.

Paul's songs of alienation were rapidly defining Simon and Garfunkel's unique niche in the marketplace. But they knew it would also take practical skills to stay on top once they got there. Paul said, "What separated us from the rest of the folkies, and a fact that was completely ignored, was that we had had experience in the recording studio."

Their early experience in the music business had toughened them professionally. Paul noted, "We knew about the studio, we knew about sounds, textures, voices, overdubbing. We really came out of the rock 'n' roll of the fifties, although the music we were singing was the folk-rock of the early sixties. But I think that's why we had the hits."

The whirlwind of activity did take an emotional toll, and Art seemed better equipped to deal with the rapid changes than Paul. Art had again enrolled at Columbia and was determined to continue with graduate school. He got an apartment near the school and maintained his circle of close friends and family. His life-style was hectic, but he managed to organize his schedule to accommodate recording dates, concert performances, and school-work. With the exception of newfound fame, his life seemed in control.

It wasn't as easy for Paul. He had been living in England, where he thrived on the easy-going life-style of the folk-club circuit. When he returned to New York on the heels of a hit record, he admitted, "I became very insecure. I didn't know what to do with myself. I had never even lived in Manhattan. I'd been washed away from the friends I had before the success. The success was pushing me into money and places I wasn't prepared to deal with. I didn't know who to be friends with or where to live or where to go." It seemed that his love affair with Kathy was now over, although it would continue to provide material for song lyrics in later years.

Paul found an apartment on the East Side and saw Art almost

daily. On a typical evening, they visited clubs to see other new performers, or ended up in one of their favorite cheap restaurants for a burger, before they headed back to Paul's to listen to music on the stereo or to the new tune Paul was working on. They talked, listened, sang, smoked dope sometimes, and talked some more.

They recognized that music was the central focus of both their lives and that the relationship they had with each other was more important than any other. There wasn't much room for women amid the hustle of supporting and promoting their hit albums and singles.

Often the music seemed the least important component of success: There were photo sessions and endless meetings with publicists, agents, and lawyers, and, of course, a string of record executives to cope with. They began to realize they needed someone to look after their interests, so they started searching for a personal manager. Meanwhile, Columbia Records and Simon and Garfunkel's agents at the William Morris talent agency were busy arranging live appearances. The duo was often bunched together with several other popular but disparate acts, as was the custom, and Art grew to hate the way they were being showcased. The last straw came at a concert where they were sandwiched in among the Four Seasons, the Yardbirds, Mitch Ryder, Chuck Berry, and Lou Christie. They knew their delicate sound needed a special kind of presentation and would be lost among the other, more raucous rock 'n' roll performers.

They flexed their muscle and demanded new performance criteria. They hired Mort Lewis, a savvy show-business manager who handled only top acts, and instructed him to solve the concert format problem.

Lewis recognized the duo's symbiotic relationship with students and immediately limited their appearances to college campuses, where songs of alienation and isolation were welcome, and where sympathetic reviewers breathlessly spread Simon and Garfunkel's fame. Lewis thought it was a mistake to bury the team's clean-cut, buttoned-down image by booking them into traditional night-clubs, so he limited appearances to the respectful, hushed collegiate crowd, which strained to hear every meaningful word. In addition, the weekend college dates interfered less with Art's school schedule.

Columbia Records was also eager to book Simon and Garfunkel

on television, but Lewis wisely limited appearances to a select few, like "The Kraft Music Hall" and NBC's popular "Hullabaloo," which, in 1966, was the principal showcase for the introduction of new musical talent.

Lewis's brilliant strategy of underexposure meshed perfectly with the aloof, faintly mysterious image the duo had established for itself. Columbia's next single release from *Sounds of Silence,* "I Am a Rock," further emphasized the aura of rebellious outsiders that hovered around the duo's unsmiling image. In June 1966, the song rose to number three.

The somewhat petulant tone of "I Am a Rock" may have been a sign of the pressure Paul felt to submit immature work to feed the voracious appetite of the music business. Even Paul acknowledges the song's failings. He thought, "Oh, man, I can't be this sick!"

But the song became the third straight Simon and Garfunkel hit. Both Art and Paul began to feel the turmoil subside as the frenetic race to solidify their position in the business finally ended. Three hits in a row proved that their success was no fluke. They could, seemingly at will, duplicate and even surpass their last hit.

Meanwhile, other groups had begun to record Paul Simon's songs. "Red Rubber Ball," which Paul coauthored with Bruce Woodley while in England, was a hit for the group Cyrkle both in the United States and in Great Britain. The Bachelors' version of "The Sounds of Silence"— not Simon and Garfunkel's—scored a bit hit in England. But Paul and Art finally topped the English charts with their renditions of "Homeward Bound" and "I Am a Rock."

Now audiences overseas demanded to see Simon and Garfunkel in concert. Lewis and Columbia organized a European tour for June and July of 1966. Before the tour began, Paul and Art found time to get into a studio to lay down tracks for their next single. The string of hits had bolstered their confidence, and they approached the recording with cocky assurance. Paul was sure the song he had been working on was his best ever.

"The Dangling Conversation" evolved from a memory of a girl Paul once knew. Images of the relationship had come flooding back to Paul as he sat alone on the floor of his bathroom—his favorite songwriting space. It was dark, and as he listened to the faucet drip, he recalled the hours he and his lover had spent reading the poetry of Emily Dickinson and Robert Frost. He wrote, "We note our place with bookmarkers / That measure what we've lost."

The lines lodged in his mind but developed no further until a few months later, when, on a Jamaican vacation, he read Saul Bellow's novel *Dangling Man,* and the word "dangling" stuck with him. The fragmentary moments finally came together one afternoon as he drove through upstate New York. The bits and pieces shaped themselves into a story. Two people sit in the late afternoon sunlight. One is working a crossword puzzle. The other reads the *New York Times,* and they are both contemplating the same unhappy thought: They have come to the end of their relationship and have nothing more to say to each other. Paul captured the delicate and painful feeling of emotional dislocation in the lines: "Yes we speak of things that matter / With words that must be said / Can analysis be worthwhile? / Is the theater really dead?"* Within a spare framework of elliptical images he managed to communicate a universal emotional experience instantly recognizable to his listeners.

Paul took "The Dangling Conversation" to Art. The two worked out the harmony, and within a few hours it was ready to record. The song developed so rapidly because at this point the two were in perfect sync personally and professionally. With the single goal of making Simon and Garfunkel even more successful, they couldn't afford ego problems. Art was the only one Paul trusted to give an honest evaluation of his work, and when Art liked a song Paul's spirits soared. The relationship had developed an unspoken but rigid pattern of advice and consent. As always, Art passively waited until Paul presented his ideas, and then the two would come to terms. Each had equal veto power, and that kept the partnership delicately balanced.

In March 1966, the Simon and Garfunkel team entered a studio to begin work on the song. A witness to the recording, Paul's brother Eddie, said it was a typical Simon and Garfunkel session. Paul laid down track after track in the studio while Art remained in the glass booth. Art pushed hard for perfection and rejected take after take, suggested nuances, asked for changes in pitch, intonation, and rhythm. Eddie, who had observed the two men for years, described the relationship in terms of teamwork: "Paul

* "The Dangling Conversation" © 1966 by Paul Simon

works a record like a pitcher who's working a batter. And Artie's like the smart catcher who knows just what to call."

The veteran Columbia engineer Roy Halee, who by now had become an integral part of the team, entered the creative mix to offer his suggestions, and the collaborative process became more complex. Often Paul wound up outvoted on issues, usually those related to technical purity. Paul would argue for a particular take because he thought it had the right emotional feel, while Art and Roy would overrule him in favor of a cleaner or more precise take. In these early days, the process seemed to be a positive arrangement. But unconsciously, Paul's old, competitive instincts stirred, and he began to keep score.

"The Dangling Conversation" was released in July and, to everyone's surprise, didn't do nearly as well as Simon and Garfunkel's previous three songs. Paul was particularly upset since he had been so certain it was the best he had to offer.

He later said of it, "Why it wasn't a big hit is hard to know. It probably wasn't as good a song. It was too heavy." Even though the song didn't do quite as well as the other three singles, it did reach number twenty-three on the charts. Simon and Garfunkel's amazing track record made their own expectations impossibly high.

They resumed their busy concert schedule and, although they had had three successive hit songs, were still occasionally booked as an opening act. In June of 1966 Simon and Garfunkel opened for the reigning royal family of rock, the Mamas and the Papas, at a concert in Los Angeles. The Mamas and the Papas—John Phillips, Denny Doherty, Cass Elliot, and Michelle Gilliam, who married John and became Michelle Phillips—had had a big hit earlier in the year with "California Dreamin'," the quintessential anthem of the laid-back, California life-style. They followed it with "Monday, Monday" and "I Saw Her Again." Their trademark mellow vision of life and love was similar to that of the immensely popular Lovin' Spoonful, but their soaring, pure harmonies were matched only by those of Simon and Garfunkel. John Phillips's songs were popular but ultimately lacked Simon's lyric gift, which blended melody, voice, and meaning.

Because Simon and Garfunkel's string of hits had finally established them as genuine stars, it was inevitable that their past life as teenage rock 'n' rollers Tom and Jerry would come back to haunt them. Pickwick Records obtained several of the tracks they had made as struggling teenagers and released a quickie album to exploit their newfound success. Deceptively called *Simon and Garfunkel,* the album sported a recent color photo of the duo in keeping with their carefully crafted current image as offbeat, faintly intellectual types. The cover shows the pair ready to mount the stairs to an airplane. Paul, wearing a cape, stands next to Art, who holds a book in his hand. Both glare sullenly at the camera.

Although the liner notes trumpeted the album as "a generous sampling of the two stars of tomorrow who are the talk of the record world today," no mention was made of the fact that the songs were recorded eight years earlier and that the duo's style of music had changed dramatically. There was also no mention of Tom and Jerry.

Furious at Pickwick's obvious misrepresentation, they were powerless to stop the album's sale since the tracks had been legally sold. Paul's old employer, E. B. Marks, controlled the publishing rights to several of his old songs and also tried to capitalize on the new Simon and Garfunkel popularity. Marks released a promotional, one-sided demo recording Paul had done as Paul Kane and publicized it as a Paul Simon album. The album contained early versions of "He Was My Brother," "Bleecker Street," "Carlos Dominguez," "Benedictus," and "This Side of a Hill."

The rip-off albums created a brief reminder of the duo's rock 'n' roll past, but true folk believers quickly forgave them, and the albums disappeared quickly. Through the years, other attempts to resurrect the old sounds prompted Paul and Art to incorporate versions of their teenage tunes into performances to give the audience a laugh.

Meanwhile, "The Sounds of Silence" filled the airwaves and soon caught the attention of theater and film director Mike Nichols, who needed a soundtrack for his new movie, *The Graduate.* Nichols's first motion picture had been an ambitious adaptation of playwright Edward Albee's *Who's Afraid of Virginia Woolf?,* which starred Elizabeth Taylor and Richard Burton. The somber exploration of marital strife did surprisingly well at the box office. This time, Nichols would use his satiric comic skills to explore contemporary American values. Humorist Buck Henry was hired to turn the Charles Webb novel into a film script.

The plot of *The Graduate* concerns the adventures of young

Benjamin Braddock, a college graduate who returns to his upscale California home to ponder his future. Benjamin looks to the adults around him for guidance but finds only materialism, venality, and lust—the latter appearing in the seductive form of one of his parents' best friends, Mrs. Robinson. The film's theme—youth's alienation from the values of an older generation—was perfectly in tune with the concerns of a younger generation of moviegoers. Nichols saw Simon and Garfunkel's music as a perfect match for the material.

Paul and Art had recently returned from a European tour which was warmly received, especially in England, where Paul's work was familiar. Barely a year had passed since his last appearance on the English folk-club circuit, and several of the songs he had sung as a solo act made it to the top of the British charts as Simon and Garfunkel hits.

When they returned to the States, Mort Lewis told them Nichols wanted to talk to them about a soundtrack for *The Graduate*. They both liked the idea of branching out into films, and Columbia Records was thrilled at the prospect of vastly increased exposure for their young stars. Nichols made it clear that deadlines in the film business were much more stringent than in the recording industry. Not only would Paul be required to write to the specific needs of the film story line, he would have to do it on time. The ego boost of writing for Mike Nichols dislodged any initial misgivings and they signed the contract.

The soundtrack wasn't due for several months, so Paul and Art squeezed in recording sessions for their next album. Then they faced a mounting list of concert dates. With so many demands, there wasn't much time for a social life.

Both Simon and Garfunkel enjoyed the company of Mort Lewis and saw him and his wife, Peggy, frequently. But work was the real center of their lives. Art lamented, "We work constantly. All I think about is records." But he found the work exhilarating and added, "The best thing about us is the material."

With several solid hits behind them, they now had real artistic clout. Neither of them had even been present for the final mix of the *Sounds of Silence* album, and they both vowed not to repeat this mistake. On the new album, *Parsley, Sage, Rosemary and Thyme*, they intended to use every ounce of their hard-won creative control. They were pleased with the lush string sounds on

"The Dangling Conversation" and looked forward to experimenting with other unusual arrangements and accompaniments.

The new attitude was not lost on Columbia, but record executives could only stand by helplessly and watch the hours turn into days and months as production costs mounted. Executives were heard muttering in the hallways, "Boy, you guys really take a lot of time," as they shot nervous glances at the time sheets. The album would eventually cost in the neighborhood of thirty thousand dollars, an unheard-of sum for such deceptively simple music.What Columbia hadn't really considered was that Simon and Garfunkel wasn't a performance group in the classic sense. Unlike an act that polished material night after night in performances and brought it into the studio as a finished product, Paul and Art only outlined vocals, harmonies, and guitar accompaniments before they entered the studio. Simon's music wasn't simple. Finding just the right combination of lyric and melody was an exploratory process. The two often adapted and rewrote on the spot; then the musicians had to learn and practice the changes and additions. New ideas about tempo, rhythm, or phrasing sometimes bubbled up from the musicians, from the engineer Roy Halee, or from the work itself.

The duo pushed the technical limits of the studio as well, making demands few other Columbia artists had the know-how to request. The solid base of expertise they'd acquired as demo-song hucksters paid off. For example, they insisted that *Parsley, Sage, Rosemary and Thyme* be recorded using the latest eight-track technology—meaning they would require eight separate tracks to capture the sounds they wanted. Simon and Garfunkel then mixed the tracks together, carefully shaping and balancing every sound to create the total effect they so single-mindedly sought. They took on the role of sound engineer and chatted knowledgeably in the arcane language of "punching in" and "laying down tracks."

It was unlike any previous production experience Columbia had encountered. The executives, though worried, gave the team all they asked for. Simon and Garfunkel luxuriated in the lavish expenditures of time and money. They were "studio artists," and, as Art Garfunkel would later say, paraphrasing Orson Welles, "The studio became the biggest toy a boy could ever have."

Paul drew the material for *Parsley, Sage, Rosemary and Thyme* from his shrinking cache of polished songs. Most, including the title cut, "Scarborough Fair/Canticle" (commonly known as "Parsley, Sage, Rosemary and Thyme"), dated from his days in England. He and Art loved the delicate structure of the old English folk song and reworked it, finding within it the tensile strength to bear a bold antiwar message. "Cloudy" captures a delightful, fleeting, uncertain mood conveyed through literary allusions ranging from Tolstoy to Tinkerbell. "A Poem on the Underground Wall" and "The Big Bright Green Pleasure Machine" have as a common subject the seductive power of advertising and its negative effect on society, but they are in sharply contrasting moods.

"A Simple Desultory Philippic" is a satire, a humorous tip of the cap to Paul's archrival, Bob Dylan, written in a perfect imitation of Dylan's signature staccato style. Paul wrote, "I knew a man, his brain so small / He couldn't think of nothing at all / He's not the same as you or me / He doesn't dig poetry."* The inclusion of this song indicated the team's more relaxed attitude now that their place in the music world seemed more secure. They could afford to be gracious to their competition.

The hit single "Homeward Bound," with its perfect evocation of the lonely life of the artist on the road, was also included. "7 O'Clock News" consists of a straightforward recitation of news events on any day in 1966—events which rubbed the nation's nerves raw: civil-rights struggles, mass murders, Vietnam, and the death of iconoclastic comedian Lenny Bruce (to whom they dedicated the album). The song calmly juxtaposed the chaos of the world against the peaceful, healing lyric of the Christmas carol "Silent Night."

The mood shifts dramatically to one of pure exuberant fun in "The 59th Street Bridge Song," better known as "Feelin' Groovy." On that cut Paul asked Joe Morello and Gene Wright, members of the Dave Brubeck group, to do backup. Paul was beginning to feel more comfortable with collaborations, and he enjoyed experimenting with musicians and styles different from his own. The mellow tone of "Feelin' Groovy" was an immediate hit with a generation of young people who strongly identified Paul's buoyant mood with a marijuana high.

Despite the happy tone of "Feelin' Groovy," the album's over-

---

*"A Simple Desultory Philippic" © 1965 by Paul Simon

riding mood was serious, and the theme again was alienation, a subject Simon and Garfunkel's audiences didn't seem to tire of. In some measure, it was Art Garfunkel's angelic harmonies that kept audiences interested in Paul's somber messages.

Paul would often defer to Art when it came to harmony. Art reached back to the Everly Brothers for inspiration and for technical models. From them he learned how to hold notes and the mechanics of articulation and diction. He poured all he knew about chord structure into the arrangements, using them to squeeze the most meaning out of every song. He was a genius at harmony. Paul knew that without Art, his songs would never have found such a vast audience.

The team spent many of the waning months of 1966 completing the cuts for the album. Columbia waited patiently, knowing their previous two albums and four singles had already sold millions.

Their reputation as singers who actually said something worth thinking about propelled them into classrooms all over the country. Teachers from junior high to college played Simon and Garfunkel songs and analyzed the lyrics as if they were poems.

Teachers were creating a new generation of Simon and Garfunkel fans, and the two were uncomfortable about their growing influence. Garfunkel has said, "We would never call our music teaching." Similarly, Simon has noted, "I write and perform to entertain, not to teach or preach. I would much rather a concert-goer say: 'I had a great evening' than 'I learned a lot.' If we make them think, okay—it's an added dimension. We are just creating doubts and raising questions. There are doubts in every area."

To leaven a too-serious image, the duo often included a light-hearted version of Paul's hit for the Cyrkle, "Red Rubber Ball," at their college concerts. But their next single release continued to build their reputation for melancholy. In October 1966, Columbia released "A Hazy Shade of Winter," a moody rumination on the fleeting passage of time. Both the company and the performers hoped it would do better than "The Dangling Conversation."

Paul and Art were now almost constantly on the road, frequently shuttling back and forth between New York and California. On the West Coast they noted that the influence of drugs and money, especially in the music world, was much more obvious. They got their first real taste of Hollywood extravagance when they visited the Mamas and the Papas, who were then living in

Jeanette MacDonald's old mansion in Bel Air. John Phillips remembered Paul's reaction: "The opulence and spectacle of the place shocked him." Art and Paul were just beginning to see really large sums of money flood into their bank accounts, and they still lived relatively simply. The excesses Paul witnessed in California stunned him, prompting a droll remark to Phillips when he strolled through the cavernous mansion: "You'd have to say this is a very big house you've got here, John." Paul teased Phillips about his business acumen while he and Art were still "like, out of England. We're folk. We're pure." The joking hid the fact that both Paul and Art were appalled at the thought of throwing money around with such breathtaking abandon.

Simon and Garfunkel were both making huge sums of money, but Paul was earning considerably more than Art because he had retained ownership of his songs. In addition to the songwriting royalties, he also received 75 percent of Simon and Garfunkel's concert income.

Paul was reluctant at first to become actively involved with the management of his money. In those heady days, he preferred to turn financial matters over to his lawyer. His disdainful attitude toward the evils of capitalism echoed those of much of his generation, but as his wise lawyer pointed out, Paul had a lot more to lose than most people. Eventually he began to take a more active role in managing his financial future.

"A Hazy Shade of Winter" registered on the charts in November, peaking at number thirteen. The *Parsley, Sage, Rosemary and Thyme* album, released that same month, was an immediate critical and popular success. As music critic Ralph Gleason said on the liner notes, "The voices blend, separate, interweave, and sing counter to one another with the delicacy of a clear glass etching. *Parsley, Sage, Rosemary and Thyme* finds them most perfectly in tune with one another as artists and as friends. They radiate confidence in themselves and in their material."

For Art, the album was a vindication of the team's stubborn insistence on its own high standards of excellence. Art said that in many ways the making of *Parsley, Sage, Rosemary and Thyme* signaled the true beginning of Simon and Garfunkel's recording career.

Again, Columbia applied pressure to support the album's release with a concert tour. Mort Lewis stepped up his booking efforts, and the team hit the concert circuit. By now, Columbia was besieged with questions about the slightly mysterious pair. Fans wanted to know more about them as individuals and continued to ask questions about who did what in the partnership.

Art Garfunkel's contribution to the songs of Simon and Garfunkel has always been a matter of public speculation. People who witnessed recording sessions contend that the close harmonies derived from a complete musical interdependence. In the course of interpreting the material, both Art and Paul were seen to advise, praise, goad, and nourish each other, and this process resulted in a unique creation neither could have produced alone.

It was a subtle and complex relationship—well beyond the scope of the Columbia publicity mill to portray accurately. Paul Simon's disenchantment with the record company intensified as its publicists habitually clouded the issue, but Paul himself was party to the disinformation. Conflicting reports contended Simon wrote the lyrics, they both wrote the music, or Simon wrote the music and Garfunkel arranged it. In later years, Simon was bitter about the public's lingering perception that Art was equally responsible for the music. About this period Simon later said, "I lied. He lied. We said, 'We're Simon and Garfunkel; I write the songs, Artie arranges them.' We would parade that. It was a joint statement all through the sixties. Everyone believed it, and, of course, it was never true."

Garfunkel was always more generous in recalling this period: "People always asked why I didn't write songs. It was because Paul was so good. It seemed foolish to go for equal time." But according to Simon, "He felt, even more than I did, the frustration of having people ask 'Did you write the words or the music?' I used to feel, Oh, Christ. But at least I could say, 'I wrote both.' And that's a drag if people keep asking you. Because there's a sense of competition between us that dates from the beginnings of our friendship."

Competition had always been a significant factor in their relationship. But at this juncture, one thing they did not compete for was women, especially female fans. Paul, now split from Kathy, said, "Simon and Garfunkel had a peculiar type of groupies. We had the poetic groupies. The girls that followed us around weren't necessarily looking to sleep with us as much as they were looking to read their poetry or discuss literature...I wasn't into picking up girls on the road. Couldn't do it. Too embarrassing for me. I wasn't interested in their poetry, either."

Art, too, wasn't interested in steady female companionship. Even after his success, he said his romantic life was still simple: "Maybe some girl will call up and drop by. I mean I never have dates or call up a girl and meet her and take her out, that whole bit. It's completely out of my behavior pattern. I can't plan and I don't want to commit myself." Their seeming uninterest in these girls, and in the more sophisticated women available to them, gave rise to rumors that their primary relationship was with each other.

While touring throughout 1966, they spent most of their time together—working, getting high, enjoying their success, and trying desperately to keep perspective. Their senses of humor kept them sane. Simon has recalled, "In hotel rooms, after the shows, we'd get stoned and make up album titles, like *So Young and So Full of Pain*. We were going to do one album cover, Beach-Boys-style, with bathing suits and surfboards."

Over the years, both Paul and Art developed a love-hate relationship with the road and with the very idea of live performance. But in those early years, Paul, in particular, looked forward to performing if he could do so within the scope of an excellent sound system and a full house. His moodiness and depression, exacerbated by the frequent use of drugs, was never evident on stage. Both he and Art seemed to savor the moment they walked on stage and felt that magical bond with the audience.

In January of 1967, the duo performed at a sold-out concert in New York's Philharmonic Hall. They basked in the adoration of the East Coast, hometown crowd. When they launched into Paul's "59th Street Bridge Song/Feelin' Groovy," the crowd roared approval of its native sons. A new group, Harpers Bizarre, had a recent hit single of the tune. While the song was written about a landmark site in New York, its breezy, mellow attitude was distinctly West Coast, where "feelin' groovy"— especially from drugs—was a way of life. Fascinated by drugs and their growing influence on America's pop-music scene, which had shifted from New York to Los Angeles and San Francisco, Art and Paul turned their gaze from Manhattan's skyline toward the shimmering psychedelic colors on the California horizon.

5

In March 1967, Simon and Garfunkel released a clever tune with a catchy lyric that told of strange goings-on "At the Zoo" (the flip side was their own version of "Feelin' Groovy" from their latest album). True to form, "At the Zoo" climbed quickly to number sixteen on the charts. This single was the first clear indication that Paul's enchantment with drugs was spilling over into his work. While "Feelin' Groovy" might be interpreted as a natural high, the lyrics of "At the Zoo" about hamsters turning on seemed to be an open invitation to join the drug party sweeping the nation.

Paul wrote about drugs because they had become an important influence on his personality and work habits. The constant pressure to produce original songs forced him to search his current life experience for new material; his store of carefully polished songs from the England years was gone, and he needed more in a hurry. He used drugs to speed up the writing process, so it wasn't surprising that several of his new songs had allusions to drugs. Paul was very much a part of his generation's freewheeling and casual experimentation with a staggering variety of mind-altering drugs.

Both Paul and Art had been smoking marijuana for years. Paul also liked to smoke hashish, a preference he picked up in England where it was easy to come by. Since their teenage years, they had inhabited the world of professional musicians, where drugs were commonplace. As drug use spread through every strata of American society, Paul and Art escalated their use of, and experimentation with, drugs, keeping pace with much of their youthful constituency.

In January 1967, San Francisco was the scene of the first "Human Be-In," soon to be followed by the much heralded "Summer of Love." The Be-In was the natural evolution of a hippie rite fondly observed within the Haight-Ashbury neighborhood as well as in other hippie enclaves in the city. At the drop of a soap bubble or a tab of acid, on any sunny afternoon, hippies gathered to celebrate their spiritual communion with the universe.

These dropouts from middle-class society passed their days painting their vans and their faces, studying Native American and Oriental religions, or rummaging among street vendors who offered crafts, psychedelic drugs, and occult trappings for sale. Above all, they listened to music.

The *Oracle,* a San Francisco newspaper devoted to the hippie scene, had suggested a massive get-together (dubbed "A Gathering of the Tribes") to be held on January 14, 1967, on the polo field of Golden Gate Park. The Be-In was originally proposed to heal a rift between two warring factions of the Bay Area hippie scene—the San Francisco acid heads and the Berkeley Free Speech radicals led by Jerry Rubin. A notice for the event read, "A new concept of human relations being developed within the youthful underground must emerge, become conscious and be shared so that a revolution of form can be filled with a Renaissance of compassion, awareness and love in the Revelation of the unity of all mankind."

In a country beset with violence—both at home, with the ongoing civil-rights struggle and growing antiwar activism, and abroad, with the ever-worsening Vietnam conflict—the Be-In was to be a jubilant endorsement of peace and love. And rock 'n' roll. Favorite area bands such as the Grateful Dead, Big Brother and the Holding Company, Quicksilver Messenger Service, and the Jefferson Airplane—prime exponents of the new, psychedelic wave of rock 'n' roll called "acid rock"—agreed to perform without charge. The Be-In drew upwards of twenty thousand people to revel in the unseasonably warm California sun and the astonishing idea that love and flowers could save and renew the world. The news media found the sight irresistible and beamed countless images of young people with long, shiny hair dancing in the sun, and of spaced-out hippies bedecked with flowers, panhandling and selling drugs.

The drug trade was the economic base of the hippie culture. Master of San Francisco's lucrative acid commerce was a shadowy man known as Augustus Stanley Owsley III, who, it is estimated, manufactured more than four million doses of acid over the course of his reign. Owsley had acquired a reputation for integrity and the purity of his product, and dyed each of his acid batches a different psychedelic color so that his was easy to identify. He is said to have given away as much as he sold, and to have been particularly generous to musicians he favored. Owsley became a common sight backstage at the city's rock shows.

Paul found drugs useful in the creative process, saying, "[drugs help] to get the stuff out of you—especially if what you're dealing with is yourself—requires you to open up and touch tender spots. And to touch those tender spots, you have to be anesthetized a little bit."

He saw the heavy price of spurring creativity through drugs: early burn-out, loss of health or even life itself. But he was caught in a riptide of the popular demand for new songs, and drugs seemed to ease the pressure.

The flower children exerted increasing influence on the direction of popular music, and Paul was given a chance to study the new sounds first hand. In April, John Phillips of the Mamas and the Papas asked Paul to serve on the steering committee for the Monterey Pop Festival scheduled for June 1967. The event was to be patterned after the annual Newport, Rhode Island, jazz and folk festivals which Paul and Phillips attended in their days as folksingers.

At Monterey, music managers Ben Shapiro and Alan Pariser wanted to stage a "music mart," a three-day event that would feature up-and-coming rock groups. They confidently reserved the Monterey County fairgrounds just outside the quiet seaside community, a ninety-minute drive down the California coast from San Francisco. There, they hoped the usual arena for prize heifers and hog-calling would provide a stage for the music world's most adventurous new performers.

As a start, they booked Shapiro's longtime client Ravi Shankar, the eminent Indian sitarist, Beatle inspiration, and darling of the flower children, as their first, and only, headliner. Originally conceived of as a profit-making venture, Shapiro and Pariser discovered they were woefully undercapitalized at fifty thousand dollars, not nearly enough money to pay for three days of big-name acts. Even the Mamas and the Papas rejected Shapiro's initial five thousand dollar offer. But Phillips was intrigued with the idea of a showcase for adventurous music. He had been impressed a few months earlier with the impact of the Human Be-In's free music policy and its ensuing exposure for some of pop music's most exciting new sounds.

Paul and Art were especially curious about the new music emanating from California because they feared their own delicate sound might soon be obliterated by the high-decibel, high-energy rock 'n' roll they heard there.

Phillips, his manager Lou Adler, Simon, Garfunkel, and Los Angeles producer Terry Melcher (Doris Day's son) bought out the original organizers and set up their own board of directors.

Board members began to line up other acts and to establish guidelines for spending hoped-for profits, most of which were earmarked for music scholarships. Simon wanted fifty thousand dollars for a music workshop in Harlem.

Adler took over the monumental organizational task. Just six weeks before thousands would descend on Monterey, he worked frantically to arrange for a stage, sound systems, food, portable toilets, security, and a thousand other things. Adler found additional working capital by selling the film rights to ABC-TV for four hundred thousand dollars. He and his board, which by now included some of pop music's biggest names—Paul McCartney, Brian Wilson, Mick Jagger, and Smokey Robinson—feverishly begged the music world's premier acts to work for expenses as a gesture of their support for the new music scene.

The organizers knew they were dealing with a potentially explosive situation. Assembling thousands of young people, many high on drugs, for a day of incendiary rock 'n' roll music demanded some kind of internal control. Phillips decided to write a song to defuse the situation. He said, "I thought we should somehow put the word out to the kids that if they were going to San Francisco, they should come in peace and stay cool during the festival. We did not want riots and violence and insanity on our hands there." He wrote "If You're Going to San Francisco (Be Sure to Wear Flowers in Your Hair)" in half an hour. Phillips had said, "I didn't want to be as transparent as to name Monterey, but we did get the point across." "All across the nation, there's a strange vibration / There's a whole generation with a new explanation...For those who go to San Francisco / Summertime will be a love-in there," sang Scott McKenzie.

Paul Simon's special role was to help select performers acceptable to the hostile northern and southern factions of the California music scene. He was seen as a neutral party because of his identification as a New Yorker. His mission took him on a memorable visit to the Grateful Dead's mansion in San Francisco's Haight-Ashbury section. He called it "the spookiest place I've ever seen. Jerry Garcia, Bob Weir, Pigpen—man, it's strange up here. I'm sure they're all stoned. They sit around and riff all day. The girls do the chores, and the guys work on the music. It's like they're suburban kids underneath it all, which is mysterious enough for us right there. Artie and I are New York City kids. This stuff hasn't hit the city yet."

Paul was amazed at the free and easy drug use: "Everybody's smokin' right on the street. When we're on the road in hotels, if we smoke we drape towels in the doorway to keep the fumes in so we won't get busted. This place is unbelievable."

While both Art and Paul had trouble getting used to some aspects of the life-style, they were powerfully attracted to the chemical substances that were clearly giving many successful musicians a creative edge. The Beatles had released their *Sergeant Pepper's Lonely Hearts Club Band* album in May, just weeks before the Monterey Pop Festival. Its bizarre cover promised a psychedelic trip of unprecedented proportions. It was one of the first "concept" albums, and its unified theme and seamless blend of songs signaled yet another new direction in popular music. Concurrently, new groups were introducing strange and exciting hybrids of rock 'n' roll: David Bowie, Jimi Hendrix, the Doors, and Traffic vied for attention with remarkably imaginative new albums. Simon and Garfunkel seemed somewhat quaint and genteel among the mind-bending, gaudy visions on display.

In the spring and summer of 1967, both Paul and Art embraced the drug scene with even more enthusiasm, although both felt like rank amateurs among the heavyweights. Paul remembers that everyone on drugs flashed a mysterious, knowing smile. He felt like an outsider just like he had in grade school, and was determined to gain entry into the inner circle. In an encounter with San Francisco's notorious Owsley, Paul pretended to know all about LSD, even suggesting he dropped acid every day. He took some LSD with him when he returned to New York and swallowed it in the safety of his own apartment. Soon strange things began to happen. He remembers a play of shadow and light and a feeling of being able to sense plants growing next to him. That trip resulted in a summons to Columbia Records engineers to come to his apartment to record random sounds which fascinated him. They caught Paul sipping his coffee, then later relieving himself in the bathroom. He also demanded they capture the sounds of birds singing outside his window. "Remember, I was selling, with Artie, millions of records, so whatever I'd say, they'd do." The LSD trips continued, and Paul estimated he was continually stoned for six months of 1967.

Art was also experimenting with acid, but they said they didn't trip together. Art said acid gave him a powerful sense of his own life force. The drug offered interesting insights, especially about his musical talent. On one occasion, he felt God was taking him to task about his singing gift. He claimed he surfaced from that trip with a renewed sense of responsibility to his audience and resolved to be more serious about the development and use of his talent. He has said of this time, "The insights I got had a lot to do with seeing the real me from the not-real, and the real pushed me on to concentrate on what I can do and try to see noise for noise's sake. Because what you can do, you should do. What else are you supposed to do with your time on earth?"

One of Paul's trips frightened him into realizing he was taking acid to short-circuit the normal path of self-discovery. As he put it, "I thought I was going to get some big chunk of information for free. I was going to learn something about myself chemically, rather than learning something through my life. I thought I'd get this tremendous insight, that glint, that San Francisco something." He felt himself splitting into two halves, one delighted with the acid high, and the other disapproving and fearful of losing control—and his talent—to a chemical. Paul became alarmed at his retreat from reality. Worse, he began believing he couldn't write without drugs. He also realized that his writing emphasized pain and sorrow to an abnormal degree. He found himself depressed most of the time because he was high most of the time, a vicious cycle that the touring life-style only exacerbated.

The Monterey Pop Festival finally got underway on June 16, a cool Friday night. Earlier in the week, a steady stream of Volkswagen buses, pickup trucks, bicycles, and sports cars filled with young people in flowing, brightly tie-dyed granny dresses, blue jeans, and steel-rimmed glasses began to arrive. By Friday morning, the friendly invasion had overwhelmed the twenty-six thousand inhabitants of the peaceful peninsula town. Adorned with stovepipe hats, billions of beads, and hair down to there, the invaders drifted in a great, colorful tide toward the stage, above which a banner proclaimed the festival's theme: "Love, Flowers and Music."

They built makeshift camps with blankets and picnic coolers, and marked them with fluttering flags emblazoned with astrological signs. Tattoo artists set up shop alongside dealers in incense, barbecued tofu, and candles. A colorful tent city blossomed, a signal that the organizers had made a dreadful mistake. Phillips lamented, "The fairgrounds held only five thousand for each show—twenty-five thousand for all five shows. We could have sold out a football stadium. But it was too late. We were locked in—literally imprisoned by the hippie hordes."

Phillips was still concerned about the potential for serious drug problems. He discovered that the ubiquitous Owsley had concocted a particularly potent batch of acid and had been spotted hawking the specially dyed "Monterey Purple."Ensuing accounts of freaked-out kids on bad acid trips enraged Phillips. So far, his gentle exhortations had worked to keep the peace, but he finally had to hunt down the psychedelic Santa Claus and eject him from the scene.

After Owsley's removal, the mellow mood resumed. Chords of music wafted periodically from the guitars, flutes, and steel drums that dotted the audience. The crowd patiently waited its chance to merge with the music on stage.

The festival's headliners represented an astonishing variety of musical styles, few of which resembled the intimate, reflective songs that were Paul and Art's signature. In the absence of any true black soul and blues singer except for Otis Redding, a young Texan from Port Arthur named Janis Joplin, a member of Big Brother and the Holding Company, filled that gap. At that time, Joplin was virtually unknown outside San Francisco. She ambled across the Monterey stage clad in an outrageous gold lamé miniskirt, occasionally pulling on a bottle sporting a Southern Comfort label that actually contained a potent brew of cough syrup laced with codeine. Her performance electrified the audience and established her as, one critic commented, "the best white woman blues singer on earth."

Columbia Records' Clive Davis watched her in awe and decided on the spot to sign Joplin to a long-term contract. Davis, a young lawyer on the music-business fast track, had been recently promoted to president of the company. He was searching for a way to increase Columbia's profits while, at the same time, struggling with a musically conservative faction within the company which was led by producer Mitch Miller. Davis was aware of the huge audiences for new rock groups and sensed a seismic shift in the direction of popular music toward acid rock. Monterey proved to him that a social as well as musical revolution was underway. He decided to gamble his company's future and bet heavily on the new rock groups. He later called the Monterey festival "the creative turning point of my life."

Columbia still had Dylan and Simon and Garfunkel, but Davis felt he needed to sign more musically progressive acts. Davis restlessly prowled backstage, making a list of the strangely dressed, wild-haired musicians who might be potential gold mines.

Paul and Art also wandered around backstage, blissfully taking in the chaotic scene that Paul later called "a jubilee." He sat rapt in conversation about music with Jimi Hendrix. Noticing someone strange even by Monterey standards, he asked Phillips, "Did you see that chick walking around backstage who looks just like Brian Jones?" Phillips replied laconically, "Yeah, you mean the one with the lipstick and mascara and the frock that looks like a Moroccan caftan? Oh, yeah. That was Brian."

The English group the Who punctuated their set with smoke bombs and concluded by smashing their instruments to bits. Jimi Hendrix played guitar with his teeth and for an encore set it afire. The Grateful Dead, Country Joe and the Fish, and the Jefferson

Airplane weren't far behind in efforts to dazzle the audience with sound and spectacle.

Simon and Garfunkel appeared as the opening night's closing act. They did so with some trepidation. Amid the tumult, they appeared on the naked stage armed with only a single guitar and their delicate voices. They introduced "Punky's Dilemma" and sang several cuts from the new *Parsley, Sage* album as well as familiar favorites. Their understated performance riveted the attention of the huge audience and left them begging for more.

Their rendition of "Feelin' Groovy" perfectly captured the emotional tenor of that extraordinary festival. It also epitomized the feeling of happy optimism that characterized that so-called Summer of Love. Their performance in Monterey proved to the world and, more important, to themselves, that they were still a powerful force on the American music scene. There was room enough for all.

After their festival triumph, Simon and Garfunkel returned to their first love, the recording studio, to cut tracks for their next album. Columbia tried to speed up their snail-paced production by adding its most talented new producer to the mix. John Simon was not related to Paul, but he was a kindred spirit.

The new producer, a graduate of Princeton, was a musician and accomplished arranger. He understood the delicate tensions of the recording process and the special needs of creative musicians. He tried to be as unobtrusive as possible while still protecting Columbia's bottom line. John had earlier produced one of Paul Simon's songs, "Red Rubber Ball," for Cyrkle, and he looked forward to working with Paul on a Simon and Garfunkel album.

In July, Columbia released "Fakin' It," which Paul called "autobiographically interesting." The single quickly climbed the charts. Unlike most of Paul's other songs, the flip side, "You Don't Know Where Your Interests Lie," was never released on an album and has become the rarest of all Simon and Garfunkel records.

Somewhat relieved that they could still produce a hit on demand, Simon and Garfunkel focused on the film project they had agreed to do for Mike Nichols. Nichols was in the final throes of shooting *The Graduate* in Los Angeles, and his polite phone calls had become more insistent.

Simon's aversion to writing on order had created problems. Paul had already submitted "Punky's Dilemma," which focused on the issue of draft evasion and alluded to moviemaking as well as to the vanities peculiar to Los Angeles. He also gave Nichols "Overs." Both tunes were scheduled for inclusion on the duo's next album, but Nichols rejected them and pressured Simon for original material.

Dustin Hoffman, a relatively unknown stage actor at the time, had been cast as Benjamin Braddock, the recent college graduate uncertain of what to do with his life. Anne Bancroft had accepted the role of Mrs. Robinson, the rapacious older woman, after Doris Day had turned it down. Nichols's signing of Simon, the master of alienation, to write the score had seemed a stroke of genius, but Paul's delays created a new set of problems for the harried director.

Nichols desperately needed some music to work with in the editing room, so, as a stop-gap, he used four of Simon and Garfunkel's earlier recordings: "The Sounds of Silence," "The Big Bright Green Pleasure Machine," "Scarborough Fair," and "April Come She Will." He went on cutting the film using these songs—after all, they were what prompted Nichols to hire the duo in the first place.

The inexorable release date for the film loomed, but no amount of badgering seemed to move Paul Simon. The more Nichols worked in the editing room with the old music, the more convinced he became that those songs would do the job. Still, he wanted something—anything—new.

Paul promised to do more work on the score while he and Art continued their college-concert touring, the mainstay of their success. At the time, Paul shrewdly assessed one key to their continued popularity with the young audience: "In working colleges the thing to remember is that while we grow older every year, the college age stays the same. Right now we're working to our own generation, but that will change. Our biggest audience will probably always be people in our age bracket. They're the ones we're saying something to."

That audience was listening in ever growing numbers. *Parsley, Sage, Rosemary and Thyme* stayed near the top of the charts. Like Art, Paul thought highly of the album: "I think of it as our only album so far," said the ever self-critical Simon.

They heard little but praise. No less a judge of talent than

Leonard Bernstein named Simon and Garfunkel among the top 5 percent of new artists he considered "formidable."

Mainstream performers also were taking an interest in Simon's unusual but extremely popular songs. Artists who had never given rock or folk music a second thought began to cross over on Simon songs. Mel Tormé, André Kostelanetz, jazz duo Jackie (Cain) and Roy (Kral), Jane Morgan, and Ray Charles all developed an early appreciation for Simon's music and recorded his songs, increasing his royalties manyfold.

But even as critical and financial success increased, Paul was sliding into depression and growing more troubled by the public's inability to distinguish his individual, key contribution to the team of Simon and Garfunkel. In a way, the uniqueness of Simon and Garfunkel created the confusion. Audiences were used to singers who sang songs other people wrote, and they understood the worth of singer-songwriters, but this team was different. The two still heard the same tiresome question after each college concert. Inevitably a young admirer would corner them and ask, "Which do you write, the words or the music?" While no doubt Art felt awkward having to admit to less than equal creative input, he wasn't as upset by this omnipresent question as Paul. The more the fans and critics clamored to know who did what, the more upset Paul Simon became. While he should have been happy to answer that he wrote both the words and music, he hated to hear the question raised.

The wellspring of his anger lay deep in his past, in his dissatisfaction with his own physical appearance and the constant comparisons with Art he was forced to suffer through. He knew the fans would assume Art had written the songs because, in Simon's mind, Art looked like a writer, and he didn't. Art looked intellectual. He didn't. Art looked like a "star." Paul said, "I was a rock-'n'-roll star who didn't look at all like a rock-'n'-roll star. I don't know if the world said that, but I thought it did. And that's why, in my opinion, people thought that Artie wrote our songs. You know, he was angelic-looking, with fluffy blond hair. And he was tall and thin and he had this voice and it seemed right. He should have been the one who wrote the songs. That body should have contained that talent."

The height issue flared up again. That Art towered over him was a fact of life Paul should have accepted by now, but he couldn't help feeling pangs of jealousy when he read reviews that described him as "boyish and chunky" and Art as "tall, reedy and wraith-like." A typical press description of the pair read: "Paul Simon is the short, dark one, frequently called 'elfin'; Arthur is the tall one with the bouncy blond ringlets."

What was worse, Arthur's superior voice dominated the songs they sang together; Paul seemed to be there only to provide harmony. Simon has admitted that one of his disappointments in life is not having a better voice. Publicists added further insult when they revealed that in the studio Simon's voice was recorded first and then often rerecorded or overdubbed to add fullness before Artie recorded his vocals. Even his mother publicly said, "Paul has a nice voice, but Artie has a better one." With four hit singles and a newly released album already taking off, though, it was no time for conflict. Paul kept all of his grievances below the surface for the good of the team, just as Art had chosen to do during their teenage success.

Paul and Art continued to experiment with drugs, but because of their carefully cultivated clean-cut image, they were circum-spect about it. Paul said, "We took drugs, we just didn't sleep in tepees. We were quiet about it. I never wanted to be busted in Des Moines, you know? So we just played it straight, and it made life a lot easier and safer."

Back in Hollywood, Mike Nichols was still waiting for Paul and Art to record some original material for *The Graduate*. Snatches of a new song had been floating around in Simon's head for some time. The original working title was "Mrs. Roosevelt," and the song's initial theme concerned changing American values. They played around with the tune, retaining a particularly evocative baseball allusion: "And here's to you, Joe DiMaggio / A nation turns its lonely eyes to you." Paul has said, "I wrote that line and didn't really know what I was writing. My style is to write phonetically and with free association, and very often it comes out all right. But as soon as I said the line I said to myself, That's a great line, that line touches me. It has a nice touch of nostalgia to it. It's interesting. It could be interpreted in many ways. It has something to do with heroes. People who are all good with no bad in them at all. That's the way I always saw Joe DiMaggio. And

Mickey Mantle." Not content with "Mrs. Roosevelt," the duo sang the song repeatedly, trying out several different three-syllable names to fit the beats. The song was only half-finished, and one day, as they worked on it, Simon and Garfunkel began substituting "Mrs. Robinson" for the lead line.

At one session with Nichols, the three were discussing the progress of the score. Art quietly suggested, "What about 'Mrs. Robinson?'" Nichols jumped to his feet and screamed, "You have a song called 'Mrs. Robinson' and you haven't even shown it to me?" After Paul and Art calmed the director down, they explained the working title and sang the tune, although they made it clear it was still just a work-in-progress. But Nichols fell in love with the song and, according to Art, "froze it for the picture as 'Mrs. Robinson.'" Nichols went on to finish the film on schedule. He hired Dave Grusin to compose incidental music tracks for some scenes.

In the end, everyone concerned recognized that Paul had not written an original movie score, but the themes of Paul's earlier material perfectly fit Nichols's concept and accomplished the same goals. Paul noted, "In a funny way, the movie was scored around us....It was Mike's concept that we would be the voice of Benjamin, the graduate. In the film, every time you heard us, it would be as if Benjamin was speaking. A song like 'The Sounds of Silence' is really Benjamin talking about his life and his parents and where he lives and what he sees around him."

That first experience with the movies was not very satisfying for Art and Paul. Both had looked forward to using special recording techniques, but found film sound methods primitive compared to the flexibility they were used to in the recording studio. They also felt that film engineers were far less creative than their beloved recording engineers, and so were glad to finish the soundtrack. But they both remained intrigued by moviemaking.

They resumed a schedule that had Paul writing new songs while Art attended classes. Together they did concerts and laid down tracks for Simon and Garfunkel's first concept album, *Bookends*.

One observer at a *Bookends* recording session summed up Art and Paul's working relationship at this time: "The depth of their friendship is evident in the way they work together. Because Garfunkel only sings and does vocal arranging while Simon does the writing, guitar playing, and lead singing, one might think it's primarily Simon's show—until one sees their creative interdependence on a record date."

As the sessions went on, observers noted that Paul and Art listened carefully to one another's praise and criticism. Their working relationship appeared finely tuned and evenly balanced as each asked for the other's advice—and took it. They encouraged each other and boosted each other's spirits with sincere compliments. Producer John Simon occasionally made a suggestion, but the essential exchange was clearly between Art and Paul.

Although in the studio their working relationship seemed unchanged, on the road things were different. The easy camaraderie nourished by the familiar patterns of life in New York—where the two could join or leave at will—was replaced by the relentless togetherness of hotel rooms and the pressure-packed atmosphere of performing in unfamiliar surroundings.

At first, like fame, the road trips had been fun. Paul and Art had shoved towels near the foot of the hotel-room doors and gotten stoned. Everything appeared silly, and they laughed a lot at themselves. In a haze of marijuana smoke, they fantasized about changing their carefully constructed image in one devastating stroke. They had been invited to appear at a "Teens for Decency" show in Florida by a group organized in reaction to renegade rocker Jim Morrison's infamous self-exposure on stage. Paul and Art imagined accepting the invitation and suddenly, without warning, doing the same.

The road trips continued to bring out a particular class of adoring fans neither Paul nor Art found very appealing. Back in New York, Paul dated Denise Kaufman, who had recently broken up with *Rolling Stone* publisher Jann Wenner. Wenner may not have been happy about the relationship, since there is a noticeable absence of any substantial coverage of Simon and Garfunkel—one of the rock-music world's most celebrated groups—in the first several issues of the new magazine.

In New York, Paul and Art gradually began to spend less and less of their free time together. Paul remembered, "We saw each other so much on the road, by the time we got back, there was no need. We were pretty good friends then, but we saw each other several days a week because we were on the road together, so we didn't see each other when we weren't."

It took several more months of recording sessions to get the *Bookends* tracks cut. Columbia anxiously watched the process. The single "Fakin' It" peaked at only number twenty-three; Simon and Garfunkel hadn't had a hit in a long time by music-industry standards. Executives rationalized, "They're an album act. Their fans are all album buyers."

When Simon and Garfunkel had been signed to do *The Graduate*, Embassy Pictures offered the soundtrack album to Columbia Records. Clive Davis bought the rights, and now, near the end of 1967, the movie was ready for release, but there was no album to accompany it. Aside from the new song "Mrs. Robinson," which was never used in its entirety, Nichols had used only prereleased Simon and Garfunkel songs. Davis had been counting heavily on a soundtrack full of Simon and Garfunkel originals and was now extremely upset.

The film opened in New York and Los Angeles in December 1967, just in time to qualify for that year's Academy Awards. General release was scheduled for the following year, and Davis reasoned there still might be time to salvage the idea of a soundtrack album. Simon and Garfunkel's *Bookends* album would contain a version of "Mrs. Robinson," but that album's release date remained uncertain. Davis feared Columbia would miss out on a huge commercial opportunity.

Davis had always been a fan of cast albums. In his first days at Columbia, he had negotiated contracts for Broadway musical albums, and his experience told him cast and soundtrack albums could generate strong profits, especially with a potential hit single like "Mrs. Robinson." But Davis's staff told him there were only fifteen minutes of original Paul Simon material in the movie. When Davis went to see it for himself, it dawned on him that Dave Grusin's background music could also be used to fill out the album.

When Davis proposed the idea to Paul and Art, both objected vehemently. Davis appealed to Mort Lewis to persuade Paul and Art to change their minds. Lewis phoned back quickly with an unequivocal no. Paul and Art thought that any new Simon and Garfunkel album would require eleven or twelve new songs. Besides, their new album *Bookends* was nearing completion and would soon be ready for release. *Bookends* contained "Mrs. Robinson" and two other cuts Paul had written for the film but that Nichols had rejected. The duo feared a soundtrack album released simultaneously with *Bookends* would diffuse sales, and they refused to postpone release of their first concept album. They were excited about it and wanted to share it with their audience as soon as possible.

Davis told them both albums could be hits at the same time, because the soundtrack would attract a whole new audience for Simon and Garfunkel. Besides, Columbia needed a strong seller. As Davis admitted, "Columbia's profits were then shaky. I needed a blockbuster album to replace Mitch Miller and the Broadway show albums.This was no passing academic question; one good album that year could make or break the year's bottom line." But Simon and Garfunkel didn't give a damn about Columbia's profit picture and were adamant that the next Simon and Garfunkel release would be *Bookends*.

Then they were stunned to hear that Columbia intended to raise the price of their album. *Bookends* would cost a full dollar more than any other Columbia album. Executives argued that they needed to test the concept of "variable pricing." In other words, they wanted to see what the market would bear. Paul and Art thought their loyal fans would pay the extra dollar, but they were infuriated by what they perceived as Columbia's greed.

The friendly relationship that Davis had assiduously cultivated with the duo ended. Communication now was filtered through Mort Lewis while Davis relentlessly pursued the soundtrack idea. Paul continued to insist: "We're not waiting six months to release it just because of your problems." Davis promised not to delay the release of *Bookends,* but it would be released on the heels of the soundtrack.

Grusin's background music was, Davis admitted, not outstanding, but he felt it was good enough not to detract from the rest of Simon's songs. Paul finally agreed Davis had a point: "People who buy soundtrack albums are entirely different from regular record consumers. Mostly, they want to reidentify with a film they really liked." He argued, "The soundtrack would reach a vast number of moviegoers rather than just Simon and Garfunkel fans." Many moviegoers wouldn't even have heard of them. A whole new audience would open up to them.

Simon wanted assurance that the soundtrack album would be packaged differently from the *Bookends* album, and Columbia agreed. On *The Graduate* album cover, Mrs. Robinson's naked leg dominates the foreground, and in the background a pensive, barefoot Dustin Hoffman gazes at it. The liner notes summarize the movie story line and gives backgrounds on Mike Nichols and Simon and Garfunkel, but there is no photo of the two musicians. The *Bookends* album cover features a black-and-white close-up photo of the solemn-looking pair.

Once all agreed on the ground rules, Columbia rushed the albums to completion. By early spring 1968, *The Graduate* was playing in theaters across the country and racking up unheard-of grosses. It eventually earned forty-four million dollars, making it the third highest-earning film to date, doubling the gross income of the year's other major hit, *Bonnie and Clyde*. By February, the soundtrack recording was the country's number-one-selling album, and the single of "Scarborough Fair," originally cut for the *Parsley, Sage, Rosemary and Thyme* album, reached number eleven. Simon and Garfunkel did indeed become household names.

The Graduate continued to pack movie theaters. Its themes were popular with millions of young people who, like its hero Benjamin, were skeptical about the old order and unafraid to act out their rebellion in often outrageous ways. As Clive Davis had predicted, *The Graduate* soundtrack soared to the top of the album charts and stayed there for nine weeks.

Offers to write more film scores poured in. Simon turned down Franco Zeffirelli's request to write music for his film about St. Francis of Assisi, *Brother Sun, Sister Moon*. There was also talk of Simon writing a few original songs for the Broadway musical *Jimmy Shine*, which would star Dustin Hoffman. In addition, he was asked to consider doing the score for *Midnight Cowboy*, a story much more suited to his realistic style, but a project he rejected because he said he didn't want to become known as Dustin Hoffman's personal songwriter.

Leonard Bernstein asked Paul to collaborate with him on a sacred mass. Simon was flattered but once again found it difficult to write on demand, eventually managing to deliver only four usable lines to the maestro: "Half the people are stoned and the other half are waiting for the next election / Half the people are drowned and the other half are swimming in the wrong direction."

Although they didn't know it yet, Simon and Garfunkel's direction had been forever altered by their encounter with Mike Nichols and the world of filmmaking. *The Graduate* had brought them a vast new audience, but it had also set the scene for the end of their partnership.

6

On a spring day in 1968 as Art was strolling outside his apartment in New York, a limo cruised up beside him. The electric window hummed, and the smoked glass receded to reveal the smiling face of Mike Nichols, who casually handed him a script. Nichols was inviting Art to act in his next movie, *Catch-22*, a black comedy about the absurdity of war, based on Joseph Heller's 1961 best-seller. The script was loaded with eccentric characters, and Art was being considered for the role of Nately, "a sensitive, rich, good-looking boy with trusting eyes." Nately was young and naive, and the plot revolved loosely around his innocence and his love affair with an Italian prostitute (who is known as "Nately's whore" throughout the book). Nichols also wanted to cast Paul in the lesser role of Dunbar, a vague character who disappears before the story ends. The novel had been enormously popular, and it seemed certain the movie adaptation would also be a great success.

Of all the creative opportunities before them, both Simon and Garfunkel thought movies held the most interesting possibilities. They were especially sensitive to the increasing social impact films had gained in the late sixties. Working with Nichols on *The*

Graduate soundtrack had given them a chance to learn more about moviemaking, and Art, especially, had spent many hours talking to Nichols about acting.

They eagerly read the script in an early draft, and while there was no way to tell how the roles of Nately and Dunbar would finally evolve, they both eagerly accepted Nichols's offer. Simon and Garfunkel already had three phenomenally successful years in the music business, more money than they could ever need, and names that were as familiar as any in America. Now the glamour of Hollywood beckoned. Secure in each other's friendship, their lives seemed full of possibility. Paul would later describe this time as "Great...the best ever."

They were particularly delighted to see that "Mrs. Robinson" was on its way to becoming an American classic. When the Oscars were presented in Hollywood, Mike Nichols was named Best Director for *The Graduate*. Several members of the film's cast had also received Oscar nominations: Anne Bancroft, Dustin Hoffman, and Katharine Ross. Paul's songs couldn't be nominated because they hadn't been written exclusively for the film, but the movie's signature theme song, "Mrs. Robinson," punctuated the evening with its familiar strains every time anyone connected with the film made an appearance onstage.

Money, critical accolades, and popular success kept rolling in, and, just as important, Simon and Garfunkel were still local heroes in Queens. Keeping in touch with their families and friends in the old neighborhood gave them much needed perspective to cope with the dazzling, but often illusory, world of show business.

In April 1968, Paul was pleased to be asked to throw out the first ball of the season for his alma mater, Forest Hills High. That same month, the *Bookends* album was released to the delight of both fans and critics, even though many of the cuts had been released earlier as singles.

On *Bookends,* Paul's style had become more cinematic than ever, as evidenced by "Save the Life of My Child," which seems like a brief, terror-filled action movie set to music, beginning with the startling image of a boy perched on a high ledge threatening to jump. The song ends with another dramatic cut to a beautiful, yet harrowing, image of the boy as he takes flight to his death.

On the album's third cut, "America," Paul again worked like a film director to link a series of small, intimate images together until they accumulated into a powerful emotional whole. Paul drew upon his old love affair with Kathy and the cross-country trip they had taken together to convey a young love's full spectrum of feelings, from playful joy to penetrating sadness.

"Old Friends" and the brief title cut "Bookends" were the result of considerable discussion, thought, and research by both men, and the album became their most innovative musical experiment to date. The songs deal with growing old, a mature theme which had been on Simon's mind for some time.

Garfunkel's contribution—capturing actual voices of old people—grew out of a need to experience firsthand the world of the elderly. He had taken his tape recorder to several old-age homes where he found men and women willing to discuss the song's themes: the durability and fragility of friendship, and the nature of memory.

Garfunkel wasn't satisfied with using his recorded question-and-answer sessions with the old people, so he began to eavesdrop on conversations in Central Park. He bought a longer, shotgun microphone and concealed it under his arm beneath a long, narrow loaf of French bread. He remembers, "I would just sort of walk in front of old couples, I just wanted to hear what they had to say." On the cut, documentary-style voices echo Paul's delicate images and give them the weight of reality: "Old friends / Sat on their park bench / Like bookends."*

The song is also Paul's rumination on his own, enduring friendship with Art, which had already spanned eighteen years. In three spare lines toward the end of the song, Paul reveals the nature of the indestructible bond which held the team—and all relationships—together: "Old friends / Memory brushes the same years / Silently sharing the same fears."*

But Paul's lyric genius lay in his ability to take his audience far beyond his own personal experience into genuine insight about the human condition. When Paul wrote "Can you imagine us / Years from today / Sharing a park bench quietly? / How terribly strange / To be seventy,"* he certainly was writing about Art Garfunkel, but listeners knew he was talking about all of them as well.

The songs on *Bookends* signaled a major turning point in the relationship between Paul and Art and offered a vision of the

future especially meaningful to the Simon and Garfunkel generation, which had outgrown its wild, rebellious youth and was
stumbling toward maturity. The audience senses that Paul and
Art, who sang so eloquently about the adolescent feelings of
isolation and alienation, had, as always, preceded them by a few
steps and were now standing on higher ground. From their new
vantage point, the horizon looked different: The time of innocence and confidence was over. The song "Bookends" sends a
gentle but world-weary warning: "Preserve your memories /
They're all that's left to you."*

Some cuts on the album—especially the singles that had already
been released—were never among Simon's favorites. He later
dismissed "A Hazy Shade of Winter" and "At the Zoo" as the
facile by-products of his drug period.

It's easy to see how some songs of lesser quality slipped through
when they should have been shelved or overhauled before they
were offered to the public. Objective criticism of Paul's work was
hard to come by during this phase of his career. Columbia was in
the business of selling records, and so far, no matter what Simon
and Garfunkel recorded, sales skyrocketed.

Columbia had made good on its threat to raise the album price
by a dollar, but hedged its bet by including a large poster of the
cover as a bonus. It didn't matter. Sales were brisk from the start.

By May, Simon and Garfunkel had done the impossible; they
had bested themselves when the *Bookends* album displaced *The
Graduate* as number one. For several weeks, the two albums
jockeyed between the number-one and number-two spots. At the
same time, the words to "Mrs. Robinson" were on everyone's lips.
By June it had become one of the fastest-selling singles of all time.

That month, Jann Wenner, publisher of *Rolling Stone* and
arbiter of rock fame, finally recognized Simon and Garfunkel's
dominance of the music industry with an article he wrote himself
that, oddly enough, heralded Simon and Garfunkel's "comeback."
Granted, none of the pair's singles since "The Sounds of Silence"
had reached number one, but all of them had been hits. Observers
agreed that Wenner had apparently finally given up his grudge
against Simon for stealing his girlfriend, Denise Kaufman.

Now no one would argue that Simon and Garfunkel had

* "Old Friends" © 1968 by Paul Simon

attained superstar status. They enjoyed great power in the industry, and agents, musicians, publishers, and other celebrities relentlessly pursued them. Their manager, Mort Lewis, called one day with a twenty-five-thousand-dollar offer to do a Coca-Cola commercial. They talked it over and thought the fee was too low. Simon asked, "How much more?" "Maybe fifty thousand dollars," Lewis replied. "See if they'll go to fifty."

Coca-Cola quickly agreed, but the duo finally turned down the commercial. They boys didn't need the money; perhaps they had just been trying to see what people would pay them. Commercial endorsement was a game with very high stakes, a game Michael Jackson, still just a diminutive member of the Jackson 5, would push to astronomical heights with the same company twenty years later.

The duo's personal life-styles now contained some of the trappings of stardom, but were always tempered by a certain studied ambivalence about the accoutrements of great wealth. In 1968 Paul lived in a high-rise apartment on Manhattan's Upper East Side overlooking the East River. While the neighborhood was upscale, his rather modest apartment had only two rooms decorated in a severe modern style featuring bright orange-rose carpeting, a huge wooden hobbyhorse, and little else. As Paul explained, "I don't like to waste time on food, clothing, shelter, possessions—I don't even own a car."

He assiduously fostered the notion that money really didn't matter to him. The first year of his success he remembered paying income tax of $125,000, and the next year almost triple that amount (more than $300,000). Now he decided to not even notice how much he owed, leaving it to the accountants. He said he received a cash allowance from his business manager of seventy-five dollars a week and put everything else on credit cards.

Art lived an equally understated life-style in a nearby high rise. His apartment, however, some said looked like it had been designed "by an architect with unlimited funds." For the most part, his attitudes about money paralleled Paul's. Both considered earning money for money's sake a waste of one's life. As Art noted, "We've already earned more money than we could possibly need for the rest of our lives. So the money and success races are something we're not only out of but can stomp upon."

Their middle-class family values had taught them that money

was undeniably important for life's necessities: providing for a family, health care, and retirement. They also knew how very lucky they were to be above all of that, to be financially secure at the age of twenty-seven and to have the ultimate luxury of choice in almost every aspect of their lives.

They both kept their daily lives extremely low-key. According to Art: "We like to pride ourselves on how few celebrities we know." Their relationships with other people were still occasional and casual. Neither was seriously interested in marriage.

Paul discussed the idea of a relationship that could lead to marriage in coolly dispassionate terms. His business manager and accountants pointed out the tax advantages of marriage, but Paul pragmatically reasoned that he stood to lose a great deal more money if the marriage were to fail. His attitude was: "Girls are no problem; they don't bug me about marriage. And I don't have to prove anything to myself—or anybody else anymore."

About marriage, Art could be equally analytical. In discussing that possibility he also revealed his hierarchy of values which, in keeping with Jewish tradition, placed family squarely at the top. He could easily envision a time when he no longer held the attention of a vast audience. When the fun stopped, he thought he could quit and walk away because his ultimate goal was to marry and raise a family. As he revealed in a 1968 interview: "I want to clear my life for it. I see myself very caught up with my family. I want to make sure I have time for that."

From the start of the Simon and Garfunkel partnership, Art had speculated on what he might do when he and Paul broke up. Unlike Paul, Art's interests had always ranged far beyond the world of music. As a hedge against the day when the fame of Simon and Garfunkel faded, and for his own intellectual development, Art was still fitfully working on a graduate degree in mathematics at Columbia. He had vague thoughts that he might want to teach math someday.

But for now they were both stars. People stopped and stared at them as they walked the streets of New York. On buses and subways, people did double takes when they recognized the same serious faces that stared out from album covers that littered countless dorm rooms and coffee tables all over America.

At first fame was fun, but both Art and Paul were now having trouble separating themselves from the Simon and Garfunkel "act," whose fame had grown tremendously. They both began to sense that "Simon and Garfunkel" was overtaking their personal lives. Paul was constantly under pressure to create new music that would keep the act on top. He worried that with some songs on *Bookends* he had set a dangerous precedent by making artistic compromises. More and more, he found himself writing to meet arbitrary time schedules instead of waiting until the music was ready. Simon wanted time to experiment with other forms of music. He had made his reputation as a folkie, but his heart still belonged to rock 'n' roll, and he was fond of listening to other variants of African-American music like gospel and Jamaican reggae.

Paul's songs continued to gain in complexity as he matured, and he felt himself becoming a little stale within the folk-rock style he and Art had perfected. He was also developing a more direct writing style that used more colloquial language, although he still employed cinematic images.

He had come to hate the "poet" label—even though he had used the term himself in his highly personal "Homeward Bound," calling himself a "poet and a one-man band." He now railed against the tag, but he couldn't convince anyone of his disavowal. In April 1969 an article on the subject of rock lyrics and music as poetry appeared in the Sunday *New York Times Magazine*. Paul's picture was featured prominently at the top of a collage of folk-rock's most important writers. In fact, his image lies superimposed squarely on the much larger face of Bob Dylan.

Paul disliked the folk-rock label because it automatically suggested the inevitable comparisons to Dylan. Paul freely admitted that his feelings of jealousy and competitiveness about Dylan and other popular acts prevented him from gaining a clear perspective on their talents.

The folk-rock label also straitjacketed him. He knew he was capable of more, and he resisted any typecasting. As he told *Newsweek,* "I'm a songwriter who uses a guitar. I write songs that are a reflection of myself. Then both of us sing them to the accompaniment of my guitar. This gives them the feeling of folk music, but it's not folk music, and it's not rock."

Absorbed in their own careers and still taking drugs on a regular basis, Simon and Garfunkel barely noticed that 1967's Summer of Love had yielded a bitter harvest barely one year later.

In January 1968, North Vietnam's audacious and bloody Tet offensive ended the myth of American military invincibility, and, at home, the country was at war with itself. In April the brutal murder of civil-rights leader Martin Luther King, Jr., triggered violent demonstrations of frustration and rage throughout America. That summer, large sections of Los Angeles, Chicago, Cleveland, and Detroit erupted in flames, and rioters were shot in the streets.

Lyndon Johnson, wearied by escalating opposition to the Vietnam War, decided he could not govern a country so deeply divided and declined to run for reelection. That summer Richard Nixon, ever present in the political wings, gathered his forces, sensing an opportunity to capture the presidency at last.

June saw the assassination of Robert Kennedy in a Los Angeles hotel, extinguishing hopes for a viable peace candidate and, perhaps, even another Camelot in the White House.

As America watched in horror, assassins gunned down its leaders and heroes on television. The nation's long-smoldering mood of alienation and despair that Simon and Garfunkel articulated so perfectly in rhythm and rhyme erupted in a flash fire as the streets of America became battlegrounds. Radios across the country played the number-one hit tune, "Mrs. Robinson." Simon's song suddenly presented a timely and truthful snapshot of a nation as it passed through one of its darkest hours. In an eerie alignment of fact and imagination, "Mrs. Robinson" called up the image of a country yearning for leadership and mourning the absence of traditional heroes and the loss of national innocence: "Where have you gone, Joe DiMaggio / A nation turns its lonely eyes to you ... "*

Although the nation was humming "Mrs. Robinson," not everyone was captivated by the reference to Joe DiMaggio. The ex-Yankee slugger was so unhappy with the use of his name, there was talk of a lawsuit. He didn't understand why the song referred to him as "gone" when he was still very much alive, enjoying a lucrative career as a commercial pitchman for Mr. Coffee and other products. The misunderstanding was eventually cleared up when DiMaggio realized that the lyrics actually offered him homage by using him as a metaphor for an era.

*"Mrs. Robinson" © 1968 by Paul Simon

(Years later, Simon had a chance to meet another one of his boyhood Yankee heroes, Mickey Mantle. The retired slugger took Simon aside and earnestly asked why the writer chose DiMaggio's name instead of his for "Mrs. Robinson." Simon, deep in the throes of his own case of hero worship, was unprepared for Mantle's question. He blurted out, "It was nothing personal. Just a matter of syllables.")

Simon and Garfunkel were strangely removed from the unrest of that turbulent summer and fall of 1968. Seven years later, Simon admitted, "I wasn't involved in anything at the time; I was just by myself. I was crazy most of the time, high, and relatively depressed throughout those years—quite alone. I lived on the East Side, by the river, uptown. So even where I lived was not connected to anything—it was largely unaffected by the youth culture."

The Paul Simon who said he had been struck by news of the civil-rights movement while living in Paris five years earlier was now admittedly thoroughly insulated by success. He and Art were consumed by the exhausting work of maintaining their careers with a heavy performance schedule on the road.

Paul remembered the touring life as a very strange experience: "I always felt weird on the road. I was in a state of semihypnosis. I went into a daze, and I did things by rote." It seemed the road would never end, but their popularity was at an all-time high, and commitments now stretched far into the future. By now Simon and Garfunkel had become bored with their road games and with the enforced togetherness. More and more often, after the respectful hush, thunderous applause, and final encore, both headed back to their separate hotel rooms to smoke their joints alone. Paul tried to distract himself by working feverishly on songs for a new album.

In October, Paul and Art returned to the Forest Hills tennis stadium to perform at a sold-out concert not far from their boyhood homes. Just two years earlier, they had driven themselves to the stadium in a beat-up Volkswagen, but on that chilly autumn night in 1968, they emerged from a chauffeur-driven limousine. The concert typified the team's trademark performance style.

Several hours before the concert, their manager gleefully counted the house, estimating scalper prices at twelve dollars for a six-dollar seat. Meanwhile, Art scaled the heights and depths of the empty stadium, from the cheap seats to the pricey boxes, waving his arms and nodding his head as Paul and the technicians played with amps, microphones, and sound levels. Satisfied with the sound arrangements at last, the pair disappeared into a large mobile home outfitted with food and beverages. A stream of old friends, neighbors, and relatives flowed through the open door: Art's brother, Paul's father, and a handful of other people who still unselfconsciously called them Paulie and Artie. A knock on the door signaled show time, and the two quickly changed into their stage clothes—clean T-shirts and Levis—and then threaded their way onto the stage and settled into the brilliant pool of light in a sea of darkness.

Thousands of young, white, middle-class faces fixed their eyes on the singers and applauded wildly. Paul strummed his guitar and immediately began the first song. The audience's pleasure grew with each familiar tune—lips moved in unison all over the stadium.

The audience merged with the performers, and the duo played on and on until, at last, they left the stage and disappeared into the waiting trailer. The stream of well-wishers swelled to a torrent. Paul and Art were surrounded and sank happily in a sea of praise. The magic ebbed and flowed from the night.

1968 had been Simon and Garfunkel's most successful year. "Mrs. Robinson" had earned them another gold record. *Bookends* and *The Graduate* albums, as well as their singles, were among the top sellers of the year. *Bookends* would soon go platinum by selling over one million copies. Promotional activities and concert appearances left little time to develop new work, although Paul was making some headway on a long, experimental tune about a boxer.

As 1968 drew to a close, Simon and Garfunkel, at the age of twenty-seven years, dominated the popular music scene. Acclaimed as authentic American superstars, their names had become part of the language. A radio station in New York ran an ad to promote its commitment to the news no matter who made it. Beneath caricatures of French President Charles DeGaulle and Russian Premiere Aleksei Kosygin the caption read: "Simon and Garfunkel They Ain't." An entire generation looked to them to express their deepest emotions, their hopes and dreams as well as their anxieties.

In spite of the success, Paul and Art were finding it more and more difficult to communicate with each other. The polite criticisms and friendly give-and-take of earlier recording sessions now had a sharper edge. One observer recalled that although they weren't fighting yet, there was definitely a testiness between them, especially if one felt the other was wasting time. The new tension in the relationship may have been a result of Paul's having been dropped from the production of *Catch-22*. Joseph Heller's sprawling novel was jam-packed with quirky characters, and the large cast proved to be too much for the already bloated budget. In the interest of streamlining the production, several roles had to be cut, including Paul's film-acting debut as Dunbar. There was the possibility of Art's voluntary departure from the film unless a role could be found for Paul. But no one seriously thought that would really happen. As was their habit, the situation ended without a formal resolution, and despite Paul's hurt feelings, Art quietly proceeded with his plans to act in the film.

He found the complex process of making a film challenging. More important, in spite of Simon and Garfunkel's enormous musical success, Art still felt restless and creatively incomplete. Starring in a major Hollywood motion picture would be a glamorous way to prove himself as a solo artist.

7

Once the decision to go into films by himself had been made, Art seemed to ignore Paul's hurt feelings. It was apparent that Art savored the twist of fate that gave him the chance to stand in the spotlight alone. A few years later, when asked how Paul felt about being dropped from *Catch-22*, Art described the experience in childhood terms, saying Paul felt like a kid in a candy store who hadn't gotten a taste.

In the final turbulent months of 1968, Art concentrated on preparing for his role. Shooting was scheduled to begin in January 1969 and was projected to last three months. On the surface at least, Paul took his loss of the film role in stride. Both tacitly agreed they would follow their separate paths.

Paul seemed to easily adjust to the new arrangement and, to the relief of Columbia Records, once again turned his attention to his music.

It was clear that Art felt he hadn't abandoned the Simon and Garfunkel partnership. He acknowledged that the separation would mean problems, but he seemed to suggest, in public at least, that his move into filmmaking was made for the good of the team. Art said: "I felt that if Simon and Garfunkel are ever going to involve themselves in filming, this was a rare opportunity to learn."

Art was infatuated with Nichols and with the growing importance of film in American society. He had aligned himself with one of America's most respected creative talents and looked forward to learning how to act under his mentor's direction.

Nichols, fresh from the mega-hit *The Graduate*, had developed a reputation for creating box-office successes in spite of his penchant for serious content, and was in big demand in Hollywood. Still, he felt the pressure of industry cynics waiting for him to stumble. *Catch-22*, his third film, would finally confirm either his superior directing talent or his great good luck.

Insiders reported that Nichols demanded, and got, the rare privilege of having final cut on *Catch-22*. Nervous studio executives were always loath to relinquish such control, but Nichols wanted to be one of the few directors since Orson Welles (on *Citizen Kane*) to gain full artistic command of such a large-scale film. It's unlikely that Paramount actually gave up final cut, but that kind of publicity didn't hurt Nichols's career.

Ironically, the formidable Welles, who had bought the first film option on Heller's novel but had to let it expire because he couldn't secure financing, was cast by Nichols in the role of General Dreedle.

The film adaptation of Heller's complex black comedy set during World War II presented Nichols with a sizable challenge. Yossarian, the film's mad bombardier hero, was a character convinced—and rightly so—that the whole world conspired to see him dead. Nichols wanted to tell the story in an unconventional series of vivid, loosely connected scenes separated by blackouts. This approach would enable him to create on a grand scale, and he reveled in it. Location shooting began after Nichols transported 340 cast and crew members to the Playa de Cortes Hotel on Mexico's Sea of Cortez near Guymas. After only a few weeks' shooting, it became clear to Paramount that costs were spiraling out of sight, but everyone on location was having a great time.

The cast of *Catch-22* was a diverse group: Alan Arkin, Tony Perkins, Martin Balsam, Orson Welles, Norman Fell, Bob Newhart, Charles Grodin, Jon Voight, Martin Sheen, Richard Benjamin, and Paula Prentiss. Buck Henry, constantly rewriting the sprawling script to include Nichols's latest ideas, described them:

"This bunch is pound-for-pound the smartest, most likable, least hung-up group of actors I've ever known." But, he added, "Of course, they are weirdos and psychopaths, but there isn't a dummy in the bunch. Well, maybe one."

To amuse themselves during the endless breaks, cast and crew played word games—anagrams, "Dictionary," "Quotations." They also played tennis incessantly, but some didn't take the game as seriously as Art, who had studied its fine points, would have liked. They did little actual shooting of the film.

Art kept his distance from the restless, bantering crowd. His shyness may have come from his insecurity about this new career. He later admitted, "I have an inferiority complex about acting. If other actors turned on me and said, 'What exactly are you doing here?' I'd have no answer." He seemed especially aloof compared to the parade of extroverts Nichols had assembled. Most of the others whiled away the evening hours entertaining each other by playing the ukelele or the kazoo, or telling jokes. Art never sang to entertain the others, nor did anyone ask him to. But they teased Art, calling him the "second-richest man" in the company. Some went so far as to say he might even be richer than Mike Nichols. Everyone knew Nichols was getting the princely sum of five hundred thousand dollars plus 10 percent of the gross to direct the film. Art was paid a mere seventy-five thousand dollars—a sum he could have made in a few concert appearances.

The production delays grew longer. Nichols loved to improvise and often emerged from discussions with his cast or crew with elaborate and expensive production details that differed significantly from the original plan. The cast would then retreat to play their games while the directors, engineers, and set designers fabricated the new scene.

Excesses became commonplace. In one scene the director called for a full-scale bomber plane to plunge to earth in a fiery crash merely as background for a short piece of close-up dialogue. News of the extravagant production filtered out of Mexico, and the film reaped a publicity bonanza. Outrageous tales from the location sets were useful to prime the public's interest.

The publicity mill painted an intriguing picture of Art Garfunkel as a budding young film actor, and he liked his new image. When *Catch-22* opened, he would be a bona fide movie star while still remaining half of one of the most successful musical partnerships in history.

He had it all, it seemed. At last, Art had found a way to emerge from the shadow of Paul's songwriting talent. After all the years spent passively following Paul's lead, he finally had something important to do on his own.

Meanwhile, Paul's envy deepened and his mood darkened. As far as he was concerned, he was already doing more than his fair share to keep the partnership successful while still failing to get the recognition he craved. Now it looked as though Art might become a movie star while Paul continued to shoulder most of the burden of keeping Simon and Garfunkel on top with his unique songs. Paul wanted Art's full attention and was angry with Garfunkel's decision to split his time into two careers.

In March, Art left the Mexican shooting location to fly to Los Angeles where he met Paul to rehearse for the Grammy Awards show. As was the custom in 1969, Grammy organizers announced the winners in advance of the glittery, televised awards spectacle. Host Gary Owens, the Los Angeles deejay who had become a celebrity on the breakthrough comedy series "Laugh-In," announced what the crowd already knew. Competing with Glen Campbell ("Wichita Lineman"), The Beatles ("Hey, Jude"), Jeannie C. Riley ("Harper Valley P.T.A."), and Bobby Goldsboro ("Honey"), Simon and Garfunkel's "Mrs. Robinson" was voted Best Record of the Year. It also won a Grammy for Best Contemporary Pop Vocal Performance by a Group.

Knowing in advance the honors "Mrs. Robinson" would receive for the occasion, Art and Paul produced a silent, slapstick film that featured them playing baseball with Joe DiMaggio, who no longer objected to the use of his name in the song. The brief, surrealistic film was played over "Mrs. Robinson" and was a highlight of the evening.

Paul also picked up an individual Grammy for Best Soundtrack Album from a Motion Picture or Television Program. Paul and Art glowed in the recognition of their peers in the recording industry. This was the realization of the dream they had shared since boyhood.

Art returned to Mexico to complete *Catch-22*, and Paul went home to New York to continue writing songs for their new album.

He finished his epic struggle with "The Boxer," a new song more than five minutes long. Its combative tone reflected Paul's own embattled emotional state, constantly vying for Art's attention and torn by old jealousies.

Art and Paul rarely saw each other these days, and the key collaborative aspect of their partnership fell victim to Art's busy schedule. Time for their music had to be stolen from the movie. When he had a few free days he would fly to meet Paul. They laid down tracks for "The Boxer" in Nashville, New York, Los Angeles, and anywhere else a studio could be found to suit their schedules. Paul, pleased with the way the song had turned out, was eager to release it. But in April he took time out from recording for his second love: In the fulfillment of another boyhood fantasy, he threw out the first ball at Yankee Stadium on opening day.

Paul's happiness that spring was magnified by a whirlwind love affair with a Southern belle named Peggy Harper, who was married at the time to his friend and long-time manager, Mort Lewis. Paul was deeply in love, and he pursued Peggy with all the competitive zeal he could muster.

The daughter of a house painter, Peggy had grown up in the shadow of the Smoky Mountains in Tennessee. She was a former airline stewardess and not directly involved in the music business. Finally won over by Paul's unrelenting pursuit, Peggy separated from Lewis and asked for a divorce so she could marry Paul. Decades later Paul would write a song—"Train in the Distance"— about their relationship: "She was beautiful as Southern skies / The night he met her / She was married to someone."* It's a straightforward description of how Paul and Peggy met. The song continues: "He was doggedly determined that he would get her / He was old, he was young."* As Paul later explained, "That's me. I was…pretending to be sophisticated. I wasn't."

Art was also looking for a serious relationship. That spring, during a two-week hiatus in the filming of *Catch-22*, he flew to New York to work on "The Boxer" with Paul. While there, he met Linda Grossman, a former architecture student, in a memorable encounter on the streets of New York City. A few years earlier, Linda had seen the famous pair perform at Washington University

*"Train in the Distance" © 1981 by Paul Simon

in St. Louis, and now, when she caught sight of Art walking down Fifth Avenue with Mort Lewis, she stopped her cab, got out, walked directly up to him, and asked, "You're Artie, aren't you?" Her impulsiveness charmed Art, who was immediately attracted to her. He later explained, "I, of course, was ready...my rhythm was already going. I think I asked her to marry me about the second sentence." He invited Linda to accompany him to "The Boxer" recording session scheduled later that day. There he was moved by her rapt attention: "I was impressed...very flattered. I like people who third-degree me, who stare at me. I feel they're interested." Linda had given up the study of architecture and now worked in Boston as a graphic artist. Soon she started shuttling back and forth between Boston and New York to date Art, but his time was severely limited by his other new passion—the movies.

By now, Art's fascination with films left Paul feeling abandoned and betrayed. As he said of "The Boxer," "That song was about me—everybody's beating me up, and I'm telling you now I'm going away if you don't stop!" Signs of Paul's deep disaffection frequently surfaced, but no one—especially Art—paid any attention.

"The Boxer" was released in April. The single was Paul's only song that year, but it represented a stunning achievement. The song tells a touching story about a poor boy who literally fights his way out of poverty with his fists. A proud but vulnerable man buffeted by the unceasing blows of a hostile world, he is punch-drunk and weary, with only strangers and whores for company. But through the scar tissue and bruises, the fighter retains a sense of dignity that will not permit humiliation, no matter what comes his way.

Longer and more complex than any of his previous songs, "The Boxer" has a more complete dramatic framework. The accompaniment includes a sampling of Paul's musical explorations at that time: acoustic guitar, pedal steel guitar, bass harmonica, and a lush string section. The trademark Simon and Garfunkel vocal harmonies are perfectly true in spite of their long separations.

Paul has admitted that the song's edgy feel reflects his own state of mind during this period of inner turmoil. In addition to his feeling abandoned by Art, critics were beginning to zero in on Simon and Garfunkel. In the first few years of their career, the two had received almost universally positive notices. But as their popularity grew, critics scrutinized their work more closely. Some carped about their lack of authentic folk credentials, saccharine melodies, and pretentious lyrics. Most often, critics complained of predictable, soft arrangements which sometimes dulled the grittier aspects of Paul's songs.

The negative comments angered Paul, in particular, because he saw some truth in them. He worried that he had abdicated his artistic responsibility to Art and engineer Roy Halee too often, and that this had resulted in the lush, sweet sound that had come to characterize the Simon and Garfunkel style. Although millions of fans adored the sound, Paul felt limited by it and was more eager than ever to explore new musical directions.

Paul's depression, often drug-related, grew worse. He now sought comfort and relief in the Bible, a source which also yielded songwriting inspiration: "I think I was reading the Bible around that time [of 'The Boxer']. That's where I think phrases like 'workman's wages' came from and 'seeking out the poorer quarters.'" Soon after its release, "The Boxer" rose to number three.

Art's original three-month commitment to *Catch-22* doubled to six as Nichols moved the traveling carnival to Rome after completing location shooting in Mexico. In Italy, as in Mexico, the film was delayed by bad weather and massive script revisions. Finally, by summer, the production lumbered back to Los Angeles for an extensive stay to shoot interiors.

Paul, Peggy, and Art rented a house together on Blue Jay Way in Los Angeles. Peggy was waiting for her divorce to become final, but she and Paul were together constantly. Columbia stepped up the pressure on Paul for the new album, and the trio decided that shared living space might be the best way to squeeze rehearsal time for the songs from Art's schedule.

To make rehearsals easier, Paul moved an assortment of guitars, amplifiers, and tape recorders into one of the rooms of the large rambling house, which already had a grand piano. Art managed to schedule some rehearsal time while he waited for his *Catch-22* scenes to be shot, but he soon found a subtle but critical change in their recording method. Although Art still retained veto power over what material they would record, the delicate balance of power in the partnership had shifted.

Most of the ideas for the arrangements were now generated by Paul, his brother Eddie, and Roy Halee. Paul felt real progress was being made on the album, and it was clear to everyone that he was making a lot of creative decisions alone. Art and Paul did momentarily recapture the cooperative Simon and Garfunkel spirit with Paul's raucous new tune, "Cecilia."

Although the song was something of a departure from the Simon and Garfunkel style, Art was enthusiastic about its bubbly tone. Singing it recalled the joy Art and Paul had shared in the earlier years before their fame grew. The song's concept and arrangement happened in much the same way as all the best early Simon and Garfunkel music—experimenting together in a room with minimal recording equipment, with the single purpose of having fun while creating music.

Paul had casually laid down a lively string of rhythmic beats on a portable tape recorder earlier in the summer when Art was at the film studio. During the days, Paul worked to shape the new songs and rehearsed with the new musicians. Every night, he came home fascinated with the curious beats he'd recorded. He was obsessed by them although he had no lyric or idea beyond the pulsating beat. He recorded the beats and doubled the track, eventually gaining about three minutes of rhythm. He took the tape into the studio, where, Art recalled, "We dropped a batch of fifteen drumsticks on the parquet studio floor because we like that wood-crashing sound." They kept the unusual sound and looked for others to complement it.

Paul spotted a xylophone in the studio and, although he had never played the instrument before, beat out an accompanying rhythm while Art helped mix the various tracks. Roy Halee engineered the sound to form the perfect blend of percussion Paul was after. It was a rare example of the creative triumvirate working together as a real team once again.

Paul picked up a guitar and began playing along with the recorded rhythm tracks, and he remembered, "Virtually the first lines I said—'You're breakin' my heart, I'm down on my knees'— they're not lines at all, but it was right for that song." He called it "a little piece of magical fluff."

The lyrics for "Cecilia" skate lightly above the ecstatic rhythm line, but it is curious that the first words that occurred to Paul describe heartbreak and pleas to "come home." Although the song was cast in a clearly comic mode, Paul's mind was on more serious matters.

They were so busy in Los Angeles with film and album recording that they had to turn down repeated invitations to appear at what promised to be an interesting, three-day outdoor concert in a farmer's field in upstate New York. The Woodstock Music and Art Fair would feature many of the biggest names in the music business: Joan Baez; the Who; Crosby, Stills, Nash and Young; Richie Havens; Sha-Na-Na; Arlo Guthrie; Melanie; Ten Years After; John Sebastian; Jimi Hendrix; Santana; the Jefferson Airplane; Joe Cocker; and Country Joe and the Fish, among others. But Simon and Garfunkel couldn't spare the time to attend.

As if the dizzying whirl of making a new album and movie wasn't enough, the pair had also committed to making their first television special. In previous television appearances they had always been guests, but discussions with NBC and the "Bell Telephone Hour" sponsor, AT&T, led to the decision to feature Simon and Garfunkel as the show's stars. Paul and Art looked forward to being in command of their own program.

They began to work hard on the program, calling it "Songs for America," a title and concept which seemed inoffensive to AT&T. It would be an expensive, full-scale production directed by actor-director Charles Grodin, with whom Art had become friends on the set of *Catch-22*.

Simon and Garfunkel approached television production the same way they approached record production. For the two superstars, a television studio was little more than an expensive playground, and they looked forward to pushing it to its limits.

Meanwhile, Paul continued to familiarize Art with the new songs he had been working on that summer. They had been booked for a tour in the fall, and Paul saw it as a good chance to test some of the songs on live audiences before recording the final tracks.

The preliminary sessions for the new album had gotten off to a rocky start. Observers noted the new songs were much more difficult to produce than anyone had anticipated; every track became a struggle for control, occasionally ending in a shouting match. Arguments between the pair became a habit.

Many of the new songs, directly and indirectly, suggested Paul's preoccupation with the deterioration of the relationship. They

were Paul's oblique way of letting Art and the world know the
partnership was ending.

The most powerful and melancholy of Paul's new songs was
"The Only Living Boy in New York," which Paul had written
while Art was on location in Mexico. The opening line calls Art
by the name "Tom," a reference to the beginning of their
partnership as Tom and Jerry. In the lyric, Paul mentions the film
role: "I know your part'll go fine / Fly down to Mexico." Paul's
loneliness made him feel like the only living boy in New York with
"nothing to do today but smile." He knew Art was "ready to fly"
and graciously wished him well, reminding him to "let your
honesty shine." It is a fond and deeply personal farewell.

"Why Don't You Write Me" carried on in the same elegiac tone,
begging for some sign that the distance between the two could still
be bridged. It was a plea for communication: "I'm hungry to hear
you / Send me a card / I am waiting so hard / To be near you."*

In another song of farewell, Paul recalls Art's early passion for
architecture; referring to his friend and partner as "Frank Lloyd
Wright," he adds, "I can't believe your song is gone so soon / I
barely learned the tune." The parting of the ways now seemed a
certainty, and Paul vowed to remember "All the nights we'd
harmonize until dawn."†

These songs of wistful passage and parting also suggest the
themes of resignation and peace which are fully developed in
Paul's most powerful and most memorable composition, "Bridge
Over Troubled Water." In this song, originally titled "Hymn,"
Paul again calls to mind images of dissension and trouble, but this
time he manages to create a classic by rising above personal
references to strike a more universal chord. His subject is the
healing power of selfless love; the song's roots are in black gospel
music, a passion Paul had developed as a boy.

Through the years he had studied gospel closely and was
especially touched by the classic, "Oh, Mary, Don't You Weep for
Me," as sung by the Reverend Claude Jeter and the Swan
Silvertones. Jeter's recording of the song contained a line he had
added himself as embellishment: "I'll be your bridge over deep

* "Why Don't You Write Me" © 1969 by Paul Simon
† "So Long, Frank Lloyd Wright" © 1969 by Paul Simon

water if you trust in my name." The line stuck with Paul, who tucked it away to germinate for a later time when he felt a need to write his own version of gospel music.

Paul knew at once he had created something extraordinary with "Bridge Over Troubled Water." In the past, it was not uncommon for him to burst into tears of pent-up emotion at the moment he finally delivered a line or a melody for a song. That same feeling of release and relief poured over him as he wrote the line, "Like a bridge over troubled water, I will lay me down." The line came out as a complete thought and even surprised him with its simple power. He has said, "I didn't know it was coming. What I was saying was, 'I'm going to do this act of generosity for you.'" Unlike the rest of the album's songs, he was not thinking only of Art when he wrote this one. He was also thinking about Peggy, his soon-to-be wife.

Paul remembered the moment of triumph and relief when Peggy finally yielded to his pursuit and agreed to marry him. He used the song to plumb the depth of his love, to articulate his willingness to sacrifice anything, even himself, for Peggy's sake.

In a second major gesture of selflessness, he decided the song would be Art's to sing solo. Originally written for guitar accompaniment in the key of G, Paul had "Bridge" transposed for Art, who sang it in the key of E-flat. Paul instinctively felt "Bridge" was the best song he had ever written.

But when Simon played it for Art, he was disappointed by Art's tepid reaction. Art remembers, "Paul showed me 'Bridge Over Troubled Water,' and he felt it was his best song. I felt it was something less than his best song, but a great song." At first, Art didn't even want to sing it. After hearing Paul's rendition, Art felt he could do no better with it than Paul as a solo. Paul sang the song in a high falsetto, very different from his usual sound, and Art was impressed with the effect and encouraged Paul to take the song himself. Paul said, "No, you should do it. I wrote it so that you would do it." At last, Art reluctantly agreed.

Paul was wounded by Art's rejection of what he thought was his finest work. Although disappointed, Paul was not surprised. Throughout the preparation for the new album, Art had less creative input than ever before, and communication between the two was waning. Art's acting career had distracted him from music for months at a time, and when he did find time for Paul, he found a man whose singular obsession was still music. Paul tried repeatedly to involve Art in the development of the new songs, but by the time Art became involved, Paul had often passed through the critical phase of Art's contribution and had gone beyond it on his own. More often than not, he now brought completed songs to the update sessions.

The residual strain, growing ever since Art decided to change his career focus to acting, increased. With Paul's new aggressive stand on music decisions, there was little common ground left. Music, which had once been the cornerstone of the relationship, now had become a battleground. Paul remembered, "There were a lot of times when it just wasn't fun to work together. It was very hard work and it was complex...and I know I said I felt that if I had to go through these kinds of personality abrasions, I didn't want to continue to do it."

Art's cool reaction to "Bridge" wasn't the first sign of the estrangement, but it was the most serious, because it confirmed the widening gap in matters of musical taste. Paul felt Art had misjudged his song and that this was a telling sign of how far apart the two had drifted. The tension which had been building all summer was nearing the breaking point.

Something else was happening that affected the relationship. Paul had given up drugs. The dope he had used for years to encourage his creative flow had become more of a liability than a help, and now he vowed to change.

It wasn't an easy decision. His conflicts ran deep. He had depended for so long on drugs to enable him to write that abandoning them took an extraordinary act of will—and an ultimatum from a psychiatrist, who refused to start treatment unless Paul gave up drugs. He decided to go cold turkey, but couldn't resist a final blaze of hallucinatory glory. On the night before his first therapy session, he systematically ingested or smoked every ounce of drugs in his apartment. It would be his last taste for eleven years. Analysis and introspection would become Paul's new method of freeing his creative impulses.

Paul was also strongly influenced by Peggy, who had replaced Art as principal confidant and sounding board. Peggy encouraged Paul to seek his own individual path, and her support gave him the strength he needed to go it alone.

Paul's anger grew as he itemized his grievances: throughout the career of Simon and Garfunkel, he had suppressed his ego many times as an act of selfless dedication to the partnership; his meticulously crafted and singularly original songs were what first attracted Mike Nichols and what gave Art entré into the movie business; Art shared fully in the rewards of musical success no matter how unequal his creative contribution. And now the final blow—Art placed a higher value on movies than on the music. In Paul's mind, Art had made his choice.

Paul poured out his anger and hurt to his analyst and to Peggy. As he explored his feelings, he realized that his need for partnership was a means of dealing with his own insecurities. Beneath his aggressive, confident façade, Paul Simon was afraid to stand alone in the spotlight. He surrounded himself with a singing partner, other musicians, and engineers. Though he saw himself as the creative core of the process, he spread the responsibility for success or failure among the group. Embedded within the talents of others, he couldn't be singled out for full blame or praise.

Art's defection to the movies had given Paul time and opportunity to assess his own talents. It gradually dawned on him that his ambivalence about a solo career contributed to the depression that had plagued him for years. This key insight, and Peggy's support, gave him the courage to free himself from Simon and Garfunkel.

Few beyond their small circle of friends knew how strained the relationship between Art and Paul had become. They were still in demand on the concert circuit, and in October, when Art's final scenes for *Catch-22* were completed, the long-planned tour began.

On the road, the differences which had surfaced in recording sessions became more obvious. Paul had long agitated for a richer, more complex sound both onstage and on recordings, and he saw this tour, which he planned largely by himself, as a chance to experiment. Until now, the classic image of the team had been one of spare simplicity: two men and one guitar in a pool of light on an otherwise bare stage.

To polish the new songs for the album, Paul decided to take along the full backup band he had been working with in recording sessions. He thought the tour would give everyone, especially Art, a chance to get used to the new style before the final tracks had to be laid down. Art objected but, as usual, went along with Paul's decision.

Not all of the songs were unfamiliar. The old Everly Brothers standard "Bye Bye Love" was hastily recorded for the next album at a live concert in Ames, Iowa, during the tour. The song pays homage to their longtime vocal heroes and marks both the genesis of the partnership and their trademark harmony, the reason for their phenomenal success.

Between tour stops, they tried to focus on their next project, the network television special. From the start, it was a drain on energies already sapped by the frenetic touring schedule and escalating personal tensions. Work on the production began in September and continued in fits and starts almost up to its air date of November 30, 1969. When AT&T finally screened the program, the sponsor was alarmed by its political content and vehemently ordered the pair to tone down the program.

AT&T had expected to see the gentle, choirboy side of Simon and Garfunkel. The show's stars, however, were determined to follow the unorthodox path of the Smothers Brothers and deliver their music along with pointed antiestablishment and antiwar messages. Both Art and Paul had worked their way out of the self-absorbed trance of the year before and had turned their attention once again to the issues about which their audience cared passionately. They saw television as a chance to establish their positions on significant social problems through a medium more suitable to social commentary than music alone, and they were not about to let the opportunity pass. They would offer the audience a vivid impression of American popular culture, juxtaposing images of such popular icons as Mickey Mantle, the Lone Ranger, and Dick Clark with pictures of America's bad boy comedian and social satirist, Lenny Bruce, as well as that of antiwar politician Eugene McCarthy. The show would feature news footage of slain leaders Robert Kennedy and Martin Luther King, Jr., as well as footage of Cesar Chávez leading his United Farmworkers strikes, Woodstock, and bloody images of wounded soldiers in Vietnam.

The more AT&T pushed to water down the program's sharp political message, the harder Simon and Garfunkel pushed back, defending their position. Flexing their muscle had worked with other companies, and the issue this time was much more important than commercial endorsement of a product. In one tense meeting with the sponsor, the two were on the verge of withdrawing from the project entirely.

The argument escalated. AT&T threatened to pull its sponsorship unless changes were made. "Fuck you," they told the suits from AT&T. "This is the show we made. This is what we believe in. Don't put it on then." The sponsor made good on its threat and withdrew its financial backing, even though it took a considerable loss by selling the show to Alberto Culver for a fraction of the production cost of six hundred thousand dollars. The ease with which CBS replaced a major sponsor was an indication of Simon and Garfunkel's immense popularity and clout.

"Songs for America" finally aired in the form Simon and Garfunkel wished. One critic noted: "For all the pictorial montage of the disquieting events of recent years and the cinema verité exploration of their own feelings, the main appeal of Simon and Garfunkel remains their songs." Those songs included standards like "The Sounds of Silence" as well as several cuts from the new album. "So Long, Frank Lloyd Wright" was played over a montage of the duo's contemporary and mythical heroes. "Bridge Over Troubled Water" was the emotional high point of the program. It played over footage of JFK with little Caroline, Martin Luther King, Jr., Bobby Kennedy, and finally Bobby's funeral train.

"Songs for America" aired once and was never repeated, but few who saw it would forget "Bridge Over Troubled Water." Once again, Art Garfunkel's soaring interpretation of a Paul Simon song made it, almost overnight, a Simon and Garfunkel classic.

The two wearily ended their tour with two sold-out performances at New York's Carnegie Hall. The sellout was further proof of their incredible box-office power—the Rolling Stones were giving a concert in town at the same time, but Simon and Garfunkel still sold every ticket in record time. As usual, the reviewer for the *New York Times* took pains to describe both men physically: Garfunkel "... tall, slim...his hair in his customary sunburst halo, and Mr. Simon, short and dark and...impish."

The critic was less than enthusiastic about the use of an electronic band in the second half of the program. He noted that the first half, featuring only Paul's acoustic guitar and the duo's distinctive harmonies, was far preferable to the second half, when the band backed them up. He said Simon and Garfunkel with the band "might have been any anonymous contemporary group."

He found the mix of old and new songs appealing, but took exception to a new song which he called "Like a Bridge on Troubled Water": "In its mawkish, undiluted sentimentality, it was reminiscent of the songs of faith that were once great favorites on the lesser concert circuits. It seemed incredible that such an anachronism could be offered straight at a Simon and Garfunkel concert." What surprised the reviewer even more was "the enthusiastic, cheering response of the audience."

The tour helped fit all the remaining album pieces together, and when it ended they were finally ready to record the rest of the tracks they needed. But the sniping continued when they entered the studio. According to Paul: "Our patience was running out, and there was sort of vaguely the presence of Mike Nichols around, which was disconcerting to me." They tried to concentrate on recording the new songs. As with all of their albums, the tracks had been recorded in several locales over a long period of time.

"El Condor Pasa (If I Could)" was a selection gleaned from Paul's early years in Paris when he saw a group called Los Incas perform an eighteenth-century Peruvian folk song. He vowed to record the song someday, his way. Paul acquired the Los Incas tracks and dressed them up with new lyrics, a meditation on choice, limits, and possibility. "Keep the Customer Satisfied" suggests Paul's weariness with the burden of generating the unique songs which had made Simon and Garfunkel into a national phenomenon. Familiar Simon themes: the stress of being on the road and the idea of homecoming are central to the song's story line.

Paul brought an eclectic mix of song styles to these recording sessions, but he intended to showcase much more than his interest in a wide variety of musical forms. He wanted to detail the span of a relationship from beginning to end.

Paul's lyrics are typically transparent regarding the breakup in "So Long, Frank Lloyd Wright." But also typically, neither partner talked openly about the song's obvious implications. Art remembered the recording of "So Long, Frank Lloyd Wright" as one of his favorites because he, along with Paul and Roy, conspired to include an uncharacteristic playful moment that occurred during the recording. The song ends with a fade-out that Art sang alone—"So long / So long." The fade-out went on and on, and faintly in the background, the voice of Paul can be heard yelling, "So long, already, Artie." It was the first and only public record of the split.

One tune was poignantly titled "Song for the Asking," and again the theme was parting. The song is a wistful, last-ditch attempt on Paul's part to make amends and go on sharing the career that they worked so hard to build. It also suggests Paul's willingness to make changes to preserve the relationship: "Don't turn away / I'd be more than glad / To change my ways for the asking."* Paul seems to offer his most treasured possession, his music, as a peace offering, a sign of his love and friendship. But the love was unrequited.

The recording of the album's most memorable song was a formidable experience. Paul was still smarting over Art's initial reaction to "Bridge," and he wanted to vindicate himself with a perfect recording of it. Paul remembered, "It became very hard to take criticism from each other. Like I used to feel 'I don't have to audition my songs for anyone,' and I don't want to have to say to Artie, 'Would you like to sing this song?' I want to be able to say, 'Now here's the song, let's do it.'"

Although they bickered incessantly, Paul, Art, and Halee managed to channel and transform their angry energy into a positive, creative force. It was the last time the three would work together as they had in their glory days.

There was no disagreement that the genius of "Bridge" lay in its gospel flavor and that a solo piano accompaniment was required. Jimmie Haskell, an arranger who was in the room at the time and who had worked for Paul before, wrote the chords in Art's key. It was a simple task, but one which would eventually earn Haskell a Grammy, an honor Paul felt was disproportionate to the effort involved.

The piano arrangement was performed by the duo's sideman, Larry Knechtel, and it took four arduous days to complete, much longer than Paul expected. In a state of agitation, he paced the studio control room waiting for the work to be done. However, when Knechtel finally played it, Paul was thrilled with the simple, solemn sound.

When Art and Roy Halee heard the arrangement, they, too, were excited, but both felt the song needed something more. Art, at last totally involved in the production process, suggested adding a third verse to Paul's original two. The give-and-take of the old

*"Song for the Asking" © 1970 by Paul Simon

days came into play once again, and Paul reverted to his role of collaborator rather than that of sole creator. He requested: "Play the piano part for a third verse again, and…I'll write it." As he had been on "Cecilia," Paul was willing to write spontaneously, a radical departure from his customary habit.

His first thoughts turned to Peggy. She had recently found a few gray hairs and was upset at the thought of getting old. So Paul wrote, "Sail on silver girl / Your time has come to shine." Paul comforts her and his listeners with the reassurance that come what may, friendship will abide in times of trouble.

When it was done, Paul wasn't completely satisfied with the lyrics to the new verse and imagined everyone could tell it was a last-minute addition. But everyone else in the studio thought it worked. The third verse did what Art and Roy wanted it to do, and finally Paul agreed with their assessment, an indication of the respect and trust they still commanded from him.

The co-producers saw their opening and took it. Art reminded Paul of a recording of "Old Man River," by the Righteous Brothers, they had heard years ago. The record's producer, Phil Spector, had devised a spectacular ending to a rather spare version of the old standard. Art loved the way the song started slowly and, at the end, unleashed a huge finale complete with a vibrant, forceful female chorus. He wanted to try something similar on "Bridge."

Roy, Art, and Paul immediately recognized that the new concept demanded a much larger production. The trio expanded the treatment to include drums and other instruments that would give the song a larger, lusher sound. This sound ran counter to Paul's new attitude about a leaner, less polished approach for his songs, but he recognized later the decision to do the song in a bigger style transformed it from a moderate success to a huge hit. He said, "I think a lot of what people were responding to was that soaring melody at the end."

All of the instrumental tracks were completed in Los Angeles, and the team returned to New York to lay down the vocals. Art spent several days on the song, recording only small sections of it at a time so as to gain a larger measure of control over the final product in the editing booth. The whole process took roughly two weeks before the final version was mixed.

The album was meant to contain twelve songs, so Paul suggested a topical number called "Cuba Sí, Nixon No." Paul went so far as to cut an instrumental track for the song, but Art refused to do it. Art suggested replacing the tune with a Bach chorale, and Paul thought that was totally out of character with the rest of the material. The two wrangled over the issue, and Paul remembered, "We fought so much over what the last one should be. Finally we said, screw it, put it out—eleven songs. It was really tense."

Neither Art nor Paul had the energy to fight anymore. The *Bridge Over Troubled Water* album was complete, but it had drained them of every ounce of civility and friendship. In the past, working together on an album had been a source of strength. Sharing the development of the music had always given them new energy—like refilling the creative reservoir. It was a language only they shared, and now they were barely speaking. The struggle to complete the television special, the pressures of the movie, the concert tour in October and November, and the demanding work on the album finally took a toll not even music could restore. They had learned an important lesson which would alter the course of their careers and their friendship. It was possible, perhaps necessary, to live and work without each other. Paul remarked, "If this is what it's going to be like, maybe it should be our last."

According to Clive Davis, Paul and Art called him to the studio to listen to the completed album tracks. It was also a gathering of the Simon clan—Paul's brother Eddie and his parents Belle and Lou were on hand to witness the birth of the album. In his autobiography, *Clive: Inside the Record Business*, Davis takes some credit for the incredible success of *Bridge Over Troubled Water*. He claims Art and Paul had already picked "Cecilia" as the most certain single hit from the album because they thought the audience might like an up-tempo number after their last, somber hit, "The Boxer." But Davis says he surprised them all by suggesting a simultaneous release of the "Bridge" single and album. Davis's account is open to question, because Art and Paul had tested audience response to the song on their television special and in concert appearances, and there was no question the song would be their choice.

People who worked the sessions knew Paul and Art had stretched their personal and professional relationships to the breaking point. But most thought they would smooth out their differences in time. A hit single and album could have an amazingly calming effect on frayed artistic nerves.

But shortly after the album was completed, Art made a stunning announcement. He had accepted a starring role in Mike Nichols's next movie, *Carnal Knowledge*. It was the final blow for Simon and Garfunkel, although neither of them knew it yet.

8

By January 1970, both Paul and Art desperately needed a break from each other. By some estimates *Bridge Over Troubled Water* had taken more than eight hundred tension-filled hours to complete. Making music together, once so easy, had become an abrasive, divisive process, and the recording studio, once their favorite creative refuge, now seemed like a prison.

While both knew there were serious problems with their relationship, they still preferred to avoid a confrontation that might lead to permanent separation. Paul's unspoken but clearly understood strategy was to keep the horizon free of any Simon and Garfunkel project for the foreseeable future.

Both secretly looked forward to ventures of their own. With the exception of the rejected song, "Cuba Sí, Nixon No," Paul's song bag was completely empty. He needed time to gather new material and to forget about the bitter state of his relationship with Art.

Art left for Scotland, where he vacationed on a farm with his now steady companion, Linda Grossman. Simon and Garfunkel were scheduled to tour Europe and the United States to promote the new album, and later in the year, Art would begin location shooting for *Carnal Knowledge*.

Art was gaining confidence in his decision to pursue a movie career: "I had the feeling I could do more than there was room for me to do in this group." He had also found a satisfying relationship with Linda, whom he would eventually wed. Paul and Peggy had already married.

Rumors of the tension between Paul and Art had leaked out, and interviewers were probing the status of the partnership. Both men seemed to have marriage on their minds when they answered questions from the press. Art commented that relationships like theirs suffered the same wear and tear that marriages do. The one significant difference was that Simon and Garfunkel lacked the sense of enduring commitment that enables married couples to survive times of strife.

In his characteristically analytical way, Garfunkel viewed as natural the evolution which might make "Paul and Artie come to feel more different than similar." Art felt an overwhelming need to "express the thing that is uniquely you," and so his acting career now took precedence over singing. Paul warned Art to think hard about his priorities. Simon said, "Psychologically, I wasn't able to play second fiddle to the movie career. I don't know if he seriously thought out the consequences of his movie roles as regards to his career with me."

Also, Art had grown more aggressive about his music tastes, and that widened the gulf between them. He felt strongly that the duo should continue to emphasize the rich, lyrical sound that showcased his strengths as vocalist and arranger, whereas Paul wanted to experiment with radically different musical styles. Anxious to explore new territory, Paul no longer wanted or needed to negotiate the direction of his musical career with Art. More important, he had gotten over his fear of performing as a solo act.

Bridge Over Troubled Water was released in February 1970. As usual, single cuts were gradually spun off to sustain interest in the album.

By March, the *Bridge* album was number one. The reviews were almost uniformly excellent. Ellen Sander in *Stereo Review* said, "Their latest album, *Bridge Over Troubled Water,* is a model of consistency and professionalism." She spoke for many when she wrote, "Their voicing hasn't changed much over the years; it is still the sweet, two-part harmonic treatment, the aging choirboy innocence they have always infused into their songs. The sound is a pillar of contrast to the ever-changing time and temper of the rock which surrounds them. It's a relief to have some secure musicians in pop, individuals who neither feel compelled to compete with the Beatles, bulldoze the Stones, nor twist the listener's head into submission. From the start, they've had one good thing going for them, and they haven't thrown out the baby voices with the bath water. The result is a sense of distance and perspective only a mature team could produce."

Soon everyone knew both the album and the single of "Bridge" would be tremendous hits worldwide. As so often before, Simon's song managed to say exactly the right thing at the right time to a vast audience. A universal anthem of faith, the song soothed jangled nerves around the globe. People everywhere could apply it like a balm to their private pain. The record even captivated people who didn't normally buy popular records and so created yet another audience for Simon and Garfunkel.

Some felt it took a healthy dose of chutzpa for Simon and Garfunkel, two suburban white boys—and Jews at that—to bring the wonders of gospel-inspired music to millions of people worldwide.

That spring Paul was working on several new songs while he taught a songwriting workshop at New York University—and seeing his analyst four times a week. A dozen talented young songwriters had been selected through competitive auditions for the opportunity to attend Paul's workshop. In the class was singer/songwriter Melissa Manchester, who remembered, "It was a very loose situation. He came in the first day and said, 'Listen, I've never done this before, and I'm not sure I know how, but we'll keep at it until it ends itself.' We used to sit around playing our songs, and he'd play stuff he was working on, too. He'd walk around discussing our songs with us, telling us to play one passage another twenty times and then taking apart the lyrics."

Paul's sincere interest in their efforts created a lasting bond of trust and respect with everyone in the class. Manchester sensed she was in the presence of a master. She was struck by how deeply Paul's songs were embedded in his personal life and how hard he worked to free them. She summed up the experience: "In the end, I felt I only got to know a part of him, but I think he was one of the most decent, sincere human beings I ever met. As far as his songs went, he seemed to pay penance through them for all the things gone screwy in his life."

The infectiously happy "Cecilia" was released in April and rose quickly to number four. That month the duo played to a packed house in London's Albert Hall, an important stop on the *Bridge Over Troubled Water* tour. This time there was no backup band. It was vintage Simon and Garfunkel—one tall figure topped with a blond dandelion mane bent close to a short, dark man with a guitar, both encircled by a single shaft of light on a bare, dark stage.

When it came to do "Bridge," pianist Larry Knechtel joined Art onstage while Paul retreated to the wings. There he watched with barely concealed envy as Art sang the soaring lyrics and felt thunderous waves of applause wash over him.

Paul thought himself a fool to have given such a gift to someone who showed no gratitude. And each night, the song drove the wedge deeper between the two.

It became easier to let the silences grow, although a decade later Art speculated: "The two of us could've really used a compassionate, intelligent, perceptive third party—someone who negotiates. We're a perfect case of two people who communicate poorly about sensitive issues. It's a situation where the things that bug you are so idiosyncratic that you're almost embarrassed to reveal them. Paul and I have this unique friendship, in that a lot of stuff is never said."

Deprived of a mutual creative goal, the relationship drifted farther apart. In the spring of 1970, however, neither man appeared quite ready to sever the ties completely. Paul still gave interviews that held out the possibility for recording and performing as Simon and Garfunkel, but his message was loaded with ambivalence: "So whether we go back on the road in a year, I don't know. It's possible.... I've experienced this performing thing, and I can put that aside for awhile. As far as recording goes, that's a simple matter of saying, let's make another record, or saying, I'm too busy now, I want to do this thing so we won't make another record. Probably we will make another record. We've always waited a long time in between records, so we don't feel compelled to put out another one in six months or a year from now. If we want to by then. A lot depends on the songs. You get the impetus to record when you get a song that you just have to record, and there is none now."

Paul also grew more envious of Art's movie stardom: "Everybody treated Artie like a star but me. I'll tell you one thing, fame and attention are really a hothouse for feelings." He could barely conceal his anger when he told people, "The movies became the time schedule we worked around. It deprived me of the freedom I had earned by being successful...."

Throughout the spring, Art and Paul kept their distance. Being apart was easier than before. Both men had other primary relationships; each had his own set of friends. Their commitment to continue the *Bridge* tour through midsummer was the only thing they had in common at the time. Except for performances, they saw each other very little and talked less.

In June 1970, the long-delayed *Catch-22* opened. Vincent Canby of the *New York Times* was enthralled by Nichols's transformation of the unwieldy novel into film. He called it "triumphant" and praised it as "quite simply the best American film I've seen this year."

Canby was in the minority, however. Other critics across the country thought the film bore little resemblance to Heller's original vision, and they universally complained it had been vastly overproduced. Alan Arkin, who played the lead, Yossarian, was singled out for his performance, but the rest of the huge cast was generally lumped together. Canby did mention Art along with Martin Balsam, Orson Welles, and Jon Voight and said, "Each one is marvelous." One of the few reviews to single out Art's performance appeared in *Variety*. It said his "characterization might strike some as winsomely effeminate." By and large, however, Arthur Garfunkel's film acting debut went virtually unnoticed.

Catch-22 met a similar fate. Despite the enormous advance publicity, the movie failed at the box office. But it didn't seem to matter. By the time the tepid reviews and ticket sales registered, Art and Mike Nichols were deeply involved in their second film together, *Carnal Knowledge*.

Art wasn't shy about his pride in the chance to solidify his acting career with a starring role in another Nichols film. It was payback time. Paul raged at Art's superior attitude: "I felt as if Artie had fucked me over—not because he did the movies, but because part of him saw those movies as an opportunity to fuck me over. It was as if he were saying, 'Hey, I've always felt like a nobody. Now you're going to be the nobody.'"

Art discouraged Paul from visiting the movie set, refusing to share any of his spotlight or glamorous new friends like Jack Nicholson and Ann-Margret. Paul's old insecurities about Art's blond handsomeness were aroused by his acting like a "movie star."

Now it was Paul who felt betrayed. Throughout the partnership, Paul had played along with Columbia's promotional fiction that both men wrote and arranged the music. Paul felt it had been an act of generosity on his part to maintain the illusion of an equal partnership, but now all he had to show for it was Art's rejection. He decided to set the record straight.

On July 18, the last stop on the concert tour would be in Simon and Garfunkel's old neighborhood—Forest Hills tennis stadium in Queens. The first date sold out so quickly promoters hastily added a second performance and had no trouble filling the seats. Though neither Art nor Paul formally recognized it, these Queens concerts represented more than just a simple homecoming. Their spectacular career together had come full circle. Together they had ridden the arc of stardom higher and longer than either of them had ever dreamed possible. On a hot July night they returned home to the starting point, each searching for new beginnings and new directions. They were also looking for a way to say good-bye.

They took to the stage amid tumultuous applause. Art had a virus and sore throat, but no one noticed. As ever, the faithful at their feet—relaxed and happy, white middle-class collegiate types—leaned forward and cupped their ears to gather in every precious syllable. For their fans, the words meant everything. Paul and Art opened with "The Boxer," and all over the stadium lips began to move in silent unison to the tough and tender tale of the poor boy whose dignity was inviolate. They sang the litany of hits that marked their time together, from the earliest—"The Sounds of Silence," "Teen Angel," "Bye Bye Love," "I Am a Rock"—to the latest—"Mrs. Robinson" and "Cecilia." They revealed the full spectrum of their talent.

Clad in baseball caps, T-shirts, and Levis, they sang the perfect harmonies they had taught themselves in basements just a few blocks away so many years ago. The audience was high on the familiar words and melodies and the blissful unity of those voices.

Toward the evening's end the stifling air hung still and hushed, not a breeze stirring, when Art's pure solo tenor drove "Bridge Over Troubled Water" to its redemptive finale. The stadium erupted in screams of delight. Once again, Simon and Garfunkel had created a magical state of grace and left their fans glowing in its warmth. Paul and Art walked off into the shadows backstage and parted, leaving the good-byes unspoken. They would not tour together again for more than a decade.

Paul's memory of that parting was a bit melodramatic: "We did our last concert at Forest Hills tennis stadium, shook hands, and didn't speak [to each other] for a couple of years." In truth, they would continue to talk to each other, but they wouldn't discuss sensitive matters or analyze the cause of their estrangement.

Paul made his first solo appearance that August at a benefit performance in New York's cavernous Shea Stadium. The concert commemorated the twenty-fifth anniversary of the bombing of Hiroshima; its proceeds were earmarked for peace candidates in the upcoming election. The star-studded bill included Janis Joplin, Creedence Clearwater Revival, the Rascals, Johnny Winter, and John Sebastian.

His confidence at an all-time low, Paul was not reassured by what he sensed was a sloppy approach by concert organizers. He was committed to the cause, however, and eager to test the waters for his solo career. Featured among such high-powered per-formers, he thought he could ease into the spotlight as a single.

His instincts about faulty planning were correct, however, and less than twenty thousand people showed up, thirty thousand fewer than capacity. Paul gamely played a few Simon and Gar-funkel songs, but grew so frustrated with the small, rowdy crowd that he walked off the stage in the middle of "Scarborough Fair." Outraged at the poor showing, Simon regretted this debut ap-pearance. Emotionally, it was a world away from his last ap-pearance with Garfunkel in Queens just a few weeks earlier.

Meanwhile, Art was immersed in filming *Carnal Knowledge*. Nichols had collaborated with social satirist Jules Feiffer on the story of two Amherst College roommates who meet in the mid-forties. The movie follows the progress of their sexual adventures and attitudes from college to middle age in the seventies in a series of vignettes. It was a challenging and ambitious project, eagerly awaited by critics and fans alike.

Nichols cast Jack Nicholson as Jonathan, a cynical jock obsessed by women with big breasts, and Art Garfunkel as Sandy, a confused, would-be intellectual in saddle shoes who plans to read meaningful novels like *Jean Cristophe* and Ayn Rand's *The Fountainhead*.

The two Feiffer characters spend every spare minute sharing elaborate sexual fantasies while avoiding any real personal growth. Though never overtly stated, lines like "Maybe shmuckdom is what you need to stay young and open" hint that the two are Jewish, but they clearly represent a macho American male perspective on the war between the sexes. The stunningly beautiful women, played by Candice Bergen and Ann-Margret, are almost incidental to the movie.

Nichols, working under the influence of cartoonist and screenwriter Feiffer, directed the movie as if it were a series of comic-strip frames that follow the two men through several relationships doomed by an absence of trust, understanding, and love. To Sandy and Jonathan, women are no more than sex objects whom they must relentlessly and aimlessly pursue. Neither man really knows what to do when he catches one.

Sandy becomes a doctor, a husband, and a philanderer, eventually ending up in bed with a teenage hippie. Jonathan becomes a tax lawyer who spends his life searching for the perfectly formed female, whom he sees as his castrator as soon as he finds her. He eventually becomes impotent, forced to buy sexual favors from prostitutes.

The movie is a two-character study which has as its center the revelation of a friendship. Nichols knew the actors chosen for the roles of Sandy and Jonathan had to be equipped to reveal the subtle nuances of male friendship without a trace of falseness. There was no question Nicholson—an established actor with almost limitless range—could portray his end of the relationship.

Nichols, who had observed Simon and Garfunkel relate to one another during their work on the soundtrack for *The Graduate*, selected Art for the role because he felt certain Art would draw on his long-term friendship with Paul. Art and Paul could have been the film's models: bright, middle-class, upwardly mobile Jewish men with a long, complicated history between them. Nichols's hunch was right. Art played the role effortlessly and convincingly.

Filming *Carnal Knowledge* was fun for Art. The cast was much smaller then the massive *Catch-22* group. He felt he had a more direct, intimate relationship with Nichols and the rest of the cast, and the filming ran smoothly and on schedule.

Candice Bergen has recalled, "Jack, Artie, and I shared a large house in Vancouver that came to resemble the set of the Amherst dorm." The togetherness could have bred dissension, but with this group, the constant interaction generated friendship. Bergen recalled another benefit of the enforced camaraderie for Nichols: "Mike liked the cloistered atmosphere of Vancouver, which kept us a unit and focused our energies, our concentration, on our work."

Bergen called the set "a tiny utopia" and later noted: "The entire making of *Carnal Knowledge* was dreamlike, idyllic—like working in a state of grace. For all of us there was an effortlessness about the work, an ease to the acting that came from the precision and generosity of Mike's direction and the intelligence of the script." Art became close friends with Jack Nicholson, who said Art reminded him of Leslie Howard and predicted Art could have a great film career if he wanted it. Over the years, Garfunkel has maintained his friendship with Nicholson, and they often can be seen together on the slopes of Aspen.

In September 1970, the single "El Condor Pasa" was released from the *Bridge* album and quickly rose to the number-eighteen spot. Simon and Garfunkel's single was the second hit version of the song—in May, folksinger Julie Felix's recording reached the number-nineteen spot in England. With three hit singles and a hit album setting sales records, the public still thought of Simon and Garfunkel as a team, and so did Columbia Records. But in his mind, Paul Simon had already put the team aside and was eager to make a move that would publicly signal his independence.

In an emotional meeting with Clive Davis at Columbia, Paul declared that "Simon and Garfunkel" was finished and that he wished to pursue a solo recording career. Davis was shocked. He and other Columbia executives tried to talk Paul out of the split. The company had a great deal to lose, and, at first, their attitude approached paternal indulgence. Suppressing their initial panic, they reasoned that Paul was simply weathering one of his chronic depressions. They had witnessed his dark moods before, and this one, too, would soon lift. He just needed time to work through this "phase" he was going through.

Tom and Jerry, circa 1957, and Art and Paul as Simon and
Garfunkel, circa 1966.

New York Mayor Ed Koch with Paul and Art before the historic
Central Park concert in September 1981.

Art and Paul holding their Grammy awards for "Bridge Over Troubled Water." They were going through one of their non-communication periods at the time.

Pal Phil Ramone and Paul Simon both won Grammys in 1975. Paul seems happy to be "Still Crazy After All These Years."

Paul flanked by one time live-in girlfriend Shelley Duvall and "Saturday Night Live" pal Gilda Radner.

Art with girlfriend Laurie Bird in the 1970s.

Art Garfunkel sharing a drink with actress/director Penny Marshall. They also shared a five-year relationship while he recovered from the shock of his lover's suicide.

Carrie Fisher and Paul Simon on their wedding day in August 1983. Their affair had been on going for five years. The marriage lasted less than one.

Paul Simon, Carrie Fisher, and her crooner
father Eddie Fisher. Paul wrote of himself and
Carrie, "one and one half wandering Jews."

Art and wife Kim in the 1990s.

Art Garfunkel and Jack Nicholson discussing girls, and life, and girls in 1971s *Carnal Knowledge*.

Art with costar Candice Bergen in *Carnal Knowledge*.

Paul in *One-Trick Pony* (1980) with Joan Hackett playing the recording executive's wife who seduces him.

Two composers of different generations and musical styles, Paul Simon and Leonard Bernstein were discussing "worry beads" and giving up smoking in 1977.

Penny Marshall, Charles Grodin, Paul Simon, and Carrie Fisher attending memorial services for John Belushi at New York's Cathedral for St. John the Devine in March 1982.

A beaming Art Garfunkel and Paul Simon as they are inducted into the Rock and Roll Hall of Fame in 1990.

Ladysmith Black Mambaza and Paul Simon on their *Graceland* tour in Zimbabwe in 1987.

Clive Davis tried to tell Paul he was making a huge mistake. He was certain Paul didn't realize how rare it was for a team like Simon and Garfunkel to become not only a household name, but a worldwide institution. In no uncertain terms, Davis told Paul he was throwing away the career of a lifetime, and he predicted Paul alone would never match the success of Simon and Garfunkel.

Paul was deeply hurt by Davis's gloomy assessment. He had gone to Davis looking for some shred of support for his risky venture, but had found none. He left the meeting both frustrated and furious. However, Davis's wounding words became the spur that drove him on. Seething, he had told Davis, "Don't tell me that. Don't tell me that statement, that I'll never be bigger than. How do you know what I'll do? I don't even know what I'm gonna do in the next decade of my life. It could be maybe my greatest time of work. Maybe I'm finished. Maybe I'm not gonna do my thing until I'm fifty. People will say then, 'Funny thing was, in his youth he sang with a group. He sang popular songs in the sixties. Fans of rock 'n' roll may remember the duo Simon and Garfunkel.' That's how I figure it."

Paul studied the mental scorecard he had kept since the early recording days of *Sounds of Silence*. He remembered how often he had subjugated his own desires to those of the creative triumvirate for the good of the music. He had been the creative engine that drove the hugely successful Simon and Garfunkel machine, but had never received the individual praise he felt he deserved. So now he began to tell everyone that they had both lied in the sixties about Art's contribution to the team of Simon and Garfunkel.

In interviews, he was now careful to describe the partnership as a three-way collaboration: Paul, Art, and with equal billing, engineer Roy Halee. It was true that during the peak Simon and Garfunkel years Halee had had an equal vote in recording decisions. Simon later revealed the compromises he had had to make: "If Roy and Artie said, 'Let's do a long ending on "The Boxer,"' I said, 'Two out of three,' and did it their way. I didn't say, 'Hey, this is my song, I don't want it to be like that.'" He further limited Garfunkel's contribution by describing Art's and Roy's roles in terms of responsibility and not creativity.

There was never a formal announcement of the split, no messy display of angry emotion ringing with finality; the roots of their friendship ran too deep to be severed cleanly, publicly, or com-

pletely. The parting was more like a death in the family. They had
already endured the pain only close friends or lovers can inflict on
one another and had moved on to accept the loss. The quiet split
was a tacit agreement that gave them both dignity and flexibility,
especially with the press. They knew instinctively how important
the idea of their partnership was to their audience, as well as how
to manipulate their image. There would be no public scene like the
parting of their boyhood heroes, the Everly Brothers, who would,
in a few years, shock their fans in an unseemly outburst of anger
and recrimination onstage.

Neither Art nor Paul knew whether the split was permanent.
Paul remembered, "When *Bridge Over Troubled Water* was
finished, Artie was going to do *Carnal Knowledge,* and I went to
do an album by myself. We didn't say that's the end. We didn't
know if it was the end or not."

For now, Paul saw the breakup as a chance to escape the never-
ending pressure to produce Simon and Garfunkel hits. The pattern
of success had insulated him from the need or opportunity to take
risks. Unshackled, he could regain the competitive spirit of his
early days: "It was a chance to back out and gamble a little bit. It's
been so long since it was a gamble."

Adamant about his decision and determined to prove Davis and
the others wrong, Paul bristled whenever Columbia asked the
inevitable question, "When does the new Simon and Garfunkel
album come out?" Simon and Garfunkel were more than bread
and butter to the company—they had become a national and
international institution, and Columbia refused to believe its prize
pair could slip through its fingers so easily.

Paul may have been ready to sing his own songs—but would
anyone listen? Intellectually he knew the public wouldn't embrace
him at first with the same affection it held for Simon and
Garfunkel, but in his heart he hoped it would. He said, "I was
ready to be welcomed into the public's arms, as I had been in the
past." As news of the breakup spread, Paul worried that it might
cost him what mattered most: a loyal and receptive audience.
Unlike the music of other rock supergroups such as the Rolling
Stones, whose popular niche was far more specific and limited, the
gentle, elliptical music of Simon and Garfunkel encompassed the
full audience spectrum, young and old, and included vast numbers

of people new to popular music. Paul discovered far fewer people eagerly awaited his new, solo offerings.

Everyone he told about his solo plans reacted with disbelief and sadness, and he soon sensed that people were taking the split personally. A palpable grief hung in the air, and almost no one but he wanted to think about a future without Simon and Garfunkel.

One exception was ex-Beatle George Harrison. He had recently survived one of the most dramatic breakups in popular music history. The sympathetic Harrison told Paul, "Now you hear sort of what we are like individually since the group broke up, and I know what you were like together, and I'd like to hear what you're like individually."

Paul appreciated Harrison's support but was still frustrated to find that virtually no one—not even music insiders—gave him full credit as the creative force behind Simon and Garfunkel, despite his recent revelations about the true nature of the collaboration.

He was angry and hurt, and years would pass before he could acknowledge that luck and Art Garfunkel had been equal and inseparable ingredients in their success. At this moment, Paul focused his anger on the lack of recognition his songwriting skills had received over the years. He vowed these same skills would now define his genius once and for all. He could feel it in his bones—he was about to write better songs than ever, and he fantasized that his first solo album would do the impossible—Paul Simon alone would surpass the fame of Simon and Garfunkel.

The only genuine assurance Paul could find was with his old colleague, Roy Halee, who had migrated to San Francisco. Columbia, anxious to keep the talented Halee happy, had built a state-of-the-art studio around him when he expressed a desire to live on the West Coast. Halee understood Paul's impulse to leave the lush, Garfunkel-dominated orchestrations behind and move on to a simpler, less complicated sound. He promised to help.

Even more eager to keep Simon happy, Columbia ultimately concluded it was fruitless to stand in his way. They finally gave in to Paul's desire to cut a new solo album.

In San Francisco, Paul began the long, slow process of giving birth to his new songs in the recording studio. He recruited musicians he had worked with before on several Simon and Garfunkel albums and rehearsed six new songs in various stages of completion over the course of several weeks. He knew he wanted to do things differently now, but was still unsure about which direction he really wanted to take. For hours, he talked to Halee about the nuances of Jamaican rhythms—reggae and ska—and the possibilities of country/western and other trends in popular music. The habit of arguing the merits of various musical styles with Halee and other musicians was an old and reassuring one, but this time things were different. Paul no longer deferred his judgments or filtered his opinions through those of others. He was learning to make decisions alone—the first big step toward taking total responsibility for his career.

Paul ushered in 1971 on a creative high. Realizing he lacked song material, he returned to New York to write on a new wave of energy and optimism. Without the aid of drugs and uninhibited by partnership constraints, music flowed from him more easily. Since he would be singing alone, he also tried to strengthen his voice through rigorous vocal exercises. Since he had kicked the smoking habit, his vocal range had increased, and freed from the demands of harmonizing with Art's soaring tenor, he experimented with new techniques. The Simon and Garfunkel sound had dictated mathematical precision in phrasing and timing. Without these limitations, Paul was excited by the potential spontaneity of a single voice.

In March 1971, Paul took time off from working on his solo album to attend the Grammy Awards with Art, who had completed filming *Carnal Knowledge* and was teaching mathematics in a private, preparatory school in Connecticut. Only a few months—not years, as Paul once described the separation—had passed since Paul and Art had seen or spoken to each other. To the glittering Hollywood crowd gathered to honor the best in the music industry and to millions of television viewers, Simon and Garfunkel were still together.

For the first time in the awards show's history, the Grammy winners hadn't been announced in advance. The award format was now similar to the Oscars and Emmys. An air of excited anticipation hummed in the huge, star-filled Hollywood Palladium. The show, hosted by Andy Williams, was televised live on ABC.

As far as the public was concerned, it was Simon and Garfunkel's finest hour. The live audience and fans across America celebrated with them as they swept their categories. For "Bridge Over Troubled Water" Simon and Garfunkel won Record of the Year, beating out "Close to You" by the Carpenters, "Fire and Rain" by James Taylor, and "Let It Be" by the Beatles. They also won Grammys for Best Contemporary Song, Album of the Year, Best Arrangement, Best Engineered Recording, and Best Song of the Year.

The academy recognized what the world already knew: "Bridge Over Troubled Water" was the biggest hit to date in recording history. In the first year of its release, Paul Simon as writer reaped more than seven million dollars in royalties. To date, more than two hundred versions of the song have been recorded by a wide range of vocal artists. The most successful rendition other than theirs belongs to Aretha Franklin.

When "the high priestess of soul" had hit with "Bridge," Paul Simon's music finally penetrated the black record-buying audience, although years later, he realized his fame in that market was not as pervasive as he had thought. One evening he was approached by a parking-lot attendant who sensed Paul was famous but wasn't quite sure who he was. He told the man he was Paul Simon, but the name meant nothing. He mentioned the name Simon and Garfunkel, but still no reaction. Paul then said, "I wrote 'Bridge Over Troubled Water.'" And the man exclaimed, "Aretha's song! Now I know you!"

Even Paul's boyhood hero, Elvis Presley, recorded "Bridge" and included it in his stage appearances. The song can still be heard wafting through supermarkets and elevators all over the globe. Paul has long since tired of the overkill "Bridge" has received and often cringes at the mention of it. He is, however, still proud of its status as an American classic.

Paul's songs have been recorded by countless other artists, including many entertainment institutions: Barbra Streisand ("Punky's Dilemma"), the Hollies ("I Am a Rock"), Frank Sinatra ("Mrs. Robinson"), Joan Baez ("The Dangling Conversation"), and Bob Dylan ("The Boxer"). But only Harpers Bizarre ("Feelin' Groovy") charted a top-ten hit with a Simon song.

The Simon and Garfunkel triumph at the Grammy Awards was obviously bittersweet—a resounding acclamation for music and voices now stilled. At the very moment the musical world offered them its most prestigious awards, all that remained of their unique sound seemed to be a distant echo to the two recipients.

With the extravagant praise of Grammy night still ringing in his ears, Paul returned to the studio even more determined to push his way back into the winner's circle to claim a gold statuette—alone.

Paul wanted his new songs to capture the raw energy and rhythm of the streets. Free of expectations, he imagined melodies and lyrics that were simple, fast, easy, and fun. Latin beats drummed in his mind, and he toyed with the infectious, charging rhythms of bands he had watched as a boy at the Roseland Ballroom while he waited for his father to pack up his bass and go home.

He had been working on some tracks, but the lyrics wouldn't come. One evening he took a break for dinner at one of his favorite Chinese restaurants in New York, and on the menu was a chicken-and-egg dish named "Mother and Child Reunion." In an instant, Paul knew it was a concept he would use on the new album.

The new song idea had something to do with a brush with death he and Peggy had had the summer before when their favorite dog was killed by a car. Both were devastated by the loss. Neither had much experience with death, and Paul suddenly imagined how much he would suffer if his wife were to die.

The song's power comes from the simple joining of three emotion-packed concepts: love, loss, and reunion—weighty subjects borne lightly along by a bubbly, reggae beat. And its title calls to mind the most perfect of all human relationships—mother and child—the one relationship upon which all others are modeled. The lines "I've never been laid so low / In such a mysterious way,"* evoke the depth of human loss with simple eloquence. The song's title, repeated in each chorus, offers comfort by suggesting reconciliation—a kind of heaven—is "only a motion away."

Paul pored over his rhythm tracks with the intensity of a Talmudic scholar, finding ways to marry the words to them—lengthening, shortening, overdubbing, and looping—until each syllable was inseparable from the music.

Although eager to explore a looser, more spontaneous style, Paul was still at heart a consummate perfectionist. He had tried to

* "Mother and Child Reunion" © 1971 by Paul Simon

use reggae earlier on "Why Don't You Write Me" on the *Bridge* album, but wasn't satisfied with the way it worked out. He thought it sounded like a poor imititation of the real thing. This time he went to Jamaica, the home of the reggae beat, to learn its intricacies firsthand.

When Simon was in England in the mid-sixties, reggae and its variant, ska, were popular dance-music forms, especially among the white middle class. By the early seventies reggae had become the musical emblem of the skinheads, a blue-collar cult whose followers favored violence and racism as a means of asserting itself. To many musicians and critics, reggae was tainted by these unsavory racist associations. But Paul was intrigued by its driving beat and saw beyond its sometimes offensive lyrics.

Paul was especially impressed with the great Jamaican artist Jimmy Cliff. He flew to Kingston and hired Cliff's studio musicians, who were a little awed by Paul's star status and puzzled by his working methods. They were accustomed to getting paid seven dollars or ten dollars per tune and expected to churn out six or seven tunes on a good day. Paul wanted to pay them to experiment and explore music possibilities for days at a time.

Each day, he bustled through the heavy, soundproof studio door, out of the tropical sun and into the dim coolness of Dynamic Studios, and strapped on his guitar. As soon as the red light went on, his celebrity, money, and strange methods all fell away. He became one of them—the only white face in the room, bobbing ecstatically to the beat, roaming and pacing amid a thicket of guitars, xylophones, and a huge stand of steel drums.

They jammed for hours, expanding a phrase here, developing a rhythmic combination there. Sometimes Simon laid his own guitar down and just stood still—listening to the sound. He would put together the pieces to the puzzle—lyrics, vocals, piano, and other touches—in studios in New York, Paris, and Los Angeles, ending up in San Francisco with Halee.

The studio had always been Paul's natural habitat. It was a safe haven he returned to for solace and comfort, especially in times of stress. So sacred was the studio to his imaginative process that he refused to look at itemized recording charges, afraid he would be inhibited by them. He has said, "A lot of times, I don't do anything but sit in a studio for an hour or so, just talk. I like the studio to be a home, to be comfortable..."

Phil Ramone, one of the industry's most successful record producers, thought Paul acted as if he had been born and raised in a studio. When Paul hired him to produce a later album, he remembered how Paul refused to let go of even the smallest detail until he had learned to trust him completely. It was only after Ramone had worked with Simon for years that he could persuade him to leave the studio for dinner and allow Ramone to work alone on some aspects of the recording.

Ramone had heard the rumors around the industry about the unorthodox and time-consuming approach Simon took to recording. Working with Paul, he realized that what seemed at first to be "outlandish, bizarre, rebellious, against all the rules" methods were really tightly controlled, thoroughly knowledgeable experiments that eventually generated the distinctive sounds which had made Simon and Garfunkel such a unique phenomenon. Paul's disciplined love of experimentation in the studio was part of the legacy of Simon, Garfunkel, and Halee, and he would rely on it to see him through the uncertain times that lay ahead.

Paul also wanted to play with more humor in his music. He had finally shaken the doldrums of the drug years. He found joy in his marriage to Peggy, and his regular, intensive analysis persuaded him that his life contained as much goodness as sorrow. He had made a momentous, liberating career decision and now felt far less burdened by the past. It was time to leaven his image with some humor on the new album.

In this more playful mood, he adopted an ironic, witty tone in writing about the important but prosaic chore of taking care of one's health in "Run That Body Down." In the same comic vein, Paul wrote the enigmatic but buoyant "Me and Julio Down by the Schoolyard." The words "me and Julio" popped into his head one day and tickled him. He thought they were inherently funny and decided to develop a short story about the chaotic chain of events set into motion after a mysteriously shocking scene is observed— "What the mama saw." The scene is never described, and Paul himself never really knew "what the mama saw," but he always thought it was something vaguely sexual.

The song's images summoned up threats of imprisonment, radical priests, and national press coverage by *Newsweek*. Through its urban schoolyard setting, Hispanic names, driving tempo, and gritty colloquial language, Paul made good on his promise to make his new album more streetwise than sweet.

Paul journeyed to Paris to meet with Stephane Grappelli, the renowned jazz violinist who had played with guitarist Django Reinhardt. Paul invited Grappelli to join him in a studio to see what might happen. Paul lacked the confidence in his guitar skills to play Reinhardt's traditional role in the duet, so he first envisioned Grappelli as a solo. But once in the studio, the temptation to collaborate was overwhelming. Paul and Stephane jammed, making up things as they went along. The sound was a real departure, and Paul thought people might think it "corny," but he liked it so much he worked the tracks into a cut for the album *Hobo's Blues*. He knew few in his audience would know enough about music history to recognize Grappelli, but he was certain jazz-guitar connoisseurs would appreciate his contribution to the song.

When Paul reached into the past with Grappelli, it was a sign of his musical maturity and humility. His long and deep analysis helped him realize he had a great deal to learn from other more talented, but far less popular, musicians. He began to recalibrate his own sense of excellence according to new, more exacting standards. He felt he had surpassed his pop music contemporaries and now aspired to the achievements of Gershwin, Bernstein, and other musical giants.

Weeks stretched into months, and still the solo album wasn't complete. Paul was saving some of his creative energies for his marriage. Peggy was pregnant, and both were committed to the new order of married life established by the women's movement that was gaining momentum throughout the country. The couple had long, earnest discussions to negotiate equal domestic roles. Their careers were to be considered equal in importance. Each promised to meet the other halfway. Household chores and child rearing would be shared fairly. Based on such a solid, fair foundation, the relationship would surely last.

Art, too, was concentrating on his relationships, both personal and professional. He had lived with Linda Grossman on the West Coast during the filming of *Carnal Knowledge* and was seriously considering marriage, in spite of the grim picture of love Mike Nichols was painting in the movie.

Carnal Knowledge opened in 1971 amid a storm of controversy and mixed reviews. Some, like *New Yorker* film critic Pauline Kael, saw it as "a grimly purposeful satire on depersonalization and how we use each other sexually as objects." Others praised it lavishly. Vincent Canby of the *New York Times* called it "a watershed film...one of the first films to uncover some of the relevant disturbing secrets of American private life." Jack Nicholson's virtuoso performance overshadowed the rest of the cast. Reviewers spent most of their time praising him and arguing about the film's meaning and validity. Art's reviews were mixed. Stefan Kanfer in *Time* said, "With *Carnal Knowledge*, folksinger Arthur Garfunkel has become an authentic screen presence—one of the few American actors who can portray naïveté." And *Variety* noted, "Garfunkel is extremely capable and appealing and should pursue acting further." But Stanley Kaufman in the *New Republic* blasted Art: "Arthur Garfunkel, the Sandy, is not an actor at all. Nichols evidently thought his personality (which is apt enough) was worth the risk, and he has helped Garfunkel at least to behave credibly. I'd be perfectly willing never to see Garfunkel again, but Nichols makes him acceptable here."

Individual notices were, however, secondary to the controversy the film's subject generated. In *The Graduate*, Nichols had focused his satiric eye on the generation gap. In *Carnal Knowledge*, he pursued his theme of alienation into the bedrooms of middle-aged, middle-class men and women like Benjamin Braddock's parents and Mrs. Robinson. The film's concentration on the soulless sexual habits and attitudes of men was of special interest to the growing women's liberation movement. An unabashed, if highly oversimplified, moral statement, the film was, for young viewers, yet another stinging indictment of the older generation. Nichols's bold venture into the sexual realm confirmed what young people suspected all along—their parents' value system was corrupt and defunct.

Art was happy about his performance in the movie. He commented, "I'm pleased with my role. I don't mind saying I would like an Academy Award for it." He agreed to help promote the film, and he plunged bravely into the controversy it had evoked. Regarding his character's sexual mores, he offered: "Certainly men have been brainwashed into believing masculinity is based on their sexual performance. The film wasn't intended to take any position of male liberation. But I will be interested in male reaction. Like women, men have been led to believe a lot of things. I think the attitudes of Jonathan and Sandy represent millions of American males. Unfortunately, I don't think these attitudes are going to change for a long time."

Once again Art found himself at the epicenter of America's popular social scene. He should have been satisfied at last to stand alone in the full glare of the spotlight, but he wasn't. In spite of an armload of Grammys and the starring role in an important film, Art still seemed confused and unhappy. Hailed as a singer and— although with considerably less acclaim—a movie actor, he still wasn't sure he was doing the right thing with his life. He had told friends that his teaching stint the previous spring was a way of searching for his true calling, but that, too, left him feeling empty.

Most significant, it was finally clear that "Simon and Garfunkel" was finished. Garfunkel later stated "We didn't talk about the split until after the fact. What confirmed it was the absence of a new project."

Paul wouldn't let Art have it both ways: "I think that Arthur would have preferred to maintain two careers. He would like to have done films and Simon and Garfunkel. I think that's the way he would have liked it." Later, both Art and Paul claimed that breaking up the partnership was a relief. Art explained, "It had lost its sense of fun. The juices weren't flowing." At last, the shared dream of a lifetime seemed to have run its course.

Now Art's thoughts turned to recording a solo album, but the prospect of making his way alone as a singer was frightening. He said, "I didn't know if I was going to do it [the solo album]. I had shaky confidence about my ability now to do my own thing. Didn't know what my own thing was. I felt I had a minimal degree of insight into what is really going on with me and why I'm doing the things that I'm doing."

He sought to examine his dissatisfaction through analysis as Paul had, but he chose group therapy rather than individual treatment. Art began to get in touch with his true feelings for the first time. Both he and Paul had avoided open discussions of sensitive issues, preferring to ignore problems and hope they would eventually disappear. As he worked through some of these things, he came to realize that he had been struggling with the same problem for years, but had never been able to resolve it on his own. Group therapy required verbalization of what now seemed so obvious: "When I had to state the bottom line, I suddenly understood." Articulating his pain to others turned out to be incredibly liberating.

Gradually he came to see that he had, more often than not, placed himself in a subordinate position in important relationships throughout his life, especially in the most crucial one with Paul. He recalled the dreary, enervating early days, searching for the big break, suffering rejection. He wouldn't have survived without Paul, but Simon's aggressiveness complemented his passive nature so perfectly he had let his personal growth atrophy.

Since the first betrayal as boys, Art had suppressed his true feelings of being a victim of Paul's aggressive decision-making. Simon, of course, failed to understand how Art could see him as a victimizer. After all, from Paul's point of view, he had been instrumental in making Art fabulously rich and famous.

But stunning popular and financial success wasn't enough. Like Paul, Art came to realize he couldn't have a joint identity. He, too, needed to seize control of his own creative destiny. Art knew Paul was ready to release a solo album, and he decided to proceed with his own.

They both needed time and distance to heal raw nerves and adjust to their new priorities and life without Simon and Garfunkel.

9

In February 1972, Paul's first solo album, simply and une-
quivocally titled *Paul Simon*, was released. On the cover was
Peggy's close-up color photograph of Paul's head wreathed in a
huge, furry parka.

Some early reviews left Paul shaken. In *High Fidelity*, Henry
Edwards wrote, "He has spent a year and a half laboring over his
first solo effort. *Paul Simon* is a tasteful, disciplined, but disap-
pointing piece of work. That's a painful thing to have to say about
an album that displays so much hard work, but there is no song on
the LP that comes anywhere near 'The Sounds of Silence,' 'Mrs.
Robinson,' or 'Bridge Over Troubled Water.'" Edwards added,
"Simon's small, melodic, compelling voice is as engaging as ever.
The first solo attempt for any major artist can be a painfully
difficult experience. Now that Paul Simon has had his initiation,
one waits eagerly for his next album."

Paul wasn't ready to think about his next album. *Paul Simon*
was his third attempt to go solo. He didn't want to flop again. He
knew he had already placed himself and Columbia at a disadvantage because of his refusal to do a concert tour to promote the

album, but he just couldn't bring himself to face the crowds alone just yet.

Obviously Paul was feeling extremely vulnerable, believing that *Paul Simon* would be his moment of truth. Peggy's advice—to take all of the praise or all of the blame—now reverberated in his ears and kept him awake at night.

He later described having terrifying dreams about performing. In one, he walked up to the microphone to find it was mounted much too high for him to reach, but was the perfect height for Art Garfunkel. In others, there would be no microphone for his guitar, or a string might break, and he would leave the stage, screaming at his manager while the audience grew restive.

Simon had been away from the concert circuit for almost two years and felt ill-prepared for the rigors of the road. Toward the end of the team years, as the gulf between them widened, layoffs of six to nine months had allowed both men to downshift to a more normal life-style. Now Paul lacked the emotional energy and self-confidence to gear up to tour.

Aware too that he had become a much larger target for critics since the enormous success of "Bridge Over Troubled Water," he preferred to keep a low profile. He feared critical attacks, and he wanted to keep the attention focused on the new Paul Simon music rather than on his public performance. There would be comparisons enough with Simon and Garfunkel without adding the solo concert stage as well.

To Columbia executives, he protested that he lacked enough of his own songs to make a complete show, and he didn't want to sing the old ones like "The Sounds of Silence" and "I Am a Rock" or "Homeward Bound" since they were so closely identified with Art. He toyed with the idea of doing "Bridge Over Troubled Water" by himself, but the time just wasn't right. He felt nervous about the quality of his voice and candidly admitted in the *New York Times,* "I don't have the same vocal instrument Artie has."

As a way of promoting the album, Paul did agree to do an extensive series of press interviews. But he chose to start them in the British press where he thought he would find a more friendly reception.

Knowing that the first question interviewers would ask would be about the breakup, Clive Davis accompanied Paul on the press tour. Davis wanted to discourage Paul from saying anything so damaging about Art that it would then be impossible for them to reunite. Paul was circumspect, but he didn't hide his feelings. When interviewers asked if "Simon and Garfunkel" was difficult to let go, he replied, "No, it was a relief."

In time, Paul became quite adept at finessing the question of a reunion. Often when it arose, he simply said, "No...but..." and left the conversation dangling.

Davis continued to argue that while the press tour was helpful, a follow-up concert tour was necessary to boost album sales. Paul, however, remained firm about his decision.

He, as well as the executives at Columbia, knew several other factors besides his refusal to tour might inhibit album sales. The new Simon songs were not simple ballads. They were more personal and idiosyncratic than ever, and that made it difficult for other artists to record the "cover" versions that usually increased sales. In addition, Paul was also experimenting with reggae, a musical form not many other performers wanted to try. More important, *Paul Simon* had no blockbuster song like "Bridge Over Troubled Water" which could carry the album.

Much to everyone's relief, sales took off anyway. Apparently there were enough curious hard-core Simon fans to buy the album and see what he was up to. Only a month after its release, *Paul Simon* reached number four and became a top seller in England.

Generally, reviews were cautious and respectful but continued to be less than raves. Although the album eventually attained gold-disk status, it sold only one-tenth of the phenomenal *Bridge Over Troubled Water*, which had sold a million copies in England alone and more than nine million in the United States.

Usually loath to compare himself with his competition, Paul gamely measured his first solo effort against sales of the latest Rolling Stones album, *Sticky Fingers*, and politely noted that his album outsold theirs. But as time went on, sales figures ultimately confirmed his early fears—the vast majority of Simon and Garfunkel fans had not been swept away as he had hoped they would.

Still, the album was a success, especially the single cuts. In March, "Mother and Child Reunion" was released, and its happy, insistent beat carried it to number four in the United States and number five in England. In May, "Me and Julio" rose to number twenty-two in the States and number fifteen in the U.K.

Art watched Paul's successful progress as a solo act and claimed

it didn't bother him. He also claimed to be confident about his
own career: "I never approached my solo years with any worry.
I'm just too much of a New York veteran."

However, in spite of the bravado, Art was troubled: His film
career had stalled, and he couldn't seem to get started on the new
album he'd been thinking about. Group therapy had helped him
through these stressful times, but Art's confusion about which
direction his career should take had not been fully resolved. He
had turned down several acting jobs, including a starring role in
an adaptation of Kurt Vonnegut, Jr.'s *Slaughterhouse-Five*, a
decision he later regretted. Mike Nichols hadn't asked Art to
appear in his next movie, the forgettable *Day of the Dolphin*.
Without his mentor, movie acting had lost some of its charm. Art
reverted to his pattern of passively letting his career develop rather
than actively pursuing it.

Clive Davis, still eager to keep both Simon and Garfunkel
productive for Columbia, even if only as solo artists, badgered Art
to record an album of his own.

At first Art resisted the idea. Paul's songs had always been the
starting point, and without them, he wasn't sure where to begin.
He didn't want to come back as a singer merely "covering" other
singers' hit songs. Davis agreed that mere imitation would be a
disastrous career move. He encouraged Art "to sift through the
best of current writing—and also have songs written for you—to
put together a very personal album." Davis argued that the best
contemporary songwriters—Jimmy Webb, James Taylor, Paul
Williams, and Carole King, Paul Simon's old college buddy—
would jump at the chance to write for Art. After all, Garfunkel
was one of the biggest names in popular music, and, like Paul, he
had a potentially huge audience waiting to hear him. When Art
saw Paul's album recapture at least a portion of Simon and
Garfunkel's vast audience, he felt compelled to stake a claim of his
own. He decided to take Davis's suggestion and sing songs which
would, once and for all, distinguish him from Paul.

Davis wasn't the only one to give Art encouragement to
produce a solo album. Paul heard about Art's plan to record and
offered his support and good wishes. Despite the image of total
separation both men later cultivated in the press, Paul and Art
were never completely out of touch with each other for long. As
Paul revealed in February 1972, "I still see him, and we're still

friendly. In fact, I was saying to him a few weeks ago that he should go into the studio and make his own record."

The first step Art took toward a solo album was the same one Paul had taken. He went to San Francisco to enlist the help of the engineer/producer who had been with them since their first rough audition, Roy Halee.

Art carefully searched for material that suited his taste and style. At first, he considered combining classical and pop. Then his youthful enthusiasm for religious music resurfaced, and he scoured church music archives for material. For awhile, he was interested in Greek music. With every detour from contemporary music—and the tastes of Art's sizable audience—Davis grew more anxious. Art seemed to be avoiding the critical issue. He must, sooner or later, step into the recording studio and compensate for the void left by Paul. Finally, Davis prevailed, and Art laid down several tracks. After listening to a few early cuts, Davis was at last convinced that his reluctant recording star was moving in the right direction. Davis then settled back to wait. The idea of doing an album was already a year old, but he knew it would take Art Garfunkel a lot longer to complete the album.

Just as Davis and other executives at Columbia were gradually getting used to Simon and Garfunkel's split, their hopes of a reunion were suddenly rekindled. In the summer of 1972, the U.S. presidential campaign was heating up. The Democrats and their hopeful, George McGovern, were in sorry financial shape. Without an infusion of capital, it looked as though Richard Nixon would win reelection without much of a fight. Art and Paul had always detested Nixon's aggressive conduct of the Vietnam War as well as his repressive domestic policies. Their support for McGovern was widely known, and McGovern was a fan. He had recently adopted a Simon and Garfunkel concept for his campaign, proclaiming "I want, indeed, to become a bridge over troubled waters."

That spring Paul was persuaded by his friend Warren Beatty to appear in Cleveland, on May 8, at a gala fund-raising concert for McGovern. Beatty also managed to line up Joni Mitchell and James Taylor. The concert was a sellout and raised approximately seventy thousand dollars for the Democrats.

After the resounding success of the Cleveland concert, fund-raisers came up with an appealing idea for an even more elaborate benefit concert to be held in July in New York's Madison Square Garden. Echoing McGovern's campaign theme of unity, organizers planned a concert that featured acts famous for their teamwork and harmony: Peter, Paul, and Mary; Dionne Warwick and Burt Bacharach; Mike Nichols and Elaine May—and Simon and Garfunkel.

Art eagerly accepted the invitation to join forces for the McGovern benefit. He said, "It appealed to my showmanship." He, like Paul and Clive Davis, recognized the allure the idea of reunion held for the audience. Paul accepted, although he had said only recently, "I don't think Artie and I will work together again, although I'm not opposed to it if something should come up that's really interesting. But I feel emotionally that it's over." It would be their first reunion in two years. Columbia Records prepared to capitalize on the event. It was the perfect opportunity to release a compilation album of Simon and Garfunkel's greatest hits.

The concert was a sellout with more than eighteen thousand attending. Nichols and May—who hadn't performed together in many years—got the evening off to a roaring start with their classic vignettes of modern American Jewish angst. Their routines were new to many of the thousands of young people in the audience, but the rest knew them by heart. Peter, Paul, and Mary followed, and the crowd sang along with Dylan's peace anthem, "Blowin' in the Wind" and Woody Guthrie's simple reminder of American values, "This Land Is Your Land."

Simon and Garfunkel then took the stage. As if they had done it only yesterday, the two shyly loped toward the microphones, returning the waves and cheers of the audience. Even though they had rehearsed their songs, Art at first felt rusty and anxious. He hadn't joined voices with Paul in public since that night in Queens two years ago, and he wasn't sure what would happen.

But enveloped by the audience's warmth, the two soon relaxed. As Art said, "About three bars into the first song I had a very strong feeling, 'Well, here we are again. This is where I left off.'"

They sang the familiar tunes: "Mrs. Robinson," "For Emily, Whenever I May Find Her," "The Boxer," "Feelin' Groovy," and "The Sounds of Silence." They closed with the song of hope the crowd had come to hear, "Bridge Over Troubled Water." Simon chose this moment to sing a verse of "Bridge" by himself for the first time. Finally, he would stake his claim to his greatest song and, in no uncertain terms, make it clear to Art and to the audience that he was not satisfied to return to where the two had left off.

That night, at an exclusive after-concert party at the New York Hilton thrown by Clive Davis, Paul and Art circulated among the well-wishers but avoided each other. They didn't discuss their careers although they would both soon resume work on separate albums. This evening was not a reunion; it was only a one-shot event.

The reviewer for *Rolling Stone* sensed that the two were still estranged and suggested in his piece that they were only going through the motions: "They stood at their mikes looking straight ahead, like two commuters clutching adjacent straps on the morning train."

The latest sales figures on Paul's album were in, and he met with Davis to figure out why they weren't better. Clive assured him there was nothing wrong with the album, which had sold far better than those of many other popular artists. Davis still contended that the major problem with sales was due simply to Simon's refusal to tour. Paul knew he was right, and agreed to do a concert tour to promote his next release.

Davis was pleased that both Simon and Garfunkel were busy recording new albums for Columbia, but he still hoped they would come to their senses and reunite. Columbia wanted to squeeze out every last ounce of profitability before "Simon and Garfunkel" was just a fading memory. The crowd's warm and enthusiastic reception in Madison Square Garden reinforced the company's belief that the audience was still there, so it released *Simon and Garfunkel's Greatest Hits* that summer.

The album was a compilation of the team's most popular songs, but Columbia departed from the traditional approach of using only the old familiar versions the audience knew by heart by including live performances of "For Emily, Whenever I May Find Her," "Feelin' Groovy," "Homeward Bound," and "Kathy's Song." The album sparkled with the immediacy of live performances and was an especially poignant reminder of the magical spell they could cast in concert.

In September, "For Emily, Whenever I May Find Her" was released as a single and climbed to number fifty-three. *Greatest Hits* rose to number five on the U.S. charts, another strong affirmation of the audience's continuing interest in Simon and Garfunkel. The team was still together in the hearts and minds of their fans.

Meanwhile, "Duncan," Paul's third single release from *Paul Simon*, was not as successful as his earlier solo singles. While chastened by modest sales, Paul was committed to the solo path. He was already at work on his second album.

In September 1972, Peggy gave birth to the couple's first child, a son to whom they gave Peggy's maiden name, Harper. In October, Art married Linda Grossman, his steady companion of four years, in her hometown, Nashville. The Simons attended the wedding, and the two old friends chatted amiably. In a strange coincidence, two rock 'n' roll-mad Jewish boys from Queens had married two Southern belles from Tennessee, neither of whom had anything to do with music. These marriages would also run a similar course, although no one could have predicted it at the time.

In November, Paul published a comprehensive collection of his songs in book form, reaffirming once again that it was he who was responsible for the Simon and Garfunkel success. *The Songs of Paul Simon* is subtitled "as sung by Simon and Garfunkel and Paul Simon himself from 'Hey Schoolgirl' to 'Mother and Child Reunion.'" In the introduction, Simon offers remarkably detailed insight into his creative process, writing in a colloquial style strikingly similar to that of his songs' lyrics.

The book contained his entire output to date, with the exception of two songs he judged "too really bad" to include, and three songs that E. B. Marks Music, the company for which he sold tunes in college, denied him permission to republish. Simon's brief introduction ends with a firm assertion of his faith in his music-writing skills: "I think my next songs will be better."

The book is illustrated with photographs, handwritten notes, and scribbled drafts of songs that span his musical career, from Queens to the Simon and Garfunkel triumph on Grammy Awards night in May 1971. Paul dedicated the book to the two people who had contributed most to his success: Art Garfunkel and his ex-manager Mort Lewis.

Simon was living in New York, and Garfunkel was on the West Coast now. They rarely saw each other. They seemed in agreement that the reunion in Madison Square Garden had been a one-time-only event, but the memory of the crowd's warm reaction remained fixed in both their minds.

Art was still laboriously working on his album, which he named *Angel Clare,* a title he chose deliberately to bait the critics who dismissed him as "too sweet" and complained of his esoteric and precious sensibility. Angel Clare is the name of the tragic heroine's lover in Thomas Hardy's bleak, nineteenth-century English novel *Tess of the D'Urbervilles,* a fact probably known only to English majors and "Jeopardy" fans. More important, Art said he picked the title simply because he liked the sound of the words—for Art, a pleasing sound was reason enough. More self-confident now, he was willing to take responsibility for his artistic decisions.

During the album's recording, Art's confidence built slowly. At first, he craved the protective stability of working with Halee and other regular Simon and Garfunkel studio musicians. He expected the process would be similar to the moment onstage at the McGovern concert, when he suddenly felt he had returned to where he and Paul had left off two years before.

But as the sessions stretched into months and the music refused to flow, he found it more and more difficult to enter the studio. He began to look forward to lunch bre ks. What once had been such a delight became a dreaded chore.

Oddly enough, part of the problem was the total freedom Columbia allowed its recording star. The company chose to keep a respectful distance from one of its biggest all-time money-makers, imposing no budget limit or deadline. Without the anchor of Paul's songs, Art was adrift in a sea of musical possibilities.

As Paul had already discovered, learning how to work alone was more difficult than Art had imagined. Clive Davis and other Columbia executives noticed Art's floundering, but still applied no pressure. At one point Art approached Davis to explain: "Look, I just want you to know that I haven't lost my perspective. The album is taking a long time, but I'm fully in control."

He asked Davis what Columbia needed to break even on the album. When Davis told him he would have to sell a minimum of 250,000 copies, Art assured him, "Don't worry about a thing. It's in the bag." With all the money Simon and Garfunkel had earned for Columbia, Davis wasn't really concerned about the album's break-even point, but Art wanted to let Davis know

he felt responsible to Columbia as well as confident about his
new work.

Davis also kept in touch with Paul, who was working on songs
for his second solo album. Simon had announced, then canceled, a
tour for that fall, postponing it until his album could be finished
and released.

Those around Paul understood the delays—he was enraptured
with his new baby boy and spent much of his time writing and
singing nonsense songs to amuse Harper. The title of his next
album, *There Goes Rhymin' Simon*, reflects his fascination with
his child and his new role as father.

Paul, Peggy, Harper James, and their two dogs lived in an
elegant, eight-room triplex on Manhattan's Upper East Side once
owned by one of Simon's heroes, classical guitarist Andrés
Segovia. They also owned a farm in Pennsylvania where country-
bred Peggy felt more comfortable than Paul. She once noted wryly
that Paul was never in danger of getting poison ivy because he
never stepped off the roads. A city boy through and through, Paul
is reported to have once said, "Sunsets are vastly overrated." But
Paul appeared as happy and content with his life as he had ever
been. The birth of his son had brought a sense of completion to his
adult life, and he was generally satisfied with the progress of his
solo career.

The Simons soon relocated to a spacious town house on
Manhattan's Upper West Side. But after a period of adjustment to
parenthood, their marriage began to show some signs of stress.
Their "enlightened" approach to modern marriage as a fifty-fifty
proposition did not fit the reality of a relationship in which one
partner was a workaholic superstar.

As he began concentrating on his solo career, Paul found it
increasingly difficult to make the compromises necessary for the
good of the marriage. Success and the wealth it brought had given
him the freedom to do as he pleased, and he chafed at Peggy's
demand that he live up to his part of the fifty-fifty bargain.

Paul was busy finishing the tracks for his second solo album,
There Goes Rhymin' Simon. It captured the essence of Paul's
sunny mood after Harper's birth. The album is a further step
along the gospel path he began to take with "Bridge." Then he had
used gospel to communicate the healing power of reconciliation.
Now he explored its capacity to express sheer joy. He was

especially impressed by the Staple Singers and their recent hit, "I'll Take You There." Just as he had earlier traveled to Jamaica to experience reggae first-hand, he again went to the source to find the most authentic gospel sound, setting up shop at the famous Muscle Shoals Recording Studio in Alabama and hiring the Staple musicians to back him up. He also invited the Dixie Hummingbirds, a classic gospel sextet, to sing along with him on several numbers. On "Take Me to the Mardi Gras" he used a genuine Dixieland jazz ensemble, the Onward Brass Band, to replicate the excitement of a New Orleans street celebration.

Paul fell in love with these exciting Southern musicians, and was so pleased with the technical aspects of the recording he decided to do half the songs on the album at Muscle Shoals.

The album's lightness of touch was a significant departure from the more darkly shaded Simon and Garfunkel work—and from the subject matter of his first solo album. Another important change had occurred. Roy Halee was no longer the principal engineer. Halee was already committed to working on Art's still-gestating album, and perhaps Paul didn't want to get into a tug-of-war for Halee's time or loyalty. So he hired widely acclaimed producer-engineer Phil Ramone.

In the mid-seventies Ramone was a pop-record producer at the top of his form, and his clients would eventually include Billy Joel, Barbra Streisand, Chicago, and Julian Lennon. Paul's meticulous work habits were legendary in the business, and they suited Phil's own thoroughly professional approach. Paul didn't completely sever his working relationship with Halee, who worked on "Tenderness" and got a co-production credit, but the major production responsibilities were shared by Simon and Ramone.

Even more than on his previous album, Paul wanted to showcase his eclectic musical taste. Now he freely explored a variety of musical styles without fear of losing his own, individual voice.

"Tenderness" is a soft, wistful ballad to which Simon added the gospel flavor of the Dixie Hummingbirds. It's a plaintive love song that yearns for a little tenderness "beneath the honesty," words that seem to presage difficulties in Simon's own marriage. "Something So Right" is another love song with lyrics reminiscent of the turbulent times just before the split with Garfunkel. In conversations with friends, Paul gave his wife Peggy credit for settling him down during that difficult time and pointing him in the right direction, in much the same way the song recounts in lines like "And I was crazy in motion / Til you calmed me down."

For all the album's references to emotional developments in his own life, Paul hadn't abandoned his interest in the American social scene. For "American Tune," Paul took a melody from Bach's St. Matthew Passion and grafted lyrics onto it that summed up his generation's weariness with political deception and lack of vision. He talks of battered and shattered dreams, but lifts the dark mood by reminding us of the promise still offered by basic American ideals. In "American Tune," Paul directs our eyes away from lost battles and focuses them instead on that symbol of the nation's compassionate and regenerative spirit, the Statue of Liberty. He links the aspirations of boatloads of immigrants to the adventurous pioneering spirit of the space age, and reminds us that the nation draws its strength from an ability to constantly renew itself. He hoped the new song, like "Bridge Over Troubled Water," would have a profound and lasting impact on the country. Its themes of renewal, optimism, and bedrock faith in American ideals avoided any appeal to hollow patriotism and were meant as balm for the wounds of a battered nation.

"Was a Sunny Day" pays delightful, cheerful homage to Paul's rock-'n'-roll heroes while "St. Judy's Comet" is a fond father's lullaby to his first-born son. Paul pictures a baby struggling against sleep while his daddy croons to him, creating a shimmering image of a night sky cascading with the twinkling tail of a comet or the flash of fireflies. The baby resists sleep, and Paul asks his son to comply "Cause if I can't sing my boy to sleep / Well it makes your famous father / Look so dumb."

Paul appeared totally captivated by his child, and when asked in a *Playboy* interview in 1984 why he didn't continue to write songs about Harper, Paul said, "I tried to, but I was just too overcome with love to write. I couldn't think of anything to write other than, 'You totally amaze and mesmerize me, I'm so in love with you I can't contain myself.'"

The album took little more than a year to produce—a new speed record for Paul. Its rapid appearance was perhaps an indication of Paul's eagerness to establish continuity with his budding audience. Simon's happy mood is apparent at first glance at the album cover—awash in bright, primary colors and studded with personal snapshots that seem to promise an intimate journey. Starting with an image of Paul as a teenage Elvis-type, a cometlike trail of color photos traces the trajectory of Paul's life, along with an intriguing assortment of song titles and symbols, and ends with a candid portrait of the proud father cradling his infant son in his arms.

One of the snapshots shows Paul with his younger brother Eddie, to whom he bears a striking resemblance. Eddie had studied classical guitar and eventually opened a guitar school, but couldn't escape the shadow of his brother's enormous fame. Although he weighed twenty pounds less, people would often stop him in the street to ask for Paul Simon's autograph. Eddie has said, "It would really be unbearable if I didn't love him so much."

Unable to escape the gravitational pull of Paul's stardom, Eddie tried to capitalize on it, asking Paul's permission to bootleg some of his music. Unlawful duplication and sale of previously recorded music were serious problems for record companies and artists. Columbia estimated that more than a million bootleg recordings of Simon and Garfunkel albums were in existence, representing a considerable loss of profit and royalties.

Paul considered the practice theft. Understandably disappointed with Eddie's request, he refused but did feel sympathy for Eddie's situation. At the time, Eddie was, in Paul's words, "drifting around." Paul has admitted, "My brother's had a rough time because of me. It's hard. I wouldn't want that burden."

As soon as the final tracks were laid for the new album, the all-important choice of which single to release first had to be made. Paul voted for "American Tune," but to his surprise Davis argued for the upbeat "Kodachrome." He complained to Davis, "You're the one who's always talking about the importance of a ballad hit!" Paul was sure "American Tune," "a quality song with strong lyrics," could be another "Bridge Over Troubled Water."

But Columbia overruled the ballad in favor of the "safer and more obvious" choice, "Kodachrome." Paul's earlier two hit singles had not been ballads, and Columbia wanted to go with a winning formula. Paul reluctantly agreed to the choice. Simultaneously released with the album, the single of "Kodachrome" jumped to the number-two position on the charts and sold more than a million records. The first line of the bouncy

"Kodachrome," "When I think back / On all the crap I learned in high school"* gives notice of quick-witted, irreverent fun ahead. The word "crap" hadn't been used before in a mainstream pop recording, and some radio stations refused to play the song because they found it offensive. The BBC had trouble with the use of the word "Kodachrome," which they thought audiences might construe as advertising. Listeners and record buyers weren't put off by either word.

This time Simon made good on his promise to promote the album with a national and international tour. In May, he began his first solo tour in Boston. Still feeling insecure about taking the stage alone, he asked the Jesse Dixon Singers to join the tour to augment the gospel-style numbers. He also invited the South American group Urubamba, which included two players from the Los Incas group with whom Paul had worked on the adaptation of "El Condor Pasa."

Uncertain about his ability to fill large auditoriums, Simon limited appearances to halls with fewer than five thousand seats. He needn't have worried—the tour was a sellout from coast to coast. In concert, Paul sensed growing enthusiasm for his new musical directions.

Invariably, Paul was greeted with shouts of "Where's Artie?" which he tried to answer with stabs at humor, although, as his producer Phil Ramone commented, "At the time, it was never funny." By the end of the evening, however, fans had little reason for sulky comparisons to the good old Simon and Garfunkel days. The audience was eager to hear Paul and his new music. Pleased by this reception, Columbia decided to do a live album of the tour.

The gospel flavor infused new life into several of the old Simon and Garfunkel standards, like "The Sounds of Silence" and "Homeward Bound." Even "Bridge Over Troubled Water" sounded fresh with a fuller gospel treatment. With the audacious and surprising mix of style and rhythms, Paul was trying, as he once put it, to "redeem" his music from the grasp of "Simon and Garfunkel." He desperately wanted people to know Paul Simon had written those earlier songs, and he could sing them any way he chose.

In June, Paul performed at London's Albert Hall, where critics

* "Kodachrome" © 1973 by Paul Simon

praised his taste, sense of adventure, and even his solo singing on the new material. But some mourned the loss of the magical element Art brought to old, familiar songs. As one critic noted, "Garfunkel's tart harmonies brought out the full flavor in many Simon songs. 'The Boxer' loses massively when Simon alone sings it. Simon is a genius, but even he misses Garfunkel."

But Simon's hard-core fans forgave Art's absence. Only one concert had been scheduled in London, but ticket demand was so great two more were added. According to critic Tony Palmer, "To say they [the concerts] were a triumph would be an understatement. The first night was more like a séance, although a joyful one at that. Simon performs with consummate ease and evident enjoyment."

While Paul toured triumphantly, Art was putting the finishing touches on the *Angel Clare* album in San Francisco. The album consists entirely of ballads, and Art defended his choice this way: "People say, 'Look at how many ballads he does.' Well, ballads are my forte. It's the first-tie theory. If you have two ties, and one's your favorite, why go out for a major occasion wearing your second favorite? Others choose to work from a larger palette. My ear just doesn't enjoy the mix of delicate and bombastic." The remark perhaps was intended to differentiate him from Paul's most recent songs with their up-tempo rhythms and joyous lyrics.

But Art's continuing deep respect for his ex-partner's talent was evident when he asked Paul to play guitar on "Mary Was an Only Child," a song Paul had suggested.

Like Paul, Art didn't hesitate to reach into the classical repertoire for material, choosing a Bach melody for "Feuilles-Oh." (It was the same Bach piece Paul had rejected for the *Bridge* album.) Linda is credited with the lyrics for "Feuilles-Oh," and she was also involved with Art in other musical choices. Some said working together was the Garfunkels' way of trying to smooth out the wrinkles that were beginning to form in their relationship.

Art was ready to promote the album, but, like Paul, he chose not to do a concert tour his first time out as a solo. He did agree to sing a few selections from the new album at a Columbia Records convention in San Francisco a few months before *Angel Clare* was to be released.

Art sang four songs and felt uncomfortable with the first three. He hadn't performed as a solo act since his college days, but he got over a shaky start to deliver a strong version of "Bridge Over Troubled Water" as a finish.

Paul also performed at the convention and was in the audience when Art sang. He was quick to congratulate Art afterward on his performance, but he limited his comments to some helpful criticism of Art's stage patter and didn't get into a discussion of the music.

Art was so sure of his reputation as both singer and movie star that the album's front cover bears neither a title nor his name— only a close-up color photograph of Art, remarkably similar in style to the portrait on Paul's first solo album cover.

By the time the promotional interviews were in high gear, Art's confidence had reached new heights. He now denied any trepidation about releasing his own album. Paul read between the lines and sympathized with Art's anxiety. In an interview with Robert Hilburn of the *Los Angeles Times,* Paul offered a conciliatory and generous assessment of Art's talent. He was doing what he could to alert critics and the public to Art's singular gift. It was time to make amends for words spoken in anger and frustration during the arduous recording of the *Bridge Over Troubled Water* album: "I should have said how good Artie is. I said what I thought he didn't do, but I didn't say, for instance, 'Here's a guy who has one of the finest voices in popular music, who has a very intelligent mind, who was enthusiastic about his work...and who offered very useful ideas.' I didn't emphasize his legitimate strengths."

Through the years, Paul Simon has been adroit in his handling of the press, but it's been a love-hate relationship. He cooperates with endless interviews because he realizes publicity can make or break his songs and his career, but depending on his mood, he can be curt or revelatory. The *Los Angeles Times*'s Hilburn says that Simon virtually interviews himself—just turn on the tape recorder, and Paul does the rest.

While Art waited anxiously for the reaction to *Angel Clare,* he submitted to the usual barrage of questions about the split and the likelihood of a reunion. He wasn't interested in talking about that, but he did make a surprising revelation about his career choices: "Acting was just a diversion. I've always felt committed to music. I love to sing."

That summer, Columbia released Art's single of "All I Know," and it made its way up the charts to number nine. *Angel Clare* was well received by critics and the public, with generous praise for Art's singing talent and his song selection. With his stirring rendition of Van Morrison's "I Shall Sing," Art Garfunkel seemed to declare he felt comfortable at last with his career as a solo vocalist. The LP jumped to the number-five slot in the United States and to number fourteen in England.

Paul was riding high on the charts as well. The single "Loves Me Like a Rock" had hit number three and had achieved gold-record status. The song offers a giddy dose of happiness in full-blown, rocking gospel style. Paul sings of a parent, a "mama" who "Gets down on her knees / And loves me / Loves me like the Rock of Ages." The song expresses the overwhelming love Paul felt for his own child. As he had predicted, response to "American Tune" was so strong Columbia released it as a single as well. "American Tune" was voted Best Song of the Year of 1974 by *Rolling Stone* magazine.

The names of Simon and Garfunkel were again on the hit-singles and -album charts—but not as a team. Their audience had accepted them each as individual talents. The likelihood of a reunion dimmed as their solo stars brightened.

10

Tensions between Paul and Peggy had been growing, and his prolonged absences for the *Rhymin' Simon* tour made things even worse.

Paul completed the tour and returned home to New York early in 1974. He would spend most of the year writing and recording songs for his next album. The happy mood of his recent one—which observers thought to be a reflection of Paul's own domestic bliss—dissipated as rapidly as the rainbow-hued comet on its cover.

The life-style of a driven workaholic never meshed smoothly with the ground rules for domestic equality Paul and Peggy had so proudly proclaimed at the beginning of their marriage. Now it appeared that both had been naïve about the dominance of Paul's career and his ability to make compromises for the good of the relationship.

Gone were their intense, all-night conversations about the direction of Paul's career. Peggy's constructive criticism—once Paul's guiding light—now seemed relentlessly negative and more and more unwelcome. As Paul has said, "I liked that she could be critical, because I felt that I was someone who was praised too

much. And I thought, finally, someone who's honest. But I began
not to like it."

Discussions now centered on whose turn it was to wash dishes,
walk the dog, or change the baby. Given the fact that they could
afford plenty of domestic help, the arguments were clearly more a
tug-of-war over egos than over mundane domestic chores. By
night, Paul received the unalloyed adulation of thousands of fans.
By day, his "equal" domestic arrangement made too many demands on his time. The plan of their life together had once seemed
workable; Paul had thought he could handle the shift in status. He
had written his best work, "Bridge Over Troubled Water," as a
testament to his willingness to surrender his own needs for the
sake of his wife, but as time went on, he found he had little real
energy or taste for the radical role changes he had agreed to make.

Peggy wasn't particularly interested in rock 'n' roll or the
company of Paul's show-business friends, but it was tough for Paul
to spend quiet evenings at home, especially after the emotional
rush of a performance or an intense studio session. The differences
between them crystallized one evening when they were at home
alone in their apartment. As Paul described it, he and Peggy traded
their customary places because she was chilly. Paul sat down in
Peggy's chair, which happened to be between two powerful stereo
speakers. Over the booming music, Paul—delighted by the sur-
round sound that reminded him of a recording studio—remarked,
"This is just like home." Peggy icily replied, "This is your home."
As trivial as the incident seemed at the time, it defined Paul's
priorities. The gap between them began to widen, and real
communication ceased altogether. Eventually, Paul found it impossible to adjust to Peggy's emotional needs and resented the
pressure to do so. Like so many couples whose lives begin to
diverge, they no longer talked; they negotiated.

The old guilt over success and money resurfaced, but with a new
twist. He later said, "Everything I did was put down. It was as if
the fact that I'd earned all that money—that didn't entitle me to
anything. I had a sense of worthlessness." The guilt turned to
anger. Paul measured his behavior and attitudes about marriage
against those of his male friends and was satisfied with his effort.
It may not have been enough for Peggy, but he wasn't willing to do
more.

After so many years of fame, power, and control, the old habits proved impossible to break—he was simply used to having things his own way. Just as in his relationship with Art, Paul reached a point where he refused to compromise any longer. The Simons separated, and a decade later Paul said: "I wasn't ready. I didn't understand what marriage meant, really. I didn't understand that if things were uncomfortable or you were unhappy, you could work it out. I was young."

Sixteen months after the birth of Harper, Paul moved out of his elegant brownstone into a Manhattan hotel. There he sat for hours, staring out the window at the traffic below. To ease his pain, he started to write songs about the loss of love, but still spent most of 1974 in deep depression. Ironically, it turned out that Art was negotiating the same painful journey.

Art and Linda were discovering that, in spite of living together for four years before marriage, they had irreconcilable differences. They, too, found their problems too great to surmount. As their marriages disintegrated, both Art and Paul gravitated toward the safe haven of their old friendship. Together they could distract themselves with talk of music instead of divorce settlements.

Even as his personal life was falling apart, Paul started to have difficulty playing the guitar. Although he is primarily right-handed, Paul plays sports as a lefty, and in a squash game he had injured the index finger of his left hand. A calcium deposit developed, and soon he was unable to bend the swollen finger, which meant that he couldn't play certain chords on the guitar. It was painful and disturbing. One day he ran into John Lennon and Yoko Ono on the street, and Paul mentioned his problem. They advised him to try a macrobiotic diet: no coffee, tea, sugar, meat, or dairy products. He stuck to a regimen of mostly rice and vegetables, and within the next eighteen months, either the diet, or his body's natural healing process, reduced the swelling, and he regained some flexibility in the finger. Simon once said the specter of not being able to play the guitar was so frightening he had blocked out this memory almost entirely.

In the spring of 1974 Paul and Art had settled into separate bachelor quarters in New York City, with Art on the East Side and Paul in a new duplex on Central Park West near Peggy and Harper. With no one waiting at home, they could resume their old habits, including roaming the music scene in New York together.

In May, Paul heard that John Lennon was working with Harry

Nilsson on Nilsson's new album. John and Harry had taken adjoining rooms at the Hotel Pierre and held court there during the day. At night, they recorded. True to the legendary work habits of rock stars, they arose in the afternoon, ordered a breakfast of Brandy Alexanders, milk shakes, and an assortment of nibbles, and entertained the elite of the music world. Word soon got out that anyone who was anyone was welcome to join the party.

When evening came, John and Harry would amble over to a recording studio to work on the music. Often other rock stars would visit the sessions and sometimes perform. One night, Paul persuaded Art to visit the scene with him. The rare chance to work with John Lennon brought Simon and Garfunkel together to sing in a studio for the first time in four years. Observers said they both appeared nervous and rusty as they tried to lay down some background vocals. They missed cues and testily accused one another of mistakes. Nilsson, quickly losing patience with the bickering and delays, screamed at them to get on with it. Still, Paul and Art uncharacteristically blew take after take. Soon everybody in the room was hurling insults and curses. After a while, the studio settled down, and the tracks were completed, but they were never used on the album.

Clearly, the two hadn't worked out their old conflicts, but the session did signal a willingness to reestablish professional contact away from the glare of publicity.

For the remainder of 1974, Paul and Art tried to regain some measure of control over their chaotic personal lives by channeling their energies into their separate careers. Art's single release of "I Shall Sing" had been a sizable hit, and Paul's last album had increased his audience dramatically. *There Goes Rhymin' Simon* had even been nominated for a Grammy in the Best Album of the Year category, but lost to Stevie Wonder's *Innervisions*. Columbia released the concert album *Live Rhymin'* that spring, but it was only a middling hit. Paul wasn't deterred by the modest sales. He was getting used to the idea of measuring his success against standards other than the Simon and Garfunkel phenomenon.

Paul was also at work on a film score for his old buddy from the political benefits, Warren Beatty, but it wasn't going well. Beatty was producing and starring in *Shampoo*, an ambitious film about the pernicious influence of Richard Nixon on the nation. Beatty surrounded himself with the most talented cast and crew he could find. Hal Ashby, who had recently directed Jack Nicholson in the surprise success of the year, *The Last Detail,* had been signed, and Robert Towne, who had just received an Oscar for writing *Chinatown,* which also featured Jack Nicholson, was hired to do the script. *Shampoo* centers on the ambitions of an affable but inept, womanizing Hollywood hairdresser. The female leads went to Julie Christie and Goldie Hawn. It seemed like a dream project.

Although Paul's first experience with film scoring on *The Graduate* had not been creatively satisfying, he couldn't resist Beatty's entreaties and the lure of joining such a star-studded Hollywood lineup. Working on Beatty's film was also a chance to reenter the movie work on Simon's own terms. He still nursed the twin wounds of his *Catch-22* rejection and Art's simultaneous ascension to movie-star status. He had even been toying with the idea of making a film of his own. So he signed on and asked Phil Ramone to produce the soundtrack.

As before, Paul found writing to order a difficult task. To make matters worse, Beatty's creative vision of a socially relevant yet entertaining assessment of the late sixties floundered early on. Instead of a biting commentary on the corruption of political ideals, the film degenerated into an aimless, softly nostalgic rumination on the largely unfulfilled promises of the tumultuous sixties.

Neither Beatty nor Simon had a firm grasp on what the film or soundtrack should do. Paul wrote two songs—"Have a Good Time" and "Silent Eyes"—but neither was used. Ultimately, his role in creating the soundtrack was severely limited, and Beatty decided instead to use existing music by the Beatles and Buffalo Springfield, among others. "Feelin' Groovy" was the only Simon song used on the track. The movie was released to mixed reviews, but its bold depiction of explicit Hollywood sexual practices attracted a lot of publicity, and it did big business at the box office. Paul reworked the songs he'd written for Beatty and set them aside for his next album.

In March 1975, the public was treated to a surprise joint Simon and Garfunkel appearance at the nationally televised Grammy Awards. Paul Simon and John Lennon were co-presenters for the Record of the Year award. The winner was Olivia Newton-John's "I Honestly Love You," but Newton-John wasn't in the audience to accept. When the award was announced, the cameras searched the audience for the recipient and found Art Garfunkel, dressed in a T-shirt with a tuxedo painted on the front, who climbed the stairs to the podium. John Lennon backed away from the spotlight, "almost as far away as he could get without leaving the stage," said one observer. The audience held its breath until Art broke the tension with a quip: "Still writing, Paul?" That began a pattern of edgy banter about the split which tantalized Simon and Garfunkel fans who hadn't given up hope the duo would reunite. Neither Art nor Paul admitted they had planned the scene, but they liked the effect it had on the audience, and from this point on, they made public sparring a regular habit.

After the Grammys, Paul returned to the task of writing material for his next album. In addition, since he and Art had drifted closer together again, Paul decided to write a song for him, the first such offering since "Bridge Over Troubled Water."

Art was working on his second album, which would include selections from such diverse composers as Stephen Bishop, Antonio Carlos Jobim, Yvonne Wright, and Stevie Wonder. The album's title song, "Breakaway," was written by Bernard Gallagher and Graham Lyle. Art enlisted the vocal support of David Crosby and Graham Nash, Toni Tennille, and Bruce Johnston. He also chose several key musicians he had worked with before, including pianist Larry Knechtel, who had so often played the accompaniment to "Bridge Over Troubled Water." The tracks were recorded in Los Angeles, New York, and London. Richard Perry produced the album, although Art gave himself an associate-producer credit as well.

Breakaway's theme is the elusive ideal of romantic love, the same theme Paul focused on in those days. But Paul's vision includes much more of love's bittersweet flavor. As always, Simon was patiently transforming the specific experiences of his own life into truths almost everyone could relate to. As always, he was just far enough ahead of his audience to illuminate the way. The "youth generation" of the sixties—even the most antiestablishment hippies—had by now settled down, married, become parents, and had marital problems of their own. Paul had grown up with his audience and was determined to maintain his connection with them. He said, "People thirty years old wonder why they're not getting off on popular music the way they once did, and it's because nobody's singing for them."

The song "Still Crazy After All These Years" is a perfect evocation of time and place, exploring an experience the audience could instantly identify with. Paul used his own lonely vigil in the window of a Manhattan hotel, after his separation from Peggy, as the framework for the song, but he saved the scene from maudlin sentiment by giving it a dangerous edge: "Now I sit by my window / And I watch the cars / I fear I'll do some damage / One fine day." If the craziness does get out of hand, he trusts his audience will understand because they've been through the madness of loss too: "But I would not be convicted / By a jury of my peers / Still crazy after all these years."*

Eddie Simon analyzed the song: "My brother's saying, 'Look, I'm working every day; I'm trying to do the right thing and get through the best way I know how; I've been famous and not famous, badmouthed and broken up inside; I've traveled, I've seen a shrink; I've been in love and got married; and that bottomed out too. And you know something? After all that work, all that pain and trouble, all these years—I'm still crazy. Still fuckin' crazy after all these years.'"

Paul told an interviewer how closely he identified with the emotions in the song: "Once I was working on a song in the shower, singing it, a song called 'Still Crazy After All These Years,' and I started crying...I must have cried for fifteen minutes."

Another of Paul's new songs for the album, "I Do It for Your Love," is unabashedly autobiographical. He later admitted, "The whole album is about my marriage.... 'I Do It for Your Love' got it out of me—that was a very emotional song for me, a very truthful song. I was crying in the middle of that song when I was writing some of those lyrics. That's really me—I don't know how good a song it is, but it's really about my life."

A profoundly sad song, "I Do It for Your Love" begins with a bleak wedding-day scene distinguished only by the scratch of pens on legal papers. At the time he wrote the song, Paul was deeply involved in discussions with lawyers about his divorce settlement.

Even the romantic moments of the first stages of a love affair are tinged with sadness: The lovers share a cold, their cheap apartment is musty, and the colors in a rug they buy in an old junk shop, dampened by rain, bleed together.

*"Still Crazy After All These Years" © 1974 by Paul Simon

OLD FRIENDS

155

In two brief lines, he captures the powerful essence of a hopeless quarrel between lovers or ex-lovers: "The sting of reason / The splash of tears." He measures the vast distances between two people in geographical as well as emotional terms. His New York and Peggy's Southern roots become "The northern and the southern hemispheres." The song ends with a brief but complete emotional history of a broken marriage: "Love emerges / And it disappears."*

Paul again chose Phil Ramone to produce his album. By now, Ramone was used to the painstaking and time-consuming work that went into a Paul Simon album, and he had learned to adjust his pace to Paul's writing progress. As Ramone described it: "A lot of times during the album, we had to stop for a month or so because there was nothing flowing from him. Once they're written, each song matures technically at its own, individual speed."

Paul decided to use jazz-flavored arrangements for most of the songs on *Still Crazy After All These Years*. The supple, intimate feel of the electronic keyboard with other jazz instrumentation and rhythms suited the wistful, rueful tone Paul sought to achieve. Still exploring musical possibilities, he had been studying composition and arrangement in New York with jazz artists Chuck Israels and David Sorin Collyer, and he credited their influences on the record sleeve.

Paul's bittersweet tone has an edgy, brittle feel on "You're Kind." It, too, traces the downward spiral of his marriage, recalling the hopeful, early days when Peggy gave him much-needed perspective on the emotional morass of Simon and Garfunkel: "You rescued me when I was blind." But despite all the goodness and love she offered, he now must leave because, "I like to sleep with the window open / And you keep the window closed."† There is no room for compromise here. Paul later mused that the "open window" might also describe his need for freedom.

"Gone at Last," originally arranged with a Latin rhythm, was recorded by Paul and Bette Midler. It had, as Paul described it, "a street feel," but this version was never used. The official explanation was that contractual differences between their respective

*"I Do It for Your Love" © 1975 by Paul Simon
†"You're Kind" © 1975 by Paul Simon

record companies prohibited it, but music insiders say Simon and "The Divine Miss M" had a falling out. She has said she was never told Paul was going to recut the song and only found out when the album was released and she wasn't on it.

Paul rethought "Gone at Last," shifting it to a gospel-style arrangement, and asked Phoebe Snow to sing it with him. Phoebe had been a Paul Simon fan for years and had even attended his songwriting seminar at NYU five years before.

The months of work Paul had poured into the aborted Midler version of "Gone at Last" made the final recording with Snow go very quickly. For all but those who knew how slowly he worked, it seemed as if Paul Simon was back to his early days of churning out demo records at lightning speed. Once they got settled in the studio, the recording was completed in less than two hours. Snow, who had been so excited about working with Paul, was almost disappointed the session went so fast. Phoebe also sang backup on "50 Ways to Leave Your Lover," another song that came to Paul as if in a dream.

As he later described it, one day he woke up with some intriguing words floating through his head: "The problem is all inside your head / She said to me." He started playing with the line using a Rhythm Ace, an electronic drum machine with a steady, repetitive beat that he kept in his apartment. Paul's choice of the number 50 in the song's title could be a reference to his previous discussions with Peggy about ever achieving a truly equal, fifty-fifty marital relationship.

According to Paul's brother Eddie, Harper Simon also had an influence on the development of "50 Ways to Leave Your Lover." Paul had been playing one of his favorite rhyming games with Harper, teaching the boy to sing 'Fe Fi Fiddle-eye-o,' and every time the child tried to sing the words, he laughed. Paul liked the tickly feel of the nonsense rhymes. They seemed to drain the song's subject—the act of leaving a lover—of any malice or threat. The song's almost mirthful tone makes it easier to swallow the bitter pill of separation.

Blending unexpected elements and combining opposites was one of Paul's favorite techniques. He believed a musician must always find a way to create tension or surprise, or risk boring the audience—in Paul's mind, a cardinal sin. Paul had long thought Art was guilty of the slightly lesser sin of predictability. He decided to show him the error of his ways. Simon wrote "My Little Town" with his old singing partner in mind. Paul said it was "a nasty song, because he was singing too many sweet songs. It seemed like a good concept for him."

Art liked the song although he didn't agree with Paul's assessment of the sameness of his musical taste. The old habit of friendship and professional cooperation blossomed as Paul taught Art the song. The rehearsal time together had a soothing effect on their relationship.

Although Paul had originally written "My Little Town" for Art to sing alone, Art liked the way it could be harmonized, and he suggested the two record it together. The sessions had gone so well, Paul quickly agreed: "It was pleasant. Nervous and tense at first. I wondered if it would be good. It fell back into something I had done for so many years. It's easy to sing with Artie. It's something I'd done all my life."

Art then suggested they both use the same track of the song on their new solo albums, which were scheduled to be released around the same time later that year. Art argued that it wouldn't be fair to the fans of either to release it on only one album: "We figured there would be a certain amount of commotion about our not having sung together in the studio for five years. We decided if people wanted to buy 'Simon and Garfunkel,' they should not have to buy one album as opposed to the other album."

In addition, Art was aware of Paul's long-smoldering resentment about his "Bridge Over Troubled Water" solo. He also knew that Paul was struggling to reclaim the song, and he didn't want either of them to repeat the mistake with "My Little Town."

"My Little Town" carries a dangerous threat. The themes of alienation and repression from Paul's early work take on a more ominous coloration. "The Sounds of Silence" and "I Am a Rock" seem merely pouty compared to the gritty tone of "My Little Town." The disarming title line leads to a series of increasingly threatening images—someone on a bike flying past the gates of grungy factories, a mother hanging clothes in the dirty breeze, a black rainbow—which build to a madman, loose in the streets, who's about to explode: "Twitching like a finger / On the trigger of a gun."* This song makes the threat found in "Still Crazy"—"I

* "My Little Town" © 1975 by Paul Simon

fear I'll do some damage / One fine day"*—seem mild by comparison.

While Paul admitted the autobiographical influences on most of *Still Crazy After All These Years,* he vehemently denied "My Little Town" had anything to do with his own past: "That song isn't about me. The song is about somebody who hates the town he grew up in. Somebody happy to get out. I don't know where the idea came from ..." When the album was released, Paul reminded his audience and critics that he hadn't discarded his English-major roots. On the album sleeve, just above the lyrics for "My Little Town," he paid homage to contemporary British poet Ted Hughes by quoting lines from a Hughes poem: "To hatch a crow, a black rainbow / Bent in emptiness / Over emptiness / But flying." Out of the emptiness beneath the "black rainbow," Paul creates his malevolent little town and someone flying out of control. It is a revealing insight into one source of Paul's inspiration and his writing method.

The duo knew the promotional drill and prepared to submit to its demands. The first step was a trip to Toronto in July to showcase the tune at a convention of Columbia executives. They performed "My Little Town" and two other numbers—their second appearance as a team in five years. The audience received them affectionately and enthusiastically, like returning prodigal sons.

Columbia's national singles promotional director, Bob Sherwood, tested "My Little Town," and his results indicated it would get the necessary airplay to become a hit. Sherwood exulted: "Everywhere we tested it, people said, 'Boy, radio sure needs a Simon and Garfunkel record.' The minute 'My Little Town' came out we had airplay."

Both Art and Paul recognized the huge commercial potential of "My Little Town" for each of their careers. They were by now savvy show-business veterans with a keen appreciation of the dollar value of a Simon and Garfunkel tune. As Clive Davis and others had predicted, neither solo career had risen to anywhere near the heights they had achieved as a team. Perhaps it was time for a dual career jump-start. Maybe it was time to tap into the vast

*"Still Crazy After All These Years" © 1973 by Paul Simon

reservoir of pent-up longing their audience felt for their reunion. No more potent burst of energy could be found than the release of a duet of a Paul Simon song. But they needed a showcase to launch the reunion record.

Paul had been spending his bachelor nights prowling trendy New York night spots with his new friend, Lorne Michaels, the Canadian whiz kid NBC had signed in the spring of 1975 to produce a revolutionary new comedy series called "Saturday Night Live." Michaels was an offbeat, but very successful, producer of Hollywood television specials, including several for Lily Tomlin. When NBC executive Dick Ebersol went looking for someone who could make waves, Lorne Michaels's name headed the list.

NBC was willing to take chances with "Saturday Night Live" because the stakes were astronomically high. Television demographics suggested a large, untapped market of aging hippies looking for something new in American television. This audience had grown up in a time when every middle-class living room had a television glowing with the same indelible messages and events. They had seen Ed Sullivan bug-eyed at the ecstatic reaction received by Elvis and the Beatles. They had witnessed a riderless black horse with empty boots parade by in the first of many national funerals. They had seen Selma and Cicero, Kent State and Vietnam, and an Eagle landing on the moon. Television had brought it all home. These television viewers had become upwardly mobile professionals, slightly embarrassed to find themselves locked in the embrace of their parents' values after all. They remained, however, not yet too far removed from their anti-establishment, protestor-activist, irreverent roots.

"That Was The Week That Was," a British satirical import hosted by David Frost, provided an interesting model, but it hadn't drawn a huge audience. Some suggested it was too brainy. Michaels proposed a comedy series unlike anything that had ever been tried on a large scale before. It would feature socially relevant material that challenged the establishment and exuded an air of unpredictability. It would also include the sure-fire magnet for the "old" youth movement: rock 'n' roll and other pop music on the cutting edge.

The program was scheduled to air live, late at night, a time when young married couples had put the kids to bed but still wanted to do something that would make them feel hip and relevant.

Michaels quickly recruited the best improvisational comedians he could find. He formed the Not Ready for Prime Time Players, with John Belushi, Dan Aykroyd, Chevy Chase, Jane Curtin, Garrett Morris, Gilda Radner, and Laraine Newman.

The program's unorthodox approach to comedy extended to its behind-the-scenes organization. Writing conferences turned into all-night bull sessions; secretaries and production assistants took stabs at suggesting routines, and all manner of strange-looking guests showed up. The staff patiently listened to anyone's notion of what the show needed.

NBC executives and staff who weren't familiar with the new cast and crew of "Saturday Night Live" were incredulous at the bizarre behavior on the seventeenth floor of that bastion of conservatism, Rockefeller Center. "The crazies," as the gossip mill named them, raised a lot of eyebrows. There was talk of drugs, and the distinctive smell of marijuana hung in the air on occasion.

But the serious drug of choice for several of the creative ensemble was cocaine, and Paul's good friend Lorne Michaels was among its devotees. "Saturday Night Live" exerted tremendous pressure to create, and many needed the jolt of a cocaine high to get through the chaotic week before the show.

Michaels, as well as several other members of the cast, told Paul all about the pioneering development of "Saturday Night Live." Paul was excited about the program and told Art he thought they should consider a joint appearance on the show. Art remembered, "He become more fervent about saying 'You'll enjoy this, come.'"

Paul and Art had been arguing the merits of various reunion scenarios to promote "My Little Town" and their new albums. A simple concert, no matter how large, wouldn't spread the word fast enough, so they decided on television as the perfect medium. A daring late-night comedy series, a program that promised to deliver them instantly back to vast numbers of their no-longer-young audience, seemed exactly what they were looking for. Art finally agreed, and Michaels eagerly scheduled Simon to host the second "Saturday Night Live," with Garfunkel featured as a musical guest. The idea was to hit the audience with the heavy comedic guns on the first program and give the creative staff a bit of a breather the following week by slotting a heavily musical second show. Michaels knew the reunion angle would boost television ratings as well as album sales.

The idea didn't sit well with other members of the cast. John Belushi was outraged that so little time would be available for the Not Ready for Prime Time Players. One observer remembers that he fumed around the production offices, calling Paul Simon a "folksinging wimp" among other things.

When Paul showed up for rehearsals, no one at the guard station recognized him. He wound up frantically calling Michaels to rescue him. Paul's ego was bruised.

The production crew of "Saturday Night Live" spent a great deal of time dealing with Paul's obsession with his developing bald spot. He fixated on the monitors, craning his neck to see if it showed. The rehearsals were slowed until he and Lorne had a quiet, heart-to-heart talk about it.

Simon even joined in the loosely structured scripting process. Although he said he made a point of asking NBC to avoid promotion of the show as primarily a Simon and Garfunkel reunion, the night was almost exclusively devoted to Paul and Art.

Inveterate baseball fan Simon especially enjoyed hearing announcer Joe Garagiola's plug during a World Series broadcast for the "Saturday Night Live" Simon and Garfunkel reunion show. Garagiola offered the ultimate compliment by comparing the reteaming of Simon and Garfunkel to the resurrection of the immortal Yankee duo of Babe Ruth and Lou Gehrig.

Reunion excitement rose to a fever pitch, and both Paul and Art became concerned about meeting the high emotional expectations of their old audience. They worried their union might be perceived as a crass commercial ploy to breathe new life into their flagging careers.

Paul was convinced humor was the best way to handle the pressure and deflect charges of blatant audience manipulation. He wanted to prove to the world that Paul Simon wasn't the angst-ridden, melancholy figure he often appeared to be. He chafed at one critic's description of his "bookwormish traits" and his "prematurely gray persona." On "Saturday Night Live" he would show everyone he had a sense of humor. In a *Rolling Stone* interview he said, "To a degree, it's a setup. When groups break up, people always assume they break up in bitterness. So we play on the comic possibilities.

Stand-up comedian Richard Belzer warmed up the studio audience by saying, "For the first time in five years, Paul Simon and Art Garfunkel will be performing together." Art and Paul had performed three songs together at the Columbia Records convention in Toronto, and they had appeared together at the McGovern benefit, but those were comparatively halfhearted efforts. This time, the reunion seemed to be the real thing.

After Belzer left the stage, Paul ambled to the host position and greeted the audience with "I know this is going to come as a disappointment to you, but Art Garfunkel is not going to be here tonight. Instead, my brother is gonna give a guitar lesson on the spot."

Paul continued with a brief monologue and then sang several of his new songs. He then introduced a few bars of a new Randy Newman song, "Marie," before he brought on its composer. Next, Paul did a duet of "Gone at Last" with guest Phoebe Snow. In a comic skit that poked fun at his diminutive stature, he tried to dribble around basketball star Connie Hawkins, who stood almost two feet taller. That skit was followed by a photographic montage spanning the Simon and Garfunkel career set to the sounds of "Mrs. Robinson." At last Paul casually said, "And now my friend, Art Garfunkel."

The crowd gave them a standing ovation. When the cheering died away, Paul looked at Art and said, "So, you've come crawling back." Art blandly replied, "It's very nice of you to invite me on your show." The audience loved it.

Paul and Art then settled down to the serious work of doing a medley of their old hits before singing "My Little Town." Art followed with his new single, a remake of the Flamingos' 1959 hit, "I Only Have Eyes for You." It had already risen to a robust eighteen in the States and soared to number one in England.

Although the studio audience showered them with unalloyed affection, the reviewer for the *New York Times* remained skeptical about the team's motivation: "Art patted Paul, Paul patted Art, and all appeared once again to be seamless two-part harmony. Commercial break." He went on to describe each segment of the program, pointedly mentioning the commercial breaks after each. After Art's solo, he noted, "Commercial break and end of reunion for the time being. Watch the record charts for possible future developments."

The "Saturday Night Live" reunion raised a storm of expectation about the duo's future. Paul adamantly denied the reunion would be permanent. He told *Newsweek*, "I can't go back and do anything with Artie. That's a prison. I'm not meant to be a partner. Besides, I don't know if Simon and Garfunkel would be that popular if they did come back."

But Paul did, as always, leave the door open a tantalizing crack by remarking: "But I wouldn't mind being in the position of doing something like the single again. That's something I'd like."

Art, too, was reluctant to commit to a permanent reunion. He told *Rolling Stone*, "Paul and I are very aware of the commercial potency of Simon and Garfunkel. And this potency could be unwieldy and unwantedly weighty.... So we do think that some of the things we might do together have long shadows or larger ramifications. And because of that there's a reserve caution—a sense of 'Let's make sure we know what we're doing.'"

After the broadcast, Garfunkel also seemed to have second thoughts about the tone of the "Saturday Night Live" reunion. The show's playful chiding exposed raw nerve endings which hadn't yet healed completely. Art said, "The subject of the vibes between us is such an issue. It's all embarrassing. It caters to the immature. I grant there's a curiosity. But to make it the source of entertainment? It would drag the whole thing down."

Both knew they could extinguish the flames of public interest in their relationship with a simple declaration that their lifelong friendship was whole again, but they also knew the public would soon lose interest if the tension was gone between Simon and Garfunkel.

The possibility of rejoining for another single depended on the public's current appetite for Simon and Garfunkel. Radio programmers, the bellwether of record sales, gave "My Little Town" the immediate airplay expected. Within a few weeks of its "Saturday Night Live" debut, the song rose to number nine on the charts. It was a solid hit, but never reached the coveted number-one spot as other Simon and Garfunkel tunes had done. Some speculated that it was because Simon and Garfunkel fans were album buyers who didn't ordinarily buy singles, and the song was already on both albums.

That same month, Paul's gospel duet with Phoebe Snow, "Gone at Last," rose to number twenty-three. The single's popularity created a lot of interest in Paul's *Still Crazy After All These Years,* and by December the album was an unqualified success, selling more than a million copies.

Columbia released Art's album, *Breakaway,* shortly before *Still Crazy After All These Years.* The practically simultaneous release gave critics the chance to compare the two albums. Paul's work was almost universally praised while Art's took a thorough beating.

Critics called *Still Crazy* "food for somber thought" and hailed it as a complex, "extraordinarily moving" album. They took note of Paul's ability to weld disparate moods—amusement, depression, skepticism, and belief—into an intriguing emotional whole. Simon sang songs rooted in experience, while Art was satisfied to croon about sophomoric innocence. Paul wrote and sang about mature male/female relationships. Art sang about the girl—not the woman—who got away.

One observer traced the divergent musical paths Art and Paul had taken to earlier Simon and Garfunkel songs. Even though Paul wrote all of the songs, in retrospect Art's preference for sweet, lush arrangements stood in stark contrast to Paul's innate skepticism, even pessimism, about romantic love. Unfettered by Paul's gritty sensibility, Art's penchant for "sweetness" was now labeled "saccharine" and "treacle." One critic called *Breakaway* "a luscious ten-course meal—all desserts."

Another said, "Both records draw upon elements of the music they once made together, but the results are so dramatically different that it seems inconceivable that Simon and Garfunkel could ever rejoin forces on a permanent basis."

Paul commented: "Poor Artie. He's really depressed now. If only Artie could sing as intelligent as he is...Artie's not all romance. He's got brains, bitterness, pain, and scars. He just happens to have a voice like an angel and curly hair like a halo. But he's a grown-up." Ironically, Paul's defense of Art employed the same litany of physical characteristics that used to drive Paul wild with envy.

Paul put together a sold-out concert tour though December 1975 to back up the *Still Crazy* album. On three occasions, he responded to the inevitable calls of "Where's Artie?" by bringing Garfunkel onstage to do a few numbers as he had on "Saturday Night Live." Paul said, "The reaction was intense and astounding," but he still vehemently denied they had any plans to reunite on another album.

In fact, Paul had turned his attention away from writing a new album altogether. He was exhausted by the demands of the promotional treadmill and a round of difficult contract renegotiations with Columbia.

Paul's career was now in the hands of his lawyer and business manager, Michael Tannen, a veteran of the music business. His father, Nat Tannen, a music publisher specializing in country-and-western material, had died when Mike was five years old. Harold Orenstein, a top music-business attorney and one of Nat's friends, had helped Mike through law school. After graduation, Tannen joined Orenstein's law firm, whose client list then included Simon and Garfunkel. Mike has been described as ruthless and shrewd. According to Orenstein, Tannen "stole Paul Simon away" from the firm when he formed his own company. Throughout the 1970s, Tannen compiled an impressive list of clients, including the Rolling Stones, Billy Joel, Bruce Springsteen, and John Lennon. In 1975, Tannen was handling the contract renewal negotiations between Paul and Columbia.

Clive Davis had left Columbia in 1973, leaving Paul to deal with abrasive Walter Yetnikoff, who favored heavy-handed negotiating techniques. Yetnikoff had heard that Simon was personally involved in his contract dealings with Columbia and that he was a troublemaker, even sitting in on negotiation sessions. A source close to Yetnikoff said, "Walter hated Paul Simon's guts."

In one bargaining session, Yetnikoff grew so enraged he called Arthur Taylor, another CBS executive, and ordered him to refuse Simon future entry to the CBS building. Yetnikoff screamed at Simon, "You're out of this building until eternity—until you're dead!" After all he had done for Columbia, Paul was outraged by Yetnikoff's bullying attitude. The situation was eventually resolved, but Paul would neither forget nor forgive.

Mo Ostin, an executive at Warner Bros., heard about the nasty scenes in Yetnikoff's office and told Mike Tannen his company would be happy to sign Paul if he ever wanted to make a switch.

Paul, drained by the aftermath of his divorce and the acrimonious Columbia contract negotiations, was emotionally spent.

Art's divorce had also become final, and a settlement had been worked out. It was agreed that Linda would receive a lump sum of $150,000 plus $35,000 a year for the next six years. Some thought it was a comparatively small sum from a multimillionaire husband. Linda would later regret the settlement and contest the terms in a court battle that would ensnare Art for years in a legal morass.

Paul and Art were officially bachelors again. At thirty-four, they were famous and wealthy, and on the surface they appeared to have it all. But as a person close to both of them said, "The reality was more like one of Paul's then-recent lyrics: 'My life's a mess / But I'm having a good time.'"

11

Paul Simon, who for years had eschewed celebrity friends, now, with his pal Lorne Michaels, traveled with an elite pack of show-business personalities, and their dramatic entrances at chic restaurants and clubs turned heads. The group included Mike Nichols, Buck Henry, Candice Bergen, Steve Martin, *Rolling Stone*'s Jann Wenner, and "Saturday Night Live" stars Chevy Chase and Dan Aykroyd.

Michaels had become Paul's principal male confidant, to whom, he said, "I could talk...about anything, without any competitiveness." Michaels felt the same way. He trusted Paul because he wasn't involved in television and had no turf to protect. Michaels even moved into an eight-room apartment with a panoramic view of Central Park, in Paul's building. His kitchen door opened onto Paul's laundry room.

In the winter of 1976, Lorne Michaels was on a roll. The "Saturday Night Live" experiment had worked brilliantly; people stayed home on Saturday nights to see how close to the edge television could be pushed by a group of guerrilla comedians who could do the outrageous things viewers themselves used to do before things got more complicated—and safe. NBC renewed Michaels's contract for a second season.

Paul enjoyed the high-energy glow of the "Saturday Night Live" crowd, most of whom were young, single, and passionately committed to their mission to revolutionize television and enjoy some laughs along the way. They spent most of their time together in a kind of comedy commune, a twenty-four-hours-a-day walk on the wild side of television production.

The commitment to create the show was all-consuming and quickly took a heavy toll on the young staff. No matter how brilliantly funny the troupe might be on a particular Saturday night, success demanded they start all over again and appear even funnier just six short days later. Many on the creative staff found they needed more and more drugs to keep them up and running with the demands of the show. The cocaine habit grew more pervasive.

Paul has asserted that he maintained his sobriety through this period, but it must have been odd to be the only drug-free person in a group of cronies who saw the world through a chemical haze.

Perhaps Paul's natural distrust of easy fixes for life's problems and his old habit of introspection insulated him from the temptation to use cocaine to escape again. He had already tried drugs of all kinds and had given them up to begin his seven-year odyssey on the analyst's couch. Drugs had never solved his problems; they had only made them worse. He had come to recognize in himself a deep need for control in both his professional and personal life, and drugs meant loss of control.

Paul also feared the power of drugs, particularly cocaine, to isolate him from other people. But even more terrifying was the insidious effect drugs had on his music. And it was music that defined his personality. Now more than ever, since his splits with Peggy and Art, making music was the most important thing in his life, and he knew just how fragile and ephemeral his gift was. He has called music his real "drug," and if he had to buy it, he would probably spend his fortune on it in an instant.

Paul's musical talent was all the more precious because he had no control over it. He lived in constant fear that one day he would wake up to find the words and music that normally floated in his head missing. On his last two albums, he wrote about this deep fear in two completely different moods. On the buoyantly optimistic "Kodachrome" he sang about "sweet imagination" that gives "those nice bright colors," and he begged, "So mama, don't take my Kodachrome away." The loss of imagination means "Everything looks worse / In black and white."* On the somber "My Little Town" he sang of an ominous black rainbow drained of its color: "It's not that the colors aren't there / It's just imagination they lack."

Paul's fear wasn't new. He had wrestled with it throughout his career. He once told Robert Hilburn, "I'm neurotically driven. It has always been that way. What happens is I finish one thing and start to take a vacation. I lay off for awhile, and then I get panicky....I say to myself: 'Oh, my God, I'm not doing anything. I can't write anymore. It's over.' All that kind of thing....Then I laugh and tell myself: 'Don't be silly. This is exactly what happens every time you finish an album. So, of course, you write again.' And so I continue to take it easy for awhile. I don't write for awhile longer and then I say: 'Hey, this is no kidding. You're really not writing now.' And somewhere along the line I really believe I'm not going to write again and I get panicky and start to write. I don't want to think that I peaked in my twenties. There is so much more time ahead."

With his marriage gone, the fear he would also lose his imaginative spark became more insistent. He had finished the *Still Crazy* tour in January, and as usual it had taken him months to gear down from the high emotional intensity of concert perfor- mance. The tour was crucial to the success of the album, but Simon regretted that its hectic pace had made it impossible for him to concentrate on writing. He said, "I felt I had to spend a lot of time on tour, gaining acceptance, selling my records."

All the effort paid off, though. In February 1976, Paul had his first and, to date, only number-one hit as a solo artist with "50 Ways to Leave Your Lover."

In March, Andy Williams hosted the Grammy Awards in Hollywood. The Simon and Garfunkel duet, "My Little Town," had been nominated as Best Pop Vocal by a Group but lost out to the Eagles' "Lying Eyes." Paul Simon won two of the most prestigious awards for *Still Crazy After All These Years*, Best Male Vocal of the Year and Best Album of the Year. He had once again risen to the pinnacle of American popular music, and this time he shared the spotlight with no one. He made one of the more mem-

*"Kodachrome" © 1973 by Paul Simon

orable acceptance speeches in Grammy history, saying simply, "I'd like to thank Stevie Wonder for not recording an album this year."

The enormous success of *Still Crazy*, which had gone gold, made Paul feel good about himself and hopeful about the future. Free of the pressure of having to prove himself as a solo performer, he could now take some time to search his imagination for new ideas. The Grammy and the gold were great, but he had his own standards of excellence. In his words: "It's nice to be praised, but my eye is on a place farther down the line. It will require more work, and either I'll get there or I won't—check back in ten years and see if I've done anything."

In May, the TV Emmys were announced, and Paul was pleased when Dave Wilson won the Best Director category for the "Saturday Night Live" Simon and Garfunkel reunion show that Paul had hosted.

Art was on the charts at number seven with his *Breakaway* album. It had sold well and would eventually go gold, as had *Angel Clare*. That winter, Columbia had released the album's title cut as a third single, but it barely made the top fifty. Art was already preparing his next album. As summer approached, Paul, too, was thinking about what might come next. With his Grammys and number-one hit, he felt better about his career than he had at any time since the breakup with Art. He had gained the acceptance he had sought, and he was living the cosseted, comfortable life of a millionaire star.

He could pad around his Central Park West duplex, gazing out at the green expanse of park below, and when he grew bored, he could escape to his elegant summer home on Long Island. His every whim was fulfilled by a phalanx of deferential servants and advisors. A Czech housekeeper shopped for him, took his clothes to the cleaner, and babysat for Harper, who often spent several nights a week with him. Peggy and Harper lived just a few blocks away, so Paul could still play the doting father. He and Peggy had finally reached an amicable relationship now that the divorce was final, and he respected her talent for mothering. He also considered himself to be a good parent and still mourned the fact that the two of them couldn't have gotten along for Harper's sake. He said, "It's just too bad we weren't compatible enough to present a united nuclear family."

The housekeeper occasionally cooked food far too rich but far too delicious to refuse. Paul burned off the extra calories by running a few miles every day in the park. Although limousine service now whisked him around town in plush comfort, he couldn't quite suppress his middle-class roots. He said, "You pull up in front of a place, just like in the movies. When you get out, the driver is there waiting for you. It's the New York dream come true." Also part of the New York dream was a circle of witty, rich, and famous friends.

One of Paul's good friends at this time was comedian and filmmaker Woody Allen, who was developing a highly auto-biographical script dealing with his (Woody's) relationship with actress Diane Keaton. The film would eventually be named *Annie Hall* (Hall is Keaton's real last name). Allen asked Paul if he might be interested in playing a small, not-too-demanding part. The character, Tony Lacey, is a rock star/recording artist and denizen of the Los Angeles music scene who meets Annie and tells her she has a great voice, a come-on line he has used with great success for years. Lacey invites her to his posh Hollywood home, in a scene designed to drive the Woody Allen character, who is in love with Annie, crazy with jealousy.

Lacey supposedly lives in Charlie Chaplin's old mansion and attends only A-list parties. He disdains New York and thrives on the superficial trendiness of Los Angeles. It would be an acting stretch for inveterate New Yorker Simon. Allen assured Paul it wouldn't be a big deal, and there was no music involved. Eventually Paul agreed. He admired Allen's work and felt a kinship with his middle-class, New York, angst-ridden Jewish sensibility. Simon's scenes would be shot in both New York and Los Angeles.

Allen, as was his custom, salted the script with cameo appearances by his friends. Carol Kane portrayed Allen's neurotic ex-wife, and Shelley Duvall played a small but juicy role as an esoteric rock-music critic.

Shelley, not a typical film-star beauty, is a talented actress whose work in the early seventies attracted the attention of some of America's finest film directors. She went to New York in 1976 to do *Annie Hall* with her pal Woody Allen. Duvall and Paul had no scenes together, but Allen's small, intimate casts spend a lot of time together throughout filming. The *Annie Hall* group hung out at Elaine's, New York City's celebrity-restaurant haven.

Shelley remembered their meeting this way: "I wasn't feeling well, so I ordered an Alka Seltzer for dinner. Paul was sitting across the table, and I liked his smile. I couldn't look at him without getting embarrassed." Shelley found Paul "charming, brilliant, funny, and kind." She had been invited to spend the weekend at a friend's house on Long Island very near Paul's, so she asked him for a ride. He happily obliged.

Shelley recalled, "We talked all the way out there; we had a million things to say. Then it turned out that my friend Susan's sister had arrived and taken up the extra bed, and since it was all sort of like one big camp, we ended up at Paul's house. He has several extra bedrooms. Anyhow, we were all talking and eventually, one by one, everybody else went home. And there were Paul and I, sitting at opposite ends of the couch. We talked all night, until 10:30 the next morning. At one point, I got hungry and went out to the kitchen and took an apple out of the icebox. Paul came out and said, 'Can I have a kiss?' I said, 'I can't now...' I had a mouthful of apple. But I spit it out...and the rest is history."

About their relationship, Shelley said little to friends and less to the public. She said, "There's not much you can say about being in love that doesn't sound dumb. It's nice to be in love." And that's as much as she would reveal. But she wasn't shy about her physical attraction to Simon. She said, "The first thing I look at is a guy's face. Then his ass. I like Paul's ass...He's got a nice ass. He runs."

Shelley moved from Hollywood into Paul's Central Park West apartment. Now that Simon was on the celebrity circuit, the love affair caught the gossip columnists off guard. One skeptically proclaimed, "They're friends only. Nothing very serious."

It was Paul's first serious relationship since his divorce from Peggy, and he found it both satisfying and frustrating. He admired Shelley's innovative acting style and her ambition to produce as well as direct both film and television. Paul later said, "I really liked the way she looked. We just weren't a match in terms of personality. So I think despite my habitual looking at the negative as a form of protection, I began to get happy."

Happiness and complacency had always been twin enemies of Paul's creative process. His reputation for melancholy far outweighed the lighter side of his public image, although some of his biggest hits, like "Feelin' Groovy" and "Me and Julio," were full of joy. Even at his happiest times, themes of loss and sorrow remained principal preoccupations. Paul himself acknowledged that his reputation for melancholy was entirely justified. Writing about life's pain and sorrow was an act of exorcism that gave him relief: "If you're jubilant, there's no need to do anything."

During the autumn of 1976, Paul spent his days studying musical theory and taking voice lessons. Singing since he was a boy had taken a toll on his voice. He thought that learning proper singing techniques might extend his years as a performer. He was also concerned about how long he would be able to play the guitar. He'd been taking cortisone for swelling and pain caused by calcium deposits in his left hand, but now was forced to switch to another drug which affected his digestion. Doctors told him there was a chance he wouldn't be able to play the guitar in another five or six years. To prepare for that possibility, he was learning to compose on the piano.

These physical limitations added to his depression and growing pessimism about his ability to create anything new. As he recalled, the nagging voice inside his head was growing more insistent: "Maybe you can't write anymore; maybe what I did wasn't very good anyway." In addition, he still worried about how audiences might receive him if and when he did manage to write new material.

The music business was undergoing tremendous changes that threatened to overwhelm Paul's intimate, personal brand of music. Punk rock was on the rise: The Sex Pistols and B-52s screamed from boom boxes. Rock concerts had become heavily produced spectacles that attracted thousands of fans unfazed by decibel levels higher than jet engines. The concert stage became home to more theater than music. Jimi Hendrix's pyrotechnics at the Monterey Pop Festival a decade earlier seemed tame compared to the violent excesses of some of the newer groups.

At first Paul reacted to the new emphasis on showmanship with frustration and alarm. His beloved rock 'n' roll had taken a nasty turn, and it took a while for him to acknowledge that rock was only on a short detour back to its roots. Rock was born out of a need to shock, but Paul had grown accustomed to using it to convey a thoughtful vision of the world as well. This new music seemed to leave little room for any ideas.

Ultimately, he came to view popular music's obsession with spectacle as little more than a rite of passage for a new generation.

In an odd way, the new music validated his own distinctive style and reaffirmed the importance of his continuing presence on the scene. He lamented "So much of what I hear on the radio is so boring." He believed that since "nobody was singing for them," his generation of scarred, disillusioned, but still hopeful young adults was out there waiting to hear his more mature artistic vision.

On the "Saturday Night Live" Thanksgiving program, Paul continued his crusade to prove he had a sense of humor by appearing feathered from head to toe in a turkey costume. The program was particularly memorable because Paul's musical guest was ex-Beatle George Harrison. Paul felt a special affinity for Harrison because he was one of his few musician-friends who had expressed an interest in Paul's solo career at the time of the Simon and Garfunkel split.

To the great delight of the audience, Paul and George harmonized on "Homeward Bound" and "Here Comes the Sun." Paul sang "50 Ways to Leave Your Lover," his biggest hit since the split. "50 Ways" had gone gold and remained number one on the charts for three weeks—the first and last time to date that Paul Simon has had a single on the yearly top-ten list.

A few months later, in January 1977, the country saw the return of a Democratic administration to the White House. The Democrats had finally managed to recapture the imagination of the country with an upstart candidate who promised a return to basic American values. Paul was asked to perform at Jimmy Carter's inaugural ball in Washington. He sang "An American Tune," setting a tone of renewed optimism for the political process.

The inaugural gala was a celebratory gathering of many of Hollywood's political activists—Warren Beatty, Jack Nicholson, Mike Nichols, and Elaine May—who had organized the 1972 McGovern reunion concert. The guest list included Paul's new "Saturday Night Live" buddies Chevy Chase and Dan Aykroyd, and in the spirit of reconciliation, John Wayne also made an appearance. The entertainment featured performances by Linda Ronstadt, Aretha Franklin, and Paul Simon. Art Garfunkel, busy recording a new album, was not in attendance.

Art was also deeply in love. He had moved to the West Coast, where he shared a beach house in Malibu with the new woman in his life, Laurie Bird. She was an actress who had recently appeared with James Taylor in his movie debut, *Two-Lane Blacktop,* but was still looking for her big screen break. While Laurie searched for acting jobs in Hollywood, Art worked sporadically on a new album. They both spent a lot of time traveling, one of Art's favorite pastimes.

Garfunkel inherited his wanderlust from his traveling-salesman father. As a young boy, Art often accompanied his father on sales trips, and now, with his success, Art could indulge his every whim to see new places. He especially loved walking the towns and countryside of Europe, often strolling alone for hours, singing aloud.

Art was taking time to savor the process of recording this album. He thought he had finally discovered the songwriter to match his taste and talent. Jimmy Webb's warm, romantic lyrics and intricate, lush melodies seemed to be exactly what Art had been searching for. All but two of the songs on his new album would be by Webb. He also took back the production reins. He would produce the album himself, with Barry Beckett as associate producer.

At Paul's suggestion, some of the major recording and engineering was done at the Muscle Shoals sound studios that had made such an important contribution to Paul's successful *There Goes Rhymin' Simon* album. Both Art and Paul hoped that some of the magic might rub off on Art's endeavor.

Art liked the idea of recording in various locations and laid down tracks in New York, Los Angeles, San Francisco, and Ireland. Intrigued by the sound of an Irish folk group called the Chieftains, he asked them to do a traditional ballad, "She Moved Through the Fair," which Jimmy Webb arranged.

Within the comfortable framework of Webb's lyrical love ballads, Art felt more confident than ever about his taste and judgment. This time he made no excuses about his music: "When I got on my own, I became more selfish. I've been criticized for being too lush...but I happen to like smooth, concentrated notes more than choppy, staccato ones. I found some songs too gritty, too sophisticated."

Comfortable at last with a sympathetic songwriter, Art experimented more with his voice, lowering it from the high tenor range he employed on his first two solo albums to his more natural baritone tenor. At ease with the vocal range and at one with the music, he asserted that he was no longer as sensitive about the fact that he didn't write songs. Instead, he reveled in his role as a vocalist: "I just wanted to stand there at the mike and sing the song."

Back in New York, Paul continued to dabble in new interests which he hoped might trigger an end to his creative drought. In May, he performed two concerts with innovative American choreographer Twyla Tharp at the Brooklyn Academy of Music. Tharp was premiering her modern-dance version of Paul's "50 Ways to Leave Your Lover," and Paul agreed to accompany her onstage with his guitar for two performances. He was also planning his own TV special.

Paul's relationship with Shelley Duvall seemed truly happy. Friends who knew them were amazed at how well the moody, depression-wracked Paul got along with Shelley's cheerful, light-hearted personality.

One morning, the couple was awakened by the phone. Shelley remembered, "I was still asleep because we'd had a big night the night before. Paul answered the phone, leaned over, and gave me a hug and a great big kiss on the cheek. I'd been dreaming, and it was so strange to be wakened by a kiss and a hug, all to the words, 'You won!'" Duvall had been named Best Actress at the 1977 Cannes Film Festival for her role as Millie Lammoreaux in Robert Altman's film *Three Women*.

Paul and Shelley went to Europe to pick up her award, and there the actress got another call. This time, Stanley Kubrick wanted her to star opposite Jack Nicholson in his modern horror tale, *The Shining*.

The film Shelley and Paul both appeared in, *Annie Hall*, was ready for its New York release, and the advance reviews were excellent. *Variety* took special note of Paul's performance: "Paul Simon is a sharp caricature of a Hollywood swinger." Many observers thought Paul had been accurately typecast. In the period before Shelley, Paul's style of meeting women seemed strikingly similar to that of his character, the shallow Tony Lacey, who uses his celebrity status to meet as many women as he wants. *Annie Hall* was a great success, becoming one of the top-grossing films of the year and proving at last that Woody Allen could be funny and serious at the same time.

Although the reviews were gratifying, Paul said he was never seriously interested in an acting career. He only wanted the experience of working with Woody Allen because he thought it would be good preparation for a film of his own, which was beginning to take shape in his mind. He had kept in touch with Mike Nichols, and he and Shelley discussed the idea of Paul writing a film script which would be directed by Nichols and star him and Duvall.

But, for the moment, television offered the most immediate opportunities for testing Paul's acting talent. He had already signed with NBC to do his own hour-long special, drawing on his coterie of "Saturday Night Live" friends to help: Lorne Michaels would produce, Dave Wilson would direct, and his and Art's old buddy Charles Grodin, along with Chevy Chase and Lily Tomlin, would provide the laughs and the television-star appeal.

Paul and Lorne worked hard to put the script together. As had been his habit on "Saturday Night Live," Paul used his years on the analyst's couch as source material. Like his friend Woody Allen, Paul liked to poke fun at his own neuroses to reveal his feelings, a style that was more in keeping with his intellectual nature than was the full-blown, searing emotionalism of singers like Janis Joplin and Judy Garland.

Meanwhile Art, his acting career stalled, had taken a full year to lay down tracks for his new album, and in the fall Columbia released a teaser selection from it, "Crying in My Sleep," hoping to build audience interest. But the single failed to place in the top one hundred. Art tried to ignore the ominous sign and concentrated on finishing the album.

Columbia was looking for something to make the album more attractive and was considering another Simon and Garfunkel duet. Eventually, the duet became a trio. Columbia had recently lured James Taylor away from Warner Brothers, and he joined Paul to sing backup for Art's version of the Sam Cooke classic, "What a Wonderful World." Unlike the distinctive Simon and Garfunkel sound of Paul's "My Little Town," the song emphasizes Art's vocalizing and Taylor's harmonies.

While Columbia exulted about stealing Taylor away, Warner Brothers was wooing Paul Simon through his lawyer, Michael Tannen. Unhappy about Paul's possible defection, Columbia dragged its feet while trying to find a way to keep him in the fold. Even though Paul as a solo act hadn't earned a fraction of the Simon and Garfunkel profit, he remained a reliable, bankable name in the industry. Columbia pointed out that Paul owed them one more album before his current contract expired and that they were determined to hold him to his obligation.

Meanwhile, they released *Paul Simon—Greatest Hits, Etc.* a compilation album designed to keep the audience interested while waiting for new material. The album contains Simon's best solo work as well as two original songs. On "Slip Sidin' Away," a tart observation about the danger of investing too much hope in false illusions, Paul sings we "Believe we're gliding down the highway / When in fact we're slip slidin' away."* Those close to Paul say the lyrics of one verse, referring to a divorced father trying to form a relationship with his son, mirror that of his own with Harper. The song has a rich, country/western arrangement with backup vocals by the Oak Ridge Boys.

The other new song, "Stranded in a Limousine," is a third variant on Simon's borderline psychotic figure from "Still Crazy" and "My Little Town." This time he rides, like Simon, in a limousine: "He was a naturally crazy man / And better off left alone."† Columbia promoted the album with the phrase, "Twelve you know by heart, plus two." Even by Paul's slow standards, two new songs in eighteen months was poor progress. Simon regarded the album as a kind of summing-up of his five years as a solo artist: "I feel as if a certain part of my life and career is over. I feel like I'm about to do a whole other thing." Meanwhile, negotiations with Columbia, never easy, seemed even more difficult this time, and Paul spent a great deal of energy worrying about the outcome.

But there was also time for partying. Paul had now fallen completely under the spell of celebrity. He, like Art, had discovered the glamour of hobnobbing with stars and reveled in the trappings of wealth and fame. In the summer of 1977, prior to the start of the third season of "Saturday Night Live," Paul and Lorne Michaels decided to stage an elegant theme party similar to those instituted by the Beatles a few years earlier. The engraved invitations stipulated that everyone wear white to the all-day lawn gathering, creating a scene redolent of British aristocracy. Over a

*"Slip Slidin' Away" © 1977 by Paul Simon
†"Stranded in a Limousine" © 1977 by Paul Simon

hundred would-be sophisticates eagerly accepted the invitation to come to Long Island and wander on the grass, nibbling exotic canapés, and drinking punch, some of which was reportedly laced with drugs. For a few years the White Party became an annual affair.

Paul juggled his social calendar to make an appearance with Art. Both flew to London to appear at the prestigious Britannia Music Awards program. They felt almost required to attend since "Bridge Over Troubled Water" had been voted the best international single and LP released in the years between 1952 and 1977. They performed "Bookends/Old Friends," and because of TV technical difficulties, their patience was strained by having to do six takes before the crew got it right. The performance in Britain was a warm-up for other reunions on American television.

Paul continued to make appearances on "Saturday Night Live." In one skit, Charles Grodin appeared bedecked with a huge blond fuzzy wig to sing "Bridge Over Troubled Water" with Paul. After a few awful bars, the real Art Garfunkel emerged from the audience, yanked the wig off Grodin's head, and said, "Hand it over, Chuck!"

Art had agreed to do a cameo on Paul's upcoming television special as well. His appearance was almost mandatory since the script was built around Paul's struggle to deal with the aftermath of the Simon and Garfunkel split. "The Paul Simon Special," broadcast on December 7, 1977, centered on a novel concept: the audience was made to feel it was watching behind the scenes at the dress rehearsal for the special. In the first scene, Paul emerges from a cab to enter the NBC studio. At the reception desk, uniformed guards fail to recognize him and turn him away. The gag—which sets up the program's premise—was drawn from Simon's own experience the first time he hosted "Saturday Night Live."

On the special, Charles Grodin plays an overzealous television producer eager to add some pizzazz to the small, unassuming singer who looks so pitiful without Art Garfunkel by his side. Producer Grodin is determined to present Paul Simon as glitzy megastar.

Paul and Michaels had incorporated Simon's nightmares about performing, as well as his sensitivity about being short, into the comedy skits. In one, Paul walks to center stage and must reach high above his head to bring the microphone down to his level. He registers discomfort but proceeds with the rest of the show. His patience begins to wear thin when Grodin suggests a new title for the program, one guaranteed to capture a wide audience. Grodin wants to call the show "The Paul 'Bridge Over Troubled Water' Simon Special"—"for the recognition factor." "You don't call it 'The Barry "I Write the Songs" Manilow Special,'" counters Paul. Grodin argues, "Yes, but there's only one Barry Manilow," to which Paul answers, "There's only one Paul Simon." Grodin comes back with, "Well, there's Paul Simon the politician, Paul Simon the educator..."

Paul sings several songs backed by some of his favorite musicians. The Jesse Dixon Singers join him on "Loves Me Like a Rock," drummer Steve Gadd on "I Do It for Your Love," and saxophonist David Sanborn on "Still Crazy After All These Years."

Lily Tomlin appears in a comedy segment with Paul, and Chevy Chase does an eighteenth-century version of Johnny Carson's "Tonight Show," in which Shelley Duvall has a silent, uncredited role.

But all of the comedy and even Paul's solo singing were secondary to Art's appearance. In keeping with the low-key comic approach, Art was worked into a skit. The reunion is held in a dressing room as if the two are being observed in rehearsal. Paul enters the room to greet Art, who reads a book while waiting. The simple hellos are meant to suggest the easy familiarity customary between old and close friends. Paul suggests they rehearse in the dressing room, and Art agrees.

Grodin then appears and persuades the duo to practice a script he has written for the moment they meet on the show. Grodin is still desperately trying to dramatize the reunion with some elaborate but tiresome show-biz patter. Art and Paul roll their eyes and struggle to deliver a decent reading of "And now, my very, very, very dear friend, Art Garfunkel." Art reads his line: "Thanks for having me on your special, Paul." And Paul says: "My special wouldn't be special without you."

"Producer" Grodin isn't pleased. The two old friends are relating too simply and too naturally. Grodin wants them to pull out all the stops. He pleads and cajoles for more intensity. Finally Grodin is satisfied, and the two resume rehearsing. They then sing a letter-perfect and extremely touching "Old Friends" from the

Bookends album. With only Paul's acoustic guitar as accompaniment, they produce a rich, full sound that evokes memories of a bygone time.

At the end of the program, Grodin, frustrated in his effort to add show-biz glamour to Simon's personality, takes Paul aside for a heart-to-heart talk. In his insensitive but sympathetic way, he advises Paul that "the sound of you and Artie singing together is so much better than the sound of either one of you singing alone and that whatever petty differences you might have had in the past, I strongly urge that you take a long, hard look at them."

Paul doesn't answer but simply stares into space. Grodin's line echoes Clive Davis's painful words of warning about the consequences of the split seven years earlier. Paul had carried that hurt inside until he found a way to express it.

At the screening for family and friends, everybody said they liked the program's self-deprecating humor except Paul's mother. Belle Simon thought it was dangerous to plant the idea that either Paul or Art was anything short of terrific on his own. Paul knew his mother had a point, but he argued that the thought already existed in everyone's mind. As he reasoned, "Things like that are just below the surface anyway, and saying them is a way of dissipating them."

People close to Paul had told him he was making a big mistake in using the show to dispel the ghost of Art Garfunkel. "But he wouldn't listen," said one insider. "It was so neurotic of him to think that people really cared that much about his feelings about the split. People wanted entertainment, not analysis."

12

Television critics rejected Paul Simon's special, calling him "the victim of a miscalculated concept." John J. O'Connor of the *New York Times* sniped, "The already low-keyed Paul Simon almost disappears from his own show," and concluded: "The diminutive singer and composer, whose easy-going personality suggests the contemporary pop equivalent of Perry Como, is supposed to be worried about appearing on his first television special. That's the running gag, and is about as funny as a case of fallen arches."

Even worse, audiences weren't amused by the self-deprecating humor regarding the viability of Simon's solo career without Garfunkel. To put the final nail in the coffin, ratings were dismal, and NBC didn't ask Simon back for more.

His single of "Slip Slidin' Away" was number five on the charts, and his trio with Art and James Taylor, "What a Wonderful World," was also climbing fast, but, uncharacteristically, Paul took little comfort in the success of his music. As 1978 began, he plunged deep into depression. Winter dragged wearily on, and so did Paul's contract negotiations with Columbia Records. No progress had been made for weeks and the two sides appeared stalemated. In Michael Tannen's words, "Walter [Yetnikoff] thought we reneged on basic terms, and Paul and I believed he had reneged on basic terms.... In any case, the deal fell apart. Walter called me at one point in the middle of all this and said, 'There's no deal for Paul Simon.' I remember that very well. He said, 'Paul does not have a deal.'"

By February, Paul Simon was certain he would part company with Columbia and even more sure the leave-taking would not be friendly. Because so much money was at stake, both sides unleashed a barrage of legal briefs, suits, and countersuits.

Simon signed a new recording contract, reportedly worth thirteen million dollars, with Warner Brothers, a company which also produced movies. Paul's advisors suggested he concentrate on finishing the film script he had been working on. When the legal dust settled, there could likely be a film/album tie-in.

The film script had evolved from Paul's vague notion of doing a project with Shelley Duvall and Mike Nichols, but all that remained was the concept. Shelley had gone to London to film Stanley Kubrick's *The Shining*, and over several months of separation, the love affair died of natural causes. At the time, Shelley explained that there was "no special reason. It's just like in one of his songs. You like the window open—I like it closed. Your basic incompatibility. I still love his music. I did before I met him, but I don't feel sad when I hear a Paul song. Why should I? I'm not in love with him anymore."

Alone once again, Paul devoted himself to planning his movie. Before he'd decided on a film, he had toyed with the idea of writing a Broadway musical. Paul had often talked of his admiration for America's great popular songwriters, many of whom did their best work for the Broadway stage. He even asked Stephen Sondheim to teach him something about musicals, perhaps as a prelude to a working relationship, but nothing came of it. Paul later asserted, "I actually wanted to write a musical after the *Still Crazy* album, and I looked around for a collaborator, but I never found one, so I started jotting down ideas."

The idea of making his mark alongside composers like Cole Porter and Oscar Hammerstein appealed to his vanity, but he soon formed a more realistic assessment of his talents. Simon loved control too much to write songs for other people to sing. Besides, he couldn't be at the theater every night to make certain every detail was just as he wanted it. He chose movies over the theater because he was, at heart, a studio man, and he knew films happened in the same meticulous way as records. He could imagine himself doing take after take, until everything was perfect, and then editing the pieces to match the vision in his head.

The big screen also held the largest audience and profit potential. MTV was still three years away from creating a revolutionary blending of rock music and image, and besides, what Paul had in mind couldn't be crammed into a flashy three- or four-minute clip.

He wanted to tell the more complex tale of an aging rock 'n' roll musician whose career falls short of stardom. He tentatively titled the script *One-Trick Pony*.

Paul's new record label, Warner Brothers, was interested in the double-barreled sales potential of movie and soundtrack. Sales of Paul's soundtrack for *The Graduate* were legendary, and more recently the Bee Gees' music track for *Saturday Night Fever* had been a runaway success, eclipsing the worldwide sales of *Bridge Over Troubled Water*.

As always with Paul, the music came first. He began to develop songs and to record the tracks, but he again found it difficult to adjust to the demands of writing within the limits of a movie story line. Unlike Mike Nichols in *The Graduate*, Paul wasn't using individual songs like "Mrs. Robinson" or "The Sounds of Silence" to merely underline a character's point of view. This time his ambitions were higher. In *One-Trick Pony*, all of the songs would be used as in a Broadway show—to replace dialogue and advance the story. Paul explained, "I used the lyrics in songs to express the emotions, thoughts, and opinions of the character."

While Paul pursued a career in the movies, Art seemed to be moving in the opposite direction—from films back to the familiar world of music. He appeared happy and confident. The cover photo on his latest album, *Watermark*, released in February of 1978, showed a broadly smiling Art Garfunkel reclining in a deck chair a few yards from a vast expanse of blue ocean. The photo was taken by Art's lover, Laurie Bird, who was also partly responsible for Art's sunny frame of mind.

Art felt he was on the threshold of a new phase of his life. He was deeply in love, and his ambivalence about the direction of his career had vanished. He was certain now he wanted to be a singer. He also wanted to banish the somber, serious image of his Simon and Garfunkel days. About the album cover he said, "I was after a photograph with no mystique. I wanted to come out from the masks, to get away from the shadows, including my own."

Like Paul, Art was eager to emerge from the long shadow of Simon and Garfunkel and to find his own place in the spotlight. Art's enthusiastic embrace of Jimmy Webb's music signaled a firm rejection of Paul's theory about the need for an occasional dose of "nasty" songs like "My Little Town" to offset the monotony of sweet ballads.

Reversing the negative reviews for *Breakaway*, critics now confirmed Art's choice of Webb by praising *Watermark* as a perfect marriage of singer and songwriter. One commented, "Garfunkel has exactly the right spare, intelligent vocal style for Webb's intense, deeply felt lyrics." Hailed as a brilliant interpreter of Webb's music, Art was especially pleased with the attention critics gave his unique vocal talent. At last, it seemed he could be judged on his own merits—and the verdict was very good.

Art felt so secure in the linkage of his talents with Webb's that he reversed an earlier declaration of his independence from Paul Simon, admitting, "The loss of Paul Simon is a loss of great talent. Naturally it's something I can't enjoy dwelling on. Give me a break, and I'll take it from there."

Art was happy with the initial response and eager to do a concert tour to stimulate album sales. Up to this point, he had resisted touring because he feared he lacked enough material to present a full program. Armed with the Webb songs, he knew for the first time since the split he could give the fans the full value of their ticket.

After seven years, the return to the concert stage would be frightening, Art admitted. "For me it was a long slow process to overcome the fear to the point that I was willing to try performing again." He said that he rarely gave a thought to performing during the first four or five years of the layoff because he was busy with other interests, but that lately he had missed the pleasure of singing for a concert audience.

Art said that he especially liked to walk out onto a stage when he knew the crowd was high: "I love those shows when you come out and smell dope. It's so rare in my shows." Unlike Paul, Art had never disavowed the drugs of his youth.

In the euphoria over praise for *Watermark,* Art couldn't resist comparing his new work to that of other contemporary popular artists. True to his serious, self-critical nature, he gave both himself and the rest less than perfect marks. Unlike Paul, Art was not afraid to admit, "Frankly, my records are less than Simon and Garfunkel's. There's a certain combustible energy in partnerships, I think."

To promote *Watermark*, Art began a forty-city tour—his first since 1970—of smaller, more intimate concert halls throughout the United States. His confidence grew at every stop; the smaller concert venues meant mostly sold-out houses jammed with fans eager to hear him. Just as in the old days, he basked in the warm welcome he received each night. Occasionally, if Paul was in the vicinity, he might delight the audience by joining Art on stage to sing a few numbers. On one such evening, after receiving accolades from well-wishers, Art mused, "I'm beginning to think the duo shouldn't have split up after all. It sure is nice being stroked."

For both Art and Paul, 1978 turned out to be a creative and satisfying year. More secure in their independent endeavors, they continued to find more time for each other in their busy schedules. As Art remembered, "I started hanging out with Paul, and it seemed the most natural thing in the world. We reminded ourselves of the humor we shared, the jokes, the similar concerns, the similarity of our lives."

While on tour that spring, Art hosted a segment of "Saturday Night Live." Paul was still very close to the program's creative team, and he, too, showed up on it several times during the next few years. These occasional television appearances gave Paul a way to stay firmly fixed in the public's mind. He also appeared on other television programs. On "The Rutles," a parody of the Beatles written by Monty Python's Eric Idle, Paul spoofed himself. But "Saturday Night Live" gave Paul the best opportunity to express his funny side, something his songs just couldn't do.

The jokes about his fears and insecurities continued. In one sketch he was denied entrance to a restaurant because he was too short, and the sarcastic remarks about Simon and Garfunkel never stopped. "Saturday Night Live" also brought Carrie Fisher into Paul's life.

Carrie came from a world far different from Paul's. She had been born into show-business royalty and was used to the glare of publicity. The daughter of Debbie Reynolds and Eddie Fisher, she

had been photographed and written about from the time she was a
toddler.

Her parents' courtship and marriage was the stuff of Hollywood legend. In the mid-fifties, the adorable, innocent Debbie had
fallen in love with and married her Prince Charming, Eddie, the
boyishly handsome young singing star. For a while, they were
"America's Sweethearts," and their Protestant-Jewish union,
blessed and hyped by the movie studios, was celebrated all over the
country.

Carrie Frances was born on October 21, 1956, a little more than
a year after the marriage. All America rejoiced in the parenthood
of its pet superstars. A year and a half later, Carrie's brother Todd
joined her in the spotlight. But then the nation saw the fairy tale
come to an abrupt end when family friend Elizabeth Taylor was
seen as having lured Eddie away from domestic bliss. The divorce
made even bigger headlines all over the world than the marriage
had. Although it happened when she was only three, the Reynolds/
Fisher/Taylor affair was something Carrie couldn't escape. It had
taken on mythical proportions.

Debbie Reynolds remarried when Carrie was four, and the little
girl continued to lead the life of a pampered Hollywood princess.
At sixteen, she dropped out of high school to follow in her parents'
show-business footsteps, joining the chorus of her mother's Broadway hit, *Irene*. She left the show to return to the West Coast to
have her tonsils removed and there landed a small but memorable
role in Warren Beatty's *Shampoo*. She played a nymphet and had
only one line (of which her parents mightily disapproved):
"Wanna fuck?"

She then went to London to attend the Central School of Speech
and Drama. She remembered, "For the first time, I was with
people my own age. Twelve hours a day of acting, fencing, voice,
movement—everybody with one common interest. I was blessed.
If it hadn't been for Central, I might have stayed a Hollywood kid,
dressed in sequins and flinging mike cords for the rest of my life. I
could have ended up in the Tropicana Lounge."

While in London, she auditioned for a major role in a science-
fiction adventure film by George Lucas and won the part of the
feisty, doughnut-coiffed Princess Leia.

After *Star Wars* she returned to New York to share what had originally been maid's quarters at the Hotel des Artistes in Manhattan with her old friend Griffin Dunne. Dunne was then a struggling film director working as a waiter to support himself. He watched in amazement as Carrie became the darling of the New York in-crowd when *Star Wars* became a national phenomenon. Dunne introduced Carrie to John Belushi, whom she started to date.

Fisher and Belushi shared a fondness for drugs. As she explained, "I wanted to be accepted by people who did drugs. Drugs put me where I perceived everyone else to be. They made me relax." Through Belushi she met Lorne Michaels and, inevitably, Paul Simon. She later remembered, "I was the new girl in town....I came out into this high social intelligentsia—such as it is when it's show business."

Carrie, like Paul, fell easily into the "Saturday Night Live" orbit. She enjoyed the witty banter; she liked her men brainy but sensitive. She attributed her preference for people like Paul Simon to her parents: "I think I have a Jewish demeanor and a Protestant ethic. I think my extroversion is the Protestant manifestation, but emotionally I am Jewish, and I was always drawn to people who looked like I felt, a little upset, a little like an outcast, uncomfortable, ready to leave." It was clear she was drawn as much to Paul's melancholy as to his intelligence. Fisher recalled, "I got involved with Paul fast. I met him in April, and by the summer I was in Greece with him."

That same summer Paul was ready to offer his finished film script to the highest Hollywood bidder. He and Tannen met with executives from both Twentieth Century-Fox and Warner Brothers, then left the script, and demanded a response in twenty-four hours. The next day, both studios made offers for the project.

Simon recalled, "When both studios said they liked the script, it was a wonderful moment for me. I was happier than if someone had told me this was the best album I'd ever done. I know if my music is good or not, but this was something new for me." Paul explained that he chose Warner Brothers because he had recently signed a recording contract with them, and it seemed like a good idea to keep all of his projects under one corporate roof.

Industry insiders regarded the bidding war over Paul's film more skeptically. Everyone knew Paul signed a recording deal with Warner Bros. because of its corporate film interests, but the company had been somewhat ambivalent about Simon's movie. The offer from Twentieth Century-Fox spurred Warner Brothers to up the ante.

At first Warner Brothers felt relatively secure in backing the film. With Paul's solid-gold track record, the *One-Trick Pony* album sales could act as a catalyst at the boxoffice. Even if Paul's film experiment failed, his soundtrack could recoup the film's losses.

That September, Lorne Michaels, whose first marriage to Rosie Schuster, a producer/writer on "Saturday Night Live," ended in divorce, was marrying Susan Forristal, a model from Texas. Susan had been living with Lorne in the apartment next to Paul's and the three had become good friends. Paul described the couple as his own personal Fred and Ethel Mertz.

The wedding was held at Lorne's fashionable Long Island summer home. Lorne had asked Paul to be best man and Art to be cantor at the ceremony. Also in attendance at the star-studded affair were Jack Nicholson, Buck Henry, Lauren Hutton, Cheryl Tiegs, Jann Wenner, Bill Murray, and Gilda Radner.

John Belushi, whose cocaine habit had grown to dangerous levels, made a late and noisy arrival. Paul, upset to see Belushi in such bad shape, was determined to avoid a disruption that could ruin Lorne and Susan's big day. He hustled Belushi into a bathroom, splashed some water on him to calm him down, and shaved him. Belushi quieted somewhat, and the ceremony went on. During the reception, he finally passed out, and his friends discreetly deposited the comatose comedian behind a hedge to sleep it off.

Carrie fit right in with the "Saturday Night Live" drug scene. A self-described addictive personality, Carrie was using every available drug—legal and illegal—she could lay her hands on. Percodan was her drug of choice, although she was fond of the psychedelic colors acid could deliver as well. In her own words: "I've taken everything but Drano."

Despite her heavy drug use, her relationship with Paul deepened. According to Fisher, "High verbal skills are highest on my list of necessary qualifications for a man, for anyone, actually. I like to talk, and I don't necessarily move far, but I move fast."

Paul was equally enthralled by Carrie's wit and intelligence, even though their discussions often turned into passionate arguments. Both knew it would be a stormy, but always interesting, relationship.

Meanwhile, Paul was still fighting with Columbia; the company claimed he owed them another album under the terms of his last contract. There were reports he delivered some tracks for an album, but they were not original Paul Simon songs, so Paul's nemesis, Walter Yetnikoff, rejected them.

Relations between Paul and Yetnikoff worsened. Paul claimed Yetnikoff was out to destroy his career. He charged the company withheld his royalties, sabotaged the release of his single, "Stranded in a Limousine," by poor distribution and promotion, and pressured its other contract artists to avoid working with him. He and Tannen filed another suit to stop what Paul saw as his persecution by Columbia. To Paul the bitter struggle had become a personal vendetta against him, and his mood darkened.

Even news that he and Michaels had won an Emmy for Best Writing in a Television Special didn't lessen his misery. He still brooded over "The Paul Simon Special"'s failure to attract a big audience. He should have been thrilled with the award since the nominees included several of the industry's top writers, but nothing—not even a prestigious award—could assuage his disappointment in the program's ratings disaster. He bitterly regretted pouring so much effort into a project that the audience ignored.

He cheered himself up by plunging more deeply into work on *One-Trick Pony*. Everyone understood that as soon as the lawsuits with Columbia were settled, the project would go forward. Simon's friend and lawyer, Michael Tannen, who also handled Art Garfunkel's business affairs, would produce the film.

But the script's somber theme didn't thrill Warner Brothers. Paul named his movie's hero Jonah Levin, and like his biblical namesake, Jonah's life is being swallowed up by circumstances beyond his control. In spite of an unquenchable passion for the music, Jonah fails to grow and change with the times and winds up as a journeyman musician on the road to nowhere. It could have been Paul's own life story minus the lucky break on "The Sounds of Silence."

Like Paul, Jonah gets a mild taste of success with a hit record early in his career, but in the story ten years elapse with no sign of the dream materializing again. In the meantime, a new generation of fans and performers arrive on the scene, rudely elbowing the Jonah Levin Band into the wings.

Paul continued to refine the script. He interviewed several of his talented friends; most were fine musicians who had never quite made it to the first rank of popular music. He imagined the characters' days and nights on the road without the amenities of the first-class hotels and limousines Simon and Garfunkel enjoyed.

Although the story line isn't strictly autobiographical, Paul could imagine the emotional geography: interminable bus rides in the middle of the night, one-night stands to fill the emptiness of dingy motel rooms, the nagging feeling that somewhere along the way rock 'n' roll had become work.

Paul was most keenly interested in the toll the life-style took on marriage and family. Jonah's marriage is dissolving, and his young son, a boy of Harper's age at the time, is growing up without him.

No wonder Paul's ex-wife Peggy became anxious about the project—she knew the subject hit close to home. Paul had to constantly reassure her that he had no intention of exposing the intimate details of their relationship. He promised, "The only autobiographical elements are in the relationship between me and my son."

Paul also discussed the film's theme at length with Art Garfunkel, who found the act of probing the past very disturbing. Art said, "There was something desperate, something strung out about the time we were spending together as peers." The two saw each other often since Art and Laurie had moved back to New York. Simon was involved in his on-again, off-again affair with Carrie Fisher, but frequently the two men spent their evenings as they had in their youth, visiting mutual friends together or going to parties. These evenings sometimes stretched well into the afternoon of the following day. Art remembered, "What were we doing? Just hanging out, sharing memories, talking about rock 'n' roll...but for so many hours, as if reaching for some justification."

Paul's penetrating inquiry into the life-style of a rocker caught in mid-life crisis led Art to examine his own life: "I began to ask, 'What's going on here?' Have we been picked up and swirled into this pop world, only to be left in our mid-thirties wondering what the whole thing's about? When we had tired of the star trip, when the thrill of signing autographs wore off, and even someone as insecure as me had been praised enough, then what? Could we start traditional lives with traditional values?" In spite of his quest for a normal life-style, Art was ambivalent about marriage. He had been burned once, and his doubts about a new commitment had already become a point of contention between him and Laurie. Art was resisting Laurie's pleas to marry.

Art was also becoming convinced that, for him, rock 'n' roll was an essentially adolescent experience. He was beginning to think it absurd for people his and Paul's age to continue to make "teenage music." He agreed with Mick Jagger, who once said Elvis Presley's death—in 1977 of a drug overdose—had come at the right time, before the king grew too old to sing rock 'n' roll.

Paul held an entirely different perspective on maturing rock 'n' rollers. He thought the only thing unseemly about middle-aged rockers lay in their inability to change and grow. Paul found rock music as suitable a medium as any to communicate the emotions and ideas of mature listeners. Paul was determined to continue to make music for his generation, believing that if he continued to grow, he would never end up a has-been like Jonah.

While Paul explored Jonah's life, Art wound down his successful *Watermark* tour with a final performance at New York's Carnegie Hall, during which he quipped, "I have to stay on my toes. There's a very severe critic in the house." He then invited Paul to join him onstage to sing a duet. Initially, Paul was pleased. However, this time the evening turned out to be a reprise of the old jealous rivalry. Art brought Paul out to sing before the final encore, and after Paul left the stage, Art sang "Bridge Over Troubled Water" alone. Once again, Paul watched from the wings as Art captivated the audience with *his* magical song.

Feeling he had been used, Paul was livid. Art later acknowledged his solo of "Bridge" was a deliberate move to reassert his dominance with the audience after he and Paul had summoned up the spirit of "Simon and Garfunkel." Ironically, a song about the generosity of love and reconciliation had become the object of a continuing public tug-of-war between the two. Although they were ready to share more time together as old friends, neither was willing to share the audience.

A critic at Art's concert, however, ignored the implications and saw nothing but Art's talent. He noted, "Mr. Garfunkel has become a compelling song stylist and an understated but remarkably musical vocal technician. He has the rare ability to put a song over with a maximum of feeling, a minimum of fuss, and an admirable control of pitch, timbre, and phrasing." In spite of the sell-out tour and critical praise, the *Watermark* album sold only moderately well.

Paul carefully observed Art's progress as a singer of songs other than his own and made no secret of his disappointment with *Watermark*. Art's new vocal style didn't interest Paul. He preferred the more natural conversational style Art used on their records. Paul's public comments did little to free Art of the long shadow of Simon and Garfunkel.

Paul did give Art credit for sticking to his convictions and making the kind of music he wanted to make in spite of the inevitable comparisons. He saw it as a genuine achievement, but noted that, unfortunately, good intentions don't really count in the aggressively competitive music business.

Paul was by now secure in the knowledge he had proved his commercial viability and outgrown Simon and Garfunkel. People in small but faithful numbers seemed to be more interested in Paul's words than in Art's angelic voice. It was beginning to look as though, at long last, Paul's talent had finally eclipsed Art's.

Garfunkel decided to revive his acting career. Although he had never been totally devoted to films—he didn't have an agent actively seeking roles—he continued to read scripts that occasionally came his way. One submission, *Bad Timing: A Sensual Obsession,* to be directed by Nicolas Roeg, piqued his curiosity. Roeg had an impressive list of credits, including *Walkabout, Don't Look Now, Performance,* with Mick Jagger, and *The Man Who Fell to Earth,* with David Bowie. Roeg was fond of casting rock stars in his films because he preferred the "nonactor quality" musician/performers could give him. Roeg saw a similar quality in Garfunkel. Art agreed with Roeg's assessment: "I'd say I'm from the nonactor school of acting. The other school includes people like Dustin Hoffman and Olivier, actors who radically change by putting on a hunchback or special makeup." Roeg wanted Art to explore the depths of his own personality in order to create his character.

Art eagerly accepted the role's cerebral challenge, but he had been away from acting for eight years and knew the role would demand his full attention, leaving little time for a personal life. He was also finishing songs for a new album to follow *Watermark*. Roeg was shooting *Bad Timing* on location in London and Vienna, and Laurie reluctantly stayed behind at the New York apartment. Their relationship was becoming strained, and the separations made things worse.

Meanwhile, early in 1979, Paul and Columbia Records agreed to settle their differences out of court. Paul agreed to pay Columbia $1.5 million to essentially buy out his contract, and the company rescinded its demand for a new album. In his film script, Paul would extract a measure of revenge for the pain he suffered at the hands of Walter Yetnikoff and Columbia. With the legal battles finally over, Paul was free to move ahead with his plans for *One-Trick Pony* with Warner Brothers.

In addition to writing the script and the score, Paul had also officially taken on the lead acting role. Publicly, Paul was ambivalent about the starring role, but there was little doubt that only he could play Jonah. Because he had so little acting experience and, not incidentally, to keep the publicity flowing, he made half-hearted attempts to find another actor for the role. His options were severely limited because Jonah was not a stage singer whose songs could be lip-synched to Paul's voice, but a rock-band singer, requiring an actor who could really belt rock 'n' roll.

Later, he said he had considered Gary Busey, who had infused *The Buddy Holly Story* with such taut energy. He reportedly talked to Richard Dreyfuss but rejected that idea, saying "There was no way Dreyfuss could be in the movie and open his mouth and have my voice come out. It would be funny." For Warner Brothers, which had put up nearly seven million dollars for the picture, and for Paul, who had written a part no one else could play, there was little question about who would play Jonah.

Warner Brothers was already taking a sizable but calculated risk by bankrolling a rock 'n' roll film. Other rock stars had tried to duplicate their recording success on the screen and had failed miserably. Bob Dylan had just made the four-hour epic *Renaldo and Clara*, which promptly sank under the weight of its murky concept. Concert films and documentaries like *Don't Look Back* and *Gimme Shelter* had more, but still limited, success at the box office. A big-budget, full-scale production about the life of a musician who failed to reach superstardom sounded like risky business.

The company wanted Paul's name on, as well as his total involvement in, as many aspects of the picture as possible. Paul took the lead but refused to call himself a movie star, preferring instead to be called a "featured player."

As shooting neared, Paul was nervous but not frightened. He had added the acting challenge to his other responsibilities on the film because it was exactly the opportunity for creative growth he had been searching for. The burden of carrying the film forced him to stretch as an artist, allaying one of his worst fears. He explained, "I'm afraid to stop growing, afraid that someday I'll say, 'That's it. I've run out of ideas.' Probably all artists fear that their lives will outrun their gift. And that's a moment you don't want to face."

Too busy to face that possibility now, he plunged into high-pressure on-the-job training with some of the film industry's top professionals. He frequently discussed scriptwriting technique with screenwriter Robert Towne, a friend from the days of working on Warren Beatty's *Shampoo*. On the recommendation of Charles Grodin, he took acting lessons from Montgomery Clift's old coach, Mira Rostova. He discussed acting technique with Carrie Fisher and the "Saturday Night Live" crowd. He miraculously managed to add volume to his thinning, hair and he learned to cry menthol-induced tears on cue. He lifted weights and stepped up his running schedule, slimming down to a muscular 117 pounds so that his Jonah would have a lean and hungry look. Like Art, Paul was on his way to becoming a movie star.

Art was preparing to star in Roeg's film and was also keeping his music career alive. While rehearsing in Europe, his new album, *Fate for Breakfast/Doubt for Dessert*, was released. The music tracks had been recorded in California, but he did most of the vocals and harmonies while on location in London. The album's producer, Louie Shelton, also played guitar and added several background vocals. *Fate for Breakfast* included songs by Jimmy Webb and several other writers and featured the classic ballad, "Since I Don't Have You." True to form, all of the songs were ballads, but several had a stronger rock beat than Art's previous albums. The album got good reviews but didn't click with the public like Paul's solo efforts had.

Peter Reilly of *Stereo Review* said, "*Fate for Breakfast* is entertaining, enjoyable fun on several levels. Garfunkel doesn't patronize his material; he merely pokes some gentle, affectionate fun at our sentimental weaknesses, at the same time paying superprofessional homage to the pop-music genre itself." On a more personal note, the critic added, "There are some few performers whose work one almost automatically likes and respects. For instance, I've always liked Art Garfunkel's direct, unpretentious performing manner, and the sly wit I find mixed with a resolute integrity in his recordings inspires respect. I've found him from the first to be much more believable, somehow, both as a person and as a performer, than his one-time partner Paul Simon, and his solo career since the two split up has only reaffirmed that impression."

Although *Fate for Breakfast* became a major hit in England, it failed to stir the attention of American music fans. Earlier in the year, Art had recorded "Bright Eyes," the theme song for *Watership Down,* an animated, feature-length film adaptation of Richard Adams's novel. Although popular in England, "Bright Eyes" failed to chart in the U.S.

Paul and Carrie were also in London that spring. He was visiting her while she was filming the *Star Wars* sequel, *The Empire Strikes Back,* during which time they celebrated their first anniversary together. Paul and Carrie often jetted across the Atlantic to visit each other, as did Art and Laurie, but by now Art was consumed with the psychic pressure building on the Roeg film set. Shortly after he reported to the set, Art knew he had embarked on an exhilarating but hazardous psychological journey.

Art plays Dr. Alex Linden, a repressed professor of psychology who meets and is sexually attracted to Milena Flaherty, played by Roeg's wife, Theresa Russell. They begin a passionate and chaotic love affair which pits the doctor's possessive personality against Milena's wantonness. The film opens in an emergency room where Milena is near death in a drug-induced coma. The police are called to investigate the suicide attempt and begin to suspect they may have a murder on their hands, with Dr. Linden the prime suspect. The film consists of a series of flashbacks which delineate the oppressive relationship and build toward Milena's desperate act. The psychological detective story unfolds in Roeg's characteristic style, full of subtle inference, oblique allusions, and jumbled time sequences.

Art was excited by working with Roeg. His experience with directors had been limited to Mike Nichols, and acting for Roeg promised to be an entirely different, far more challenging, experience, because so much of the characterization depended on the actor's interpretation of the role. Art felt he was collaborating with Roeg in much the same way he had done with Paul.

The director immediately set about trying to extract the character from within Art's own personality. The two talked for hours, discussing every nuance of the role. Art described the working relationship: "From the first week, Nick began to get interested in how my character moves, speaks, ponders, asks, and the faces he makes. And I began to stretch out with this lovely feeling that he was really giving me an open shot." He added, it was "a wonderful, heightened, almost mystical experience...even more than making the *Bridge Over Troubled Water* album, this was a thrill."

Art totally immersed himself in the role and later interpreted the film this way: "Nick is saying to everybody, 'Look, haven't you ever been in a situation where you were asked to put something into words in a rational way?' Imagine you had a fight with your girlfriend, and it got really insane. The police came by and picked you up because you were disturbing the peace. You'd want to say to them, 'Haven't you ever had this yourself? C'mon, you know what it's like.' You know, touches of insanity settle in."

As Art lost himself in the role, Laurie grew more and more depressed about their long separation. The subject of marriage was a continuing source of tension between them. Art refused to make a commitment, and she brooded about their future together.

As the months wore on in London, Garfunkel narrowed the gap between his own personality and that of the character he was playing, becoming acutely aware of how close to the surface his emotions were. As he described the intense experience, "Gut-level reactions to things were like lava, and I could feel them bubbling away. My feelings were razor-sharp, and I was overly tight. I thought, 'If I come home to my woman in this shape, I'm going to be dangerous.' I had a picture of myself as if I were a blade, or as if there were a knife in my hand and the arm controlling it was randomly, loosely swinging. And I said to myself, 'I'd better take a few steps toward getting out of this whole characterization. I may look normal, but I'm anything but a normal guy now.'"

Art wouldn't have to cope with the problem of facing his lover. He never saw her alive again.

13

On June 16, 1979, while Garfunkel was in Europe, Laurie Bird died of a drug overdose in the East Side penthouse she and Art had shared. Laurie's father told reporters his daughter may have committed suicide because Garfunkel had repeatedly refused to marry her. Donald Bird had seen his daughter a week before her death, and they had talked about her depression over Art's reluctance to wed. Bird said he urged Laurie to leave Art, but she refused. Bird also said that he had tried to talk to Garfunkel, but that Art had evaded the issue.

Garfunkel later said that although he was an ocean away, he sensed the exact moment Laurie died. On the day she took the overdose, the Twenty-third Psalm popped into his head, which struck him as strange because "religion has never come to me before." He took comfort in the ancient words: "There I was, saying, 'The Lord is my shepherd, he restores me when I'm in trouble, he takes me into the valley of the shadow of death...' And I was appreciating the way it was said and the whole idea of 'We're not alone, one has a partner in life.'" Art was devastated by Laurie's death. Shortly afterward, he said, "Laurie was the greatest thing I ever knew in my life. Now I've lost it, so I've done something...rank and stupid. My priorities or something. Or I evidently have not spoken for the things I value most. There are many yearnings we have as human souls, but to me the paramount yearning is intimacy with one person."

At first, Art was too emotionally detached to absorb the enormity of his loss. It would take six months before he felt the full impact and years before he fully recovered. His single of "Since I Don't Have You" from the *Fate for Breakfast* album was released shortly after Laurie's death and getting heavy airplay in England. Sales rose sharply when news of Art's real-life tragedy spread, giving the lament for lost love poignant new meaning.

Meanwhile, Paul had finished the songs for *One-Trick Pony,* which would begin shooting that fall. Paul worried obsessively over every production detail. He wanted a gritty, realistic tone and roamed the Midwest looking for potential shooting sites in Cleveland and Chicago. He spent weeks absorbing the small-time rock-club scene, talking to the owners, waitresses, and road-weary band members, tuning his ear to their accents and attitudes. He even talked his way into a jail cell in Chicago, where he experienced the desolate feel of a lock-up for a few hours.

Filming started in November 1979 in Cleveland. Robert M. Young had been signed to direct. Years later, he described his feelings about the project: "I liked the script and the subject matter. I was intrigued by the possibility of working with Simon and his music, but I was nervous. In some ways, the situation is an advantage, but it's also a disadvantage. The advantage is that Paul, as the writer, really knows his character well. But that can make you, as the director, ask yourself, 'What am I needed for?' There was some frustration at the beginning, until I got to know Paul and found out how open he is." The cast included Blair Brown as Jonah's wife, Rip Torn as record company executive Walter Fox, and Carrie Fisher's friend, Joan Hackett, as Fox's sexy, sophisticated wife.

One-Trick Pony opens with a montage of rock life-style images propelled by the crisp, percussive sound of "Late in the Evening." The song's lyrics recall Paul's own early infatuation with music as "the first thing I can remember.../ No more than one or two.../I remember there's a radio next door / And the music's seepin' through."* He also pays homage to the street-corner a cappella groups he and Art listened to as boys.

The line between Jonah and Paul blurs when the song recounts the magic moment when, in a funky bar—underage and under the influence of a "J" (marijuana)—he picks up his guitar, turns up his amp, and in one glorious moment, "I blew that room away." It describes a moment Jonah has been trying to recapture ever since. In the last verse, Paul completes his outline of the best moments of Jonah's life when he describes his love for his wife and the pure conviction with which he pursued and won her: "When you came into my life / I said I'm gonna get that girl / No matter what I do."*

The movie's remaining songs measure the widening gap between Jonah and the realization of his elusive dream. In both "Jonah" and "God Bless the Absentee," Paul touchingly describes life on the road in a few precise images: Jonah, mindlessly replacing broken guitar strings, sizes up a dingy room before a performance, studies the blank stares of local girls, and wonders where the road leads. Weary and full of doubts, Jonah's not so sure anymore that "One more year on this circuit / Then you can work it into gold" holds any truth. The song pays tribute to the vast majority of people in Paul's profession—"Boys who came along / Carrying soft guitars in cardboard cases."† On the soundtrack album's back cover is a grainy dark photograph of Paul with one of those same guitar cases clutched in his hand.

Jonah's personal life is as unstable as his professional life. He longs for comfort from his wife, but their meetings usually end in confrontations. The ghost of Elvis divides and then reunites the couple. In one scene, she pleads with Jonah to grow up: "You have wanted to be Elvis Presley since you were thirteen years old. Well, it's not a goal you're likely to achieve. He didn't do too well with it himself." Later, Jonah reconciles with his wife by reciting Elvis's monologue from "Are You Lonesome Tonight."

Jonah realizes the loss of his family is a high price to pay for his dream. He suppresses his guilt by thinking he may still have some time before his life-style steals his boy's childhood from him. Jonah sings, "My son don't need me yet / His bones are soft."

---

* "Late in the Evening" © 1978 by Paul Simon
† "Jonah" © 1978 by Paul Simon

The preoccupation with his son echoes Paul's own. He had recently seen Harper's dental X rays and was moved by the sight. He said, "I had his whole life right there in front of me. This is my little boy, my boy, a whole life in those X rays. Yeah, it's flyin'. Time's flyin'." Normally very protective of Harper, Paul eventually allowed his son to be filmed playing Paul's character as a boy, under the movie's opening credits.

With so much narrative tied up in the music, Paul and Warner Brothers wanted to release the soundtrack album long before the movie opened to give audiences a preview of the story line. Strong advance album sales would also cross-promote the film. Phil Ramone produced the album, and Paul's recent globe-trotting recording habits weren't needed for this brand of basic American rock 'n' roll, so he mastered all but two songs in New York. The title song, "One-Trick Pony," and "Ace in the Hole" were recorded live at The Agora, one of Cleveland's small, local rock clubs Paul had visited earlier.

A scene shot at the club encapsulates the film's theme, a variant on Paul's life-long theme of alienation. Jonah's band finishes a set, and they surrender the stage to the latest popular rock-'n'-roll mutation, the B-52s (a group which also recorded for Warner Brothers). Jonah and his band, sadly bewildered, watch from the wings as the new generation of rock passes them by.

Simon took advantage of this opportunity to vent his pent-up anger about the seamy side of the music business. He had created the character of Walter Fox, an unctuous record-company president, who has been none-too-gently pressuring Jonah for new material. Played by Rip Torn, Fox holds Jonah's future in his hands.

Jonah's career seems stalled, and he needs money. His agent convinces him to appear without his band in a "Salute to the Sixties," a sad nostalgia trip for musical has-beens. There he sings his one, stale hit, an antiwar ballad, "Soft Parachutes." Jonah and the others on the bill, including the Lovin' Spoonful, Sam and Dave, and Tiny Tim, personify the movie's title: "one-trick pony" is an act that has only one number, but can coax an entire career from it.

After the show, Fox's wife seduces Jonah. The liaison gives Jonah another chance to break into the big time when Fox inexplicably renews his recording contract. Fox assigns a hot new

producer, played by rock 'n' roll star Lou Reed, to oversee the new
album, but Jonah and the band detest the lush string section and
backup singers Reed grafts onto their old sound.

But *One-Trick Pony's* ending leaves Jonah with at least a shred
of dignity. Enraged at himself for coming so close to selling out to
the record executives, Jonah sneaks into the recording studio and
destroys the tracks. He reclaims his musical integrity.

One-Trick Pony was finished on schedule and the album
readied for release. Everyone agreed that "Late in the Evening"
should be the first single cut.

While Paul completed the final scenes of his movie, Art's *Bad
Timing* opened in London to good reviews and a moderately
successful run. *Variety,* the entertainment industry trade publication whose reviews influence bookings in America, summed up its
mixed review with: "Looks nice but ultimately a downer" and said
"with only Art Garfunkel's low-key performance to go on,
alienation sets in early." It offered little hope that young audiences
would identify with these "overprivileged overdosed characters."
Variety conceded that *Bad Timing* would "doubtless be cherished
as an art film by some older buffs," but suggested the likeliest
commercial strategy for its producers would be a "hefty promotion of the star names and sex angle."

Art returned to New York in a deep depression. In addition to
Laurie's death, he was being sued by his ex-wife Linda Grossman,
now dissatisfied with the original terms of their divorce. In place
of the $150,000 lump sum and $2,917 per month for six years,
Linda now requested $5,000 per week. Linda claimed that Art had
conspired with her lawyers to "gull" her into accepting the
settlement, steering lucrative business their way as a reward for
taking his side. The acrimonious lawsuit would drag on for nearly
a decade.

But Art's far more important cause of grief was the loss of
Laurie. He examined every detail of their life together. He worked
through her death using her journals, photographs, and his own
memories, trying to come to terms with the psychic pain that had
driven Laurie to take her own life. At the time, he said, "I've been
sympathetically feeling the depth of the pain that must have led
her to take her life. I can't let it go, because I haven't cried over it
yet." With time, he could say, "I feel I've learned a lot about the

way living works on this planet. If there is an architect, I've got some clues on his moves now."

Not surprisingly, Art turned to Paul, his oldest friend, for sympathy and companionship: "I lost the center of my life when I lost Laurie. After that, I was a bachelor again and that made me more predisposed toward old friends, and one in particular." As time went on, Art began to think about the possibility of recording another album, and even became more aggressive about his acting career: "I came home after making the picture and for the first time got an agent and actively went looking for parts. But nothing came of it."

Art was still battling Linda in court, and it appeared as if he might lose. They had gotten a Haitian divorce in 1975, but a New York judge had declared it invalid. The case again went to appeal. Meanwhile, Art walked the streets to relieve his tension. In New York, he would often pick a neighborhood "where I'm not popular," put on a hat, and "go out for a sing."

Busy finishing the editing for *One-Trick Pony* and planning a concert tour for summer and fall to promote the album and film, Paul continued off and on to see Carrie. She had broken off their relationship while she made the film *The Blues Brothers* with her old buddies John Belushi and Dan Aykroyd. During the filming, she had a hot affair with Aykroyd, but broke with him too. In June 1980, Paul, Carrie, her best friend Penny Marshall, and Art went to London for the British premiere of Carrie's *The Empire Strikes Back*.

When Paul returned to New York, he began organizing the *One-Trick Pony* tour. He asked members of the band who appeared in the film—Richard Tee on piano, Eric Gale on guitar, Steve Gadd on drums, and Tony Levin (whose last name he borrowed for Jonah) on drums—to make up the nucleus of his tour band. Paul was especially excited about the tour because he would be playing as a member of a band, a role he had coveted since he was a teenager. As he explained: "It's odd to have been in rock 'n' roll all this time and never really been part of a band. I was part of a duo—a vocal duo—and I played with studio musicians."

In September, the single, "Late in the Evening," rose to number six and the *Pony* soundtrack, which fans interpreted as just another Simon LP, reached number twelve on the album charts. That was a good beginning, but the reviews for the film were yet to come. Paul and Warner Brothers waited anxiously for the movie release.

One-Trick Pony was set to premiere in New York in October 1980. Paul and Art were relaxing at Simon's summer home in the Hamptons when a call came with news that the theater next door to *One-Trick Pony* would hold the American premiere of Art's *Bad Timing*. The publicity machine couldn't resist the temptation to pair Simon and Garfunkel once again—if only on a marquee.

Bad Timing won an award in Canada but received generally tepid reviews there and in Britain. The New York reception was no warmer. Reviewers seemed generally unimpressed with Roeg's psychological study. *Newsweek* said, "Top-heavy with technique, overstuffed with tony cultural allusions, desperate to impress the audience with its multilayered significance, *Bad Timing* is an oppressively bad movie—although it is clearly the folly of a talented man." Another reviewer wrote, "Nicolas Roeg's *Bad Timing: A Sensual Obsession* could easily give you a headache. It is feverish, airless, unhealthy."

Nor was anyone impressed with Garfunkel's acting. The *New York Times* said, "Mr. Garfunkel does a very creditable job of conveying Alex's reserve, but there is little in his performance to suggest a man in the grip of an obsession."

Critics were much harsher about Paul's film and performance. *One-Trick Pony* was labeled "a vanity production" and "one of those movies which plays better as an album than it does on the screen." Another reviewer was even more blunt, calling it "a long commercial for the soundtrack."

Even worse were the reactions to Paul's acting. *Newsweek* noted, "Simon has a clenched, wary face with three expressions: poutiness, archness, and arrogance. This is a distinct drawback for a leading man."

There were a few favorable reviews. Roger Ebert, of the *Chicago Sun-Times*, and *Playboy*'s critic were enthusiastic. The *Los Angeles Times* called it "an exceptionally handsome movie…an intimate film of much wit, style, and impact. It ranks as one of the year's best." The film didn't attract particularly savage reviews. It didn't attract much of anything at all—especially an audience.

People ignored it. Along with Art's film, it sank quickly from sight.

Before the film's release, Paul had been cavalier: "If you don't risk a couple of really good audacious flops, you get fat and lazy. I'm proud that I made up a movie, that I wrote it and actually starred in it, and that's hard enough without being...good. It's actually hard to be mediocre. I have much more sympathy for mediocre movies now."

After the film's failure, however, Paul was inconsolable. He had never experienced rejection of this magnitude before. He admitted, "It was a very hard thing for me to accept. My feeling at the time was, well, I've made a failure. And here was a project that I'd put more effort into than any other project I'd ever done. I had a lot of years tied up in it, and it came and went just like that." He took some comfort in knowing the film would have a long afterlife, if only on cable television. He was most disappointed with the critics who attacked him because his central character was a failure. They misunderstood his message: "I wasn't trying to draw a portrait of a guy who didn't have any talent. He just wasn't succeeding anymore. The major difference between Jonah and Paul Simon is that I'm just lucky because people like what I do."

But this time, people didn't seem to like what he did, at least on the screen. Since the album sold moderately well, and the title song, "One-Trick Pony," rose to number forty, he decided to salvage what he could of the film's music. He was still selling out concert halls, but the costs of touring with his large entourage were becoming prohibitive, especially since he still insisted on smaller halls. Although he was destined to lose almost three hundred thousand dollars on the One-Trick Pony tour, he never considered canceling it. He said he hadn't made a profit on a concert tour since the Simon and Garfunkel years, but "I'd like to go out there. I'd like to take this band and have a record of it—you know, these guys, at this particular moment, 'cause I don't know if we'll all be together again."

Carrie celebrated Paul's birthday by flying to Fort Worth and joining him onstage to sing harmony on "Bye Bye Love." The tour, at least, seemed to be a success. But then, just before he left for the European leg, low ticket sales forced Paul to cancel a concert in the eighteen-thousand-seat Nassau Coliseum on Long Island. It was a disturbing sign that his audience was losing interest.

In Europe, Paul played a triumphant concert in Paris, where Art joined him on stage for several numbers. After the battering both had taken in their personal lives and with their films, the audience's outpouring of affection and approval had a healing effect. The spotlight seemed suddenly big enough for two once more.

Paul concluded the *One-Trick Pony* tour with a November date in London's Hammersmith Odeon theater. It was his first concert date in England in five years and he glowed in the warm homecoming the audience gave him. At the end of the evening, he was moved to make a speech of thanks to the audience, saying he wished he could do more for them than simply sing his songs. Someone yelled out that he could buy them all a drink—which he promptly did. That night, three thousand people toasted the artistry and generosity of Paul Simon.

The European tour had been successful, but when Paul and Art both returned home from Europe, they faced uncertain futures for the first time in decades.

Art was still not over the tragedy of Laurie's suicide, but he had resumed a social life. Carrie Fisher had introduced him to actress/director Penny Marshall, and the foursome began seeing a lot of each other. Marshall later joked the two couples were "the longest double date in history. Carrie and I couldn't get Sam and Dave or the Everlys." Art's low-profile relationship with Marshall would continue for several years, and they often traveled abroad together on Art's beloved walking sojourns. Although Marshall has said little about her affair with Garfunkel, she did once comment, "He opened worlds for me."

Garfunkel was ready to sing again too, but he had lost some of the confidence he exuded on *Watermark*. He stubbornly stuck to his penchant for the songs of Jimmy Webb and other contemporary ballad writers for his new album, *Scissors Cut*. Seeking the support of old friends, he invited Paul to join him on the nostalgic ballad "Cars," and enlisted the venerable Roy Halee to produce the album. As soon as it was completed, Art headed for Europe.

Still troubled by the failure of his film, Paul was especially hurt by lackluster album sales for *One-Trick Pony*. By this time, Paul Simon had sold more than forty million records in his career and had won a dozen Grammys. He was wealthy beyond his wildest dreams, and he had his health. He had a son he adored, and he traveled in an elite circle of sophisticated, talented friends, but it wasn't enough. All he could think about now was rejection. And worst of all, he was immobilized by writer's block. New songs just wouldn't come.

His depression worsened, and a friend recommended talking to Los Angeles psychiatrist Ron Gorney to find relief. Paul called Gorney from New York and was so impressed he immediately flew to California, went directly to Gorney's house, and told the psychiatrist that he couldn't fathom why being rich, famous, and healthy didn't make him happy.

Paul poured out his terror over his writer's block. He had always been able to work himself out of it before, but this time it seemed hopeless. He wasn't satisfied with his physical appearance, still obsessively self-conscious about being short. His fractured relationships with women had been frustrating and painful. He feared people wouldn't like him if he was rich, talented, and happy, too. Worse yet, happiness might snuff out his creative impulse.

Gorney listened carefully and, near the end of the conversation, as Paul got up to leave, motioned toward a guitar leaning against the wall of his living room. He asked Paul if he would like to take it with him. He suggested Paul start to write about the things he had just told him. Paul thought it was an interesting psychiatric ice-breaker, so he took the guitar to his room, but set it aside without taking it out of its case.

The next day, Gorney asked Paul about it, and Paul told him how agonizingly long it took him to write a song. But the psychiatrist insisted that he didn't expect Paul to finish a song—he only wanted him to start one. That night, Paul returned to his room and picked up the guitar. He strummed a few bars and found a simple melody he liked. Then he jotted down the words: "Allergies, maladies / Allergies to dust and grain / Allergies, remedies / Still those allergies remain."*

He took the embryonic song back to Gorney the next day. He was excited but depressed about the worth of his music. Gorney patiently pointed out his music's enormous impact, especially "Bridge Over Troubled Water." He made Paul realize that his work

* "Allergies" © 1981 by Paul Simon

made people's lives better and that he must learn to appreciate that fact.

Gorney showed Paul that his writer's block was caused by feelings of uselessness. The critics and fans had recently rendered a painful verdict—they didn't particularly like what he had to say in *One-Trick Pony*. But the rejection didn't mean Paul should stop trying. Gorney made Paul see his job was not to judge the merit of his own work, but just to write the songs.

Paul felt liberated by Gorney's insight. A few days later, he began work on the songs for his next album. His raw material would be his roller-coaster love affair with Carrie Fisher.

14

In the summer of 1981, Paul got a call from his friend, Ron Delsener, New York City's concert liaison. Gordon Davis, the city's parks commissioner, wanted to know if Paul would be interested in doing a benefit concert in Central Park that September. Paul discussed the idea with concert promoter Warren Hirsh of Fiorucci and Hirsh Enterprises. In 1979, Hirsh had organized a highly successful James Taylor benefit concert in the park. A year earlier he had brought Elton John to the crowds free of charge. There was no admission fee for the concerts, but revenues from T-shirt and memorabilia sales benefited the effort to restore Central Park's Great Lawn.

The previous concerts had been very successful, drawing hundreds of thousands of fans. Observers of the music scene knew that when either Art or Paul performed, the other often appeared as well. When he asked Paul to perform, Hirsh knew it was likely that Art Garfunkel might also become involved.

Paul agreed, although he was still reeling from the cool reception to the *One-Trick Pony* film and tour. He called Art, who was in Switzerland on one of his periodic European walking trips. Paul asked him to join him in the concert—not as a surprise guest, but as a partner.

For years, Paul had struggled to distance himself from the Simon and Garfunkel partnership. But gradually the friendship had been reborn amid lengthy heart-to-heart talks about love, life, and rock 'n' roll. With a new sense of maturity, Art and Paul could also talk about their own limitations instead of pinning blame on the other's shortcomings. As Paul said, "That sort of dialogue made us open to the idea of re-forming as a duo."

Paul's version of events is that he suggested they organize the appearance differently than they had previously. On their few concert dates during the last decade, Paul and Art had performed solo numbers and then had occasionally surprised the audience by bringing the other out to harmonize on two or three of the old Simon and Garfunkel songs. But, for the Central Park concert, Paul envisioned singing a whole set together and then doing the second half of the show alone. After some thought, he rejected that format because it offended his show-business instincts—his appearance in the second half would be anticlimactic. But then again, if he opened the show alone, he would become the opening act for Simon and Garfunkel. So he suggested he and Art do the whole concert as a duo. Art eagerly accepted.

Other reports say a reunion wasn't entirely Paul's idea alone. Garfunkel's description differs somewhat: "Instead of the usual guest shot of two or three tunes, his idea was for us to do a full second half of ten tunes. Then we went into rehearsal, friends of ours said, 'Why not a full Simon and Garfunkel concert? That's what will give the crowds the biggest kick.' Paul thought it would make sense because he didn't want to be the opening act for S and G. I was thinking that S and G didn't need an opening act—let's give them the full show! And Paul began to embrace the idea."

Both men and their attendant business managers had long been aware of the media potential of a full-blown Simon and Garfunkel reunion concert. Over the years they had been careful to keep the reunion possibility alive. In the hearts and minds of millions of fans, Simon and Garfunkel belonged together. Apparently, Paul and Art were beginning to think so too.

As soon as word of the reunion concert got out, skeptics saw it as a blatant attempt to revitalize the flagging careers of two forty-year-old singers who had lost their touch as solo performers. But

Simon defended the event: "I don't think we'd get together if the potential for a joyous reunion weren't there. We'd never decide to grit our teeth just to make a couple million dollars."

Art was in especially high spirits. *Scissors Cut* would be released a month before the concert, and he looked forward to promoting a cut from the album at the event. He was certain "Heart in New York" would be a hometown pleaser and a hit single. Written by Benny Gallagher and Graham Lyle, it would be the only new song at the concert not written by Simon.

Paul was also in a buoyant mood. His writer's block had been broken, and he was eager to record tracks for another album, but just after Labor Day, he put his own work aside to spend the next several weeks rehearsing for the concert. It had been eleven years since the last full Simon and Garfunkel concert, and both meticulous craftsmen were eager to get rid of the rust.

But the good moods rapidly dissolved. The two were barely in rehearsal when tensions developed. The concert date loomed, and unlike the elastic deadlines of studio recording, it couldn't be postponed while Simon and Garfunkel worked out their creative differences. Associates of both men saw the storm warnings and dreaded what might happen next. One said, "They took a terrible risk. They could have not agreed on anything. Everybody sort of felt at one point or another, 'God, I wish they'd never done this.' It was like going on vacation with your ex-wife."

Through the years, the relationship between Simon and Garfunkel had often been described in terms of marriage and divorce. Like many couples, it seemed that while they loved each other on some deep level, they just didn't always like each other. With only three weeks to rehearse, there was no time to explore feelings or negotiate divergent musical tastes. The song list included many of the Simon and Garfunkel standards, but several of Paul's newer songs were to be sung with updated arrangements from the *One-Trick Pony* tour. Paul had switched from acoustic to electric guitar to accommodate the band's rock style and the pain he still suffered from calcium deposits on his finger. Playing a two-hour acoustic set would be impossible. He'd also been composing on the piano recently, and several of his songs, like "Still Crazy After All These Years," were never intended to be played on a guitar. "Late in the Evening" demanded a horn accompaniment only a full, rocking band could provide.

Art didn't like the idea of using a backup band at all. He said, "I thought we'd be safer if we put all our eggs in three baskets—my voice, Paul's voice, and Paul's guitar."

Paul was adamant. It was going to be a very big outdoor show, and he couldn't imagine one guitar generating enough sound for the two or three hundred thousand people expected. "Besides," he said, "I love working with a band. I love it when it starts rocking."

The up-tempo numbers worried Art. He had never harmonized on them before and thought his voice would be lost with a hard-driving rock sound behind him. He had been singing ballads almost exclusively now and had never felt entirely comfortable with Paul's new emphasis on rock rhythms. In the words of one observer, "They fought all the time."

Paul had to constantly reassure Art that the new sounds would work by reminding him of their mutual roots in rock 'n' roll. He told friends, "Artie's worried that he can't sing rhythm, but I know he can, because that's how we grew up." And he told his anxious partner, "Artie, the band will jell, and when it does, you'll want to sing. You'll like it." A few years earlier, Paul had used virtually these same words to persuade Art that appearances on "Saturday Night Live" would also be a source of fun—and he was right. Fortunately, Art was in a trusting mood. He concentrated on learning his new material.

Art didn't resist all of the new arrangements and songs. He secretly looked forward to singing some of Paul's solo efforts. In his analytical way, he had kept a mental scorecard of Paul's songs since the split. He estimated that 70 percent of the new music could easily be adapted to the harmonies of two voices. He admitted, "I couldn't wait to get my hands on 'American Tune.'"

The classic Simon and Garfunkel songs on the program proved easier to deal with. It didn't take long before the razor-sharp harmonies settled effortlessly into place. As Paul said, "My experience with Simon and Garfunkel is that no matter how long a layoff there's been, within about an hour we can get our blend back."

Initially there was very little publicity for the concert, but news of the reunion spread like wildfire. The concert promoters took out a single ad—which did not mention a formal reunion—in the New York City papers to announce the appearance of Simon and Garfunkel. Fans didn't need to be told—the simple yoking of those two names meant a chance to recapture, if only for a moment, the glory days of their youth when the music was all that mattered.

Shortly before the concert, Paul and Art agreed to do publicity. Reporters were invited to rehearsals, but Paul and Art held interview sessions separately. Paul joked that "Simon and Garfunkel" was back from "the boulevard of broken duos." Publicly they talked of harmony and were silent about the tension of the previous three weeks. As for plans for a permanent reunion, both preferred to be ambiguous, as usual. According to Simon: "It was never meant to be a reuniting of the group. We're just going to do it and see what happens. Fun is the key to this whole thing. If this concert in Central Park turns out to be enjoyable for us and for the people who are there in the audience, then maybe we can plan to do a few more."

There was no doubt that the concert would have a very lucrative afterlife, and several ancillary productions were in the works. The concert would be videotaped for a cable television special, and Warner Brothers would record it for live album release, which Phil Ramone and Roy Halee would produce and engineer. Agents worked overtime behind the scenes to clear a legal path for Art, who was still under contract to Paul's old nemesis, Columbia Records, to perform on a Warner Brothers release.

Columbia agreed to Art's request since they knew a reunion concert would stir up interest in the old Simon and Garfunkel tracks stored in their vaults. They prepared to repackage old recordings to cash in on the wave of nostalgia the concert promised.

Paul put up nearly $750,000 of his own money to produce the video and to build an elaborate stage featuring a funky, urban rooftop setting. Stenciled on the smokestacks were the names of the concert promoters, Hirsh and Fiorucci. Lorne Michaels had formed a video production company with James Signorelli, and Paul contracted with them to handle the production and television rights. Michael Lindsay-Hogg, who had directed the Beatles' *Let It Be,* was hired to direct the video.

The day before the concert, Paul did a TV interview with Geraldo Rivera. Art was booked on the same show the day after the concert. The message in the press was clear: The Simon and Garfunkel reunion concert would be a special event—better get there early. The night before the performance, Paul said, "I think it'll be a chance for everyone to all of a sudden jump back and be eighteen years old again."

September 19, 1981, dawned overcast, but the threat of rain didn't stop the crowds. Starting early in the morning, a steady stream of fans flowed into Central Park expecting to relive, if only for an evening, the best times of their lives.

Crowd estimates at show time numbered more than half a million. Couples who had fallen in love to Simon and Garfunkel sat on blankets holding hands. Older people, swaddled in blankets against the September chill, were sprawled on beach chairs. Teenagers who had been born in the storm of social unrest that was the sixties came because, as Art pointed out, "They teach Paul Simon songs in churches and schools as part of the curriculum. It seems that part of good citizenship is the knowledge of the songs we did." They had studied the music in school, but a whole generation of fans had never seen Simon and Garfunkel perform together.

Everyone in the audience seemed to know the music by heart. Fans took for granted the perfect harmonies in some of the best-known and best-loved songs of the past twenty years, but they also came to see if harmony could be restored between friends.

The reunion of Simon and Garfunkel seemed the last chance left to prove that peace and love could heal and prevail. In December the year before, Beatle superstar John Lennon had been murdered by a crazed fan within earshot of Simon and Garfunkel's Central Park stage. Paul realized the symbolic importance of the evening: "There were really only two big reunions possible. And now one of them can't happen. And I think they probably would have done it, too, eventually."

Art, too, was tremendously excited: "I'm dying to hit the stage. I feel like a swimmer who's been on the edge of the pool for weeks. I love the event. Everything about it seems to have a positive energy."

The crowds continued to head toward the meadow as the thin September light ebbed from the sky. An hour before the concert, the skies cleared over the grassy areas now carpeted with people. Ice chests and other fortifications against the long wait anchored the blankets, transforming the field into a human crazy quilt.

The Great Lawn between 79th and 85th Streets, usually the

scene of pick-up football and soccer matches, on this night turned into an exotic market: the smell of roasted meat, beer, and marijuana hung in the air. The atmosphere conjured up an urban Woodstock. In fact, this concert drew more people than the legendary 1969 festival.

Finally, New York Mayor Ed Koch took the stage to a thunderous ovation. He was a savvy enough politician to resist the temptation to say more than, "Ladies and gentlemen, Simon and Garfunkel." The familiar figures loped toward center stage. Garfunkel triumphantly raised two clenched fists. The two then faced each other and shook hands. The crowd roared its approval. Paul strummed his guitar and smiled beatifically while the tumult swelled around them. The band began an upbeat version of "Mrs. Robinson," and soon the trademark commingling of voices rolled over the crowd in an irresistible tide of happy feelings. "Homeward Bound" followed, and the crowd knew that they were all homeward bound on a unique journey of remembrance.

When the cheers subsided, Paul spoke to the sea of faces before him, "Well, it's great to do a neighborhood concert." Paul, concerned about the sound system as always, said he hoped everyone in the crowd could hear them. He then thanked the fire department, the police department, and Mayor Koch, and then joked that they wanted to offer special thanks to a group seldom recognized for their charitable deeds for the city. He thanked "the guys selling loose joints" for donating half their proceeds to the cause.

The crowd roared with delight since most knew the police had tried earlier that morning to curb the use of "controlled substances" at the concert by conducting a drug bust at the 72nd Street Boat Basin, a well-known marijuana and drug market. There were still plenty of joints being passed around, and as the crowd swayed to the lyric "Look for America," the smell of marijuana wafted through the air. In spite of over three hundred extra policemen on duty, virtually no arrests were made.

Paul and Art then swung into the Latin rhythms and infectious good cheer of "Me and Julio," to which Art had no trouble adjusting. Paul laid down his electric guitar to accompany the duo with his acoustic guitar as they summoned up the time of innocence with "Scarborough Fair" and "April Come She Will." From the contemplative songs of the sixties, they returned to their roots in the fifties, with the Everly Brothers' "Wake Up, Little Suzie," and finally brought the crowd back to the present when Paul sang solo, "Still Crazy After All These Years." Everyone in the vast crowd could identify with the rueful lyrics. Paul and Art had gone down the road before them, and they had shown the way. Decades later—durable and resilient—here they were together again. These two white middle-class college graduates, who weren't afraid of music filled with ideas or emotions, articulated their generation's sorrows and joys as no one ever had before. These were guys from the neighborhood who found stupendous success but hadn't forgotten where they came from and what the important things were.

The magic that happened at Simon and Garfunkel concerts was a kind of transmigration of audience and performers. The crowd saw itself reflected in these two guys from Queens. It so strongly identified with Simon and Garfunkel that it blended in with them. Now, for the first time in eleven years, the magic was back for real.

Both Paul and Art were amazed at the size of the crowd. Paul later called it "numbing." He found it nearly impossible to talk to such a vast number of people, but he could feel the emotions coursing toward the stage. The audience had no trouble communicating with the two tiny figures before them. "If you thought you saw joy, you saw joy," Garfunkel later declared. Just before he sang, he told the crowd, "I am so in the mood!"

Art got his chance to sing "American Tune" with Paul, and the song's bedrock patriotism moved even the most jaded sixties refugees. On "Late in the Evening," the reference to smoking a joint produced a sympathetic roar. Art sang his new album cut, "Heart in New York," to an enthusiastic round of applause. Paul then introduced a new song, "The Late Great Johnny Ace," which dealt with the deaths of John Kennedy, John Lennon, and rhythm and blues artist Johnny Ace.

Near the end of the song, a shadowy figure from the audience vaulted past security guards and up onto the stage until he came face to face with Paul and reportedly said, "Paul, I have to talk to you." The guards hustled the man away, but the crowd was reminded once again of how easy it would be to add to the litany of tragedies this generation had already witnessed. Paul later claimed that he wasn't frightened at the time, but merely annoyed.

Paul and Art changed the mood once again with a driving

rendition of "Kodachrome" and then segued into "Maybellene" in homage to one of rock 'n' roll's progenitors, Chuck Berry. Art then brought the evening's emotions to a climax with a soaring "Bridge Over Troubled Water" that the crowd drowned out with its own harmony. "50 Ways to Leave Your Lover" and "The Boxer" closed the program. Paul's lyric "After changes upon changes / We are more or less the same"* captured the essence of reunion, for the crowd and for him and Art.

The two returned for an encore without the band and sang "Old Friends/Bookends," allowing the crowd to savor the intimate "Time of innocence / A time of confidences"† they shared with the duo. They finally closed with "Feelin' Groovy." For a few hours, Simon and Garfunkel had recreated the carefree days of the crowd's youth, and this song was perfect to sustain the buoyant mood. By then, they had given the audience all it could wish for— but one—and voices in the crowd began to shout its name.

A reverential hush fell over the crowd as Simon and Garfunkel began the song that had started it all, "The Sounds of Silence." Everyone remembered that the song marked the moment they knew they were not alone with their feelings.

After the wistful song, Paul wanted to send them off in a happier mood, so he commented that since the city wouldn't let them have fireworks as part of the show, he would invite the crowd to help them make their own glorious finale with the music. They ended the evening with a raucous reprise of "Late in the Evening," after which Paul said simply, "Thank you from the bottom of our hearts." The two figures stood side by side. Paul lightly curled his arm around Art's back, and Art did the same to Paul.

The crowd roared again as the lights came up. The half million faithful began to pack up their blankets and coolers and straggle toward the lights of the city. Soon most of the vast, teeming crowd had melted into the night.

Immediately after the concert, Art and Paul compared their reactions. Paul said, "Afterward, our first reaction was, I think, one of disappointment. Arthur's more than mine. He thought he didn't sing well. I didn't get what had happened—how big it

---

* "The Boxer" © 1968 by Paul Simon
† "Old Friends" © 1968 by Paul Simon

was—until I went home and turned on the television and saw it on all the news, the people being interviewed, and later that night on the front pages of all the newspapers. Then I got it."

Later, he also understood the potential danger he was in when the fan rushed onto the stage. Afterward, he was often haunted by the memory.

The morning after the concert, bulldozers gingerly picked their way among the tons of trash left by the concert-goers, in order to avoid running over several hundred fans who still lay rolled up in blankets covered with morning dew. The clean-up operation reportedly cost twenty thousand dollars. The front pages of the newspapers featured pictures of Art and Paul and the events of the night before. The concert attracted more people than had ever before gathered for a single-concert performance.

For several weeks, Paul reiterated that he didn't realize at the time how huge the event was: "I thought I was doing a concert, you know? But actually, what was happening was a far greater statement. I didn't perceive that statement until I came back home and saw the stuff on television. Then I realized that something extraordinary had happened."

The duo was deluged with questions about the permanence of the reunion. Both tried to deny any long-range plans to reunite. Beyond the release of the video and the concert album, both said they hadn't given much thought to the future. Paul tried to be honest about the concert's significance: It was "not a need. It was a chain of events."

He was also candid about how hard it was to work together. He pointed out that the crowd's affectionate embrace could end up choking each man's individual creativity by forcing them on an endless trip down memory lane. He recalled John Lennon talking about the impossibility of a Beatles' reunion. For Lennon, the group existed at a certain point in time, and the experience for both the group and their fans was unrepeatable. Ian Hoblyn, Paul's personal manager at that time, declared, "This was a one-time get together." But he added, "Still, they saw that crowd, and somewhere in the recesses, though not consciously, they must have felt, 'Hey, look what we could do!'" What Simon and Garfunkel could do was rekindle feelings of youth and optimism in a generation of Americans sorely in need of such comfort. A few weeks after the concert, a long poem written affectionately in the style of a Paul Simon lyric appeared in the *New Yorker* magazine. It captured the quintessential character of the Central Park concert fans: "They were feelin' sad, feelin' over thirty / Lookin' for somethin' / Lookin' for nothin' / But feelin' glad to have Paul and Artie."

Neither Art nor Paul was fully prepared to deal with the shock wave of popular interest generated by the Central Park concert. Paul may have planned to return to work on his album, and Art's future may have included a return to Europe to resume his walking tours, but the overwhelming popular approval of their reunion forced them both to reconsider their future together.

In Los Angeles, Paul's record producers Lenny Woronker and Russ Titelman waited for him to return. Because he wanted to spend a lot of time with Carrie on the West Coast, Paul had decided to record his new album there. His last record producer, Phil Ramone, was now working with Billy Joel, and Paul said that his decision to change producers was due to "scheduling problems."

Paul's friends and associates were divided on the wisdom of a reunion with Art. Several argued that a reunion made good business sense while others thought a reteaming would undermine the years of painstaking effort to establish himself as a solo performer.

Paul could have done the Central Park concert alone, but he would have been competing with the huge success of previous stars who had performed there, including Elton John, Diana Ross, James Taylor, and Barbra Streisand, all of whom drew extremely large crowds. Without Art and the extra dimension of a Simon and Garfunkel reunion, Paul hadn't been willing to risk another marginal venture like his movie and soundtrack album. Some said since the *One-Trick Pony* tour had not been drawing the expected crowds, he was worried about drawing a small crowd in his own hometown and embarrassing himself.

Art, true to his more passive pattern, accepted Paul's overture because he genuinely enjoyed the Simon and Garfunkel phase of his life and had no objections to reviving it. He saw little harm in singing the old songs. Besides, his solo career was on shakier ground than Paul's. It had been a long time since either he or Paul had tasted the undiluted success of the Simon and Garfunkel years.

The Central Park concert, however, turned out to have greater implications than either Art or Paul had considered. They felt overwhelmed by the outpouring of sentiment, and even though their deep and unresolved differences surfaced within moments of the first concert rehearsal, they now yielded to the pressure to come together. So it was that in fall of 1981 Simon and Garfunkel became a hot-selling media commodity all over again. Paul's old label, Columbia, capitalized on the popular impact of the reunion and released *The Simon and Garfunkel Collection* in England in time for Christmas. It contained seventeen of the best Simon and Garfunkel songs and was an immediate hit. In Europe it quickly sold more than two million copies. The concert album was being prepared for release by Warner Brothers, and nostalgic record buyers, caught up in the frenzy of postconcert publicity, were already demanding it in the stores.

In spite of their vows never to work together again, Paul and Art found themselves on the verge of committing to a reunion tour with dates in Europe and Japan. They also talked about another Simon and Garfunkel album. Friends and associates who knew the bitterness that existed between them were surprised at their willingness to reunite. Could the euphoria and friendship of that one magical evening in Central Park really heal the broken relationship?

Art's *Scissors Cut* album had been released that same month with its cover featuring a close-up black-and-white photo of Art in a tuxedo. Barely visible above his formal black tie is a tiny Band-Aid on his neck. The album credits included a quote from Flaubert, a note of thanks to his and Paul's longtime lawyer/ manager Michael Tannen, and a dedication to Laurie Bird.

Swept away in the aftermath of the reunion concert, *Scissors Cut* got a less than enthusiastic reception by record buyers. Despite being named one of the best albums of the year by *Rolling Stone,* it sold an anemic 130,000 units. Art later admitted: "The album came out just when we were doing the concert, and it got lost in the shuffle. When it didn't sell well, I began to bury the pain in the distraction of the show."

The reunion concert video was scheduled for broadcast in February, and tour dates were rapidly filling in. That same month, the first new Simon and Garfunkel album in twelve years was released and rose rapidly to the top of the charts. Warner Brothers released a single cut from the reunion soundtrack, "Wake Up, Little Suzie," which reached number twenty-seven and whetted the public's appetite for the forthcoming live album.

Art and Paul agreed to promote the albums, television program, and tour by doing a series of separate interviews. They cautiously evaded the inevitable question about a permanent reunion, both replying that a reteaming would be a "step-by-step" process.

Lorne Michaels, who knew the problems that existed between the two, explained the duo's reversal: "Although the concert in Central Park was very much of a one-shot, I think that by working together again, they found a lot more mutual ground. I think they both underestimated how many people cared about their reunion, how important it was to so many people. It was the right time, and they both sensed that."

For Art, the concert meant the renewal of "this most valuable personal friendship. It still means a lot—maybe everything—even after all these years." In the concert video, the camera captured the essence of that evening and the reason to continue the partnership. As Art described it, "Paul has his hand on my back for this affectionate hug, and I return the gesture. And as I looked at it, I realized both of our arms are exactly symmetrical. Both hugs, they're the same hug."

The public immediately wanted to know what plans Simon and Garfunkel had to record another original album. At first, Paul downplayed that idea, giving contractual problems as the reason: "When I left CBS [Columbia Records], there was a lot of bad blood." But he was quick to add that he and Art kept all their options open.

Paul contended his reason for sustaining the reunion had less to do with popular demand than with friendship: "It seemed like a good opportunity to repair a lot of stuff. It seemed like a chance to clean everything up. I'm a sucker for that."

Simon also saw the reunion as a way to relive and enjoy the good times of the Simon and Garfunkel years: "I wasn't really present for 'Simon and Garfunkel' the first time around. I wasn't home, the same way that I wasn't present for the concert in the park when it was happening. Because you're in the middle of it, you just think that it's your life—until it's over."

The tour may also have been a way to repeat the Simon and Garfunkel years with Paul firmly in command of the duo's destiny.

As plans for the reunion tour took shape, Paul's new solo album suffered further delays. His up-and-down relationship with Carrie had become mostly down. She was busy making movies—most recently *Under the Rainbow* with Chevy Chase. She said, "These forced separations are rough." During the filmmaking, her dependence on prescription drugs grew heavier. On March 12, 1982, her old friend John Belushi died of a drug overdose, an event which sobered Carrie along with the rest of the "Saturday Night Live" crowd. Carrie later noted, "The scariest thing Belushi ever said to me was, 'You're like me.' And then he died." What Belushi meant, Carrie knew, was that they shared an attraction to "the allure of the flame."

Paul didn't have much time to come to terms with Carrie. He and Art were trying to come to terms with their conflicts. Their personal differences seemed more manageable in light of the resurgence of their popularity. Paul said, "It got easy again. Artie and I had some heart-to-heart talks—which, amazingly, we had never had—and we just settled some things." Art attributed their past difficulties to immaturity and was confident they could iron things out. He elaborated, "For a long time, I almost needed Paul to be elsewhere. He affected me too much at a time when I needed to find my own identity. The wish to work together again evolved organically. It was the absence of stuff in the way—your ego, the need for space. I suppose we'd grown up. Paul said, 'Let's sing,' and I said, 'It's a deal.'"

They were both concerned that the reunion tour be more than just an exercise for a one-trick pony. Paul said, "It's not gonna be the same. It's gonna be something different, and let's just see what it is. I'm still not sure what the hell it means..."

They started the tour abroad because, as Art explained: "Europe is a way to build up our chops before we bring the show on home. The trick is not to give the people more nostalgia, but rather to take it further. If we're going to function again, we'll function in the present tense and draw on the old days as much as it pleases the crowd. But what would be alive for us would be whatever is new."

They headed first for Japan, then on to Spain, West Germany, France, Switzerland, Holland, Ireland, and would end up in Wembley Stadium in Britain. It soon became clear the concert crowds wanted the "old" Simon and Garfunkel, and so did the record-buying public. Warner Brothers reportedly pushed hard for a new Simon and Garfunkel album. Paul's company had lost heavily on *One-Trick Pony* and was having a poor sales year overall. Certainly Paul had no time to write ten new songs for a Simon and Garfunkel album, but Warner Brothers knew he had a lot of material already finished for his next solo album. Inquiries were made about the possibility of including Art's harmonies on Paul's work in progress.

Paul's producer at the time, Russ Titelman, later admitted, "There may have been pressure from people to make it a Simon and Garfunkel album for monetary reasons." Sources say record execs Mo Ostin and Lenny Waronker told Paul that the inclusion of Art would insure big album sales, but the decision was Paul's alone. Titleman maintained that "Paul never really decided if he wanted the record to be his or Simon and Garfunkel's."

One who worked on the album said, "The two had just come back from their Far East tour, and I guess Artie was used to being around Paul. So after a while Paul finally said to him, 'Here, why don't you go try a part of that,' or 'Maybe you could sing the bridge on this.' It was all very casual. Then it got to be more serious."

Publicly, Paul seemed to reject the idea of using Art on the album because he felt "the songs were much too personal." His new work was the expression of his most intimate relationships with the women in his life, and the material seemed to be suited for his voice alone. As he told Art, "The new songs are too much about my life—about Carrie—to have anybody else sing them." But Art responded, "Look, these aren't the events of my life, but I understand the emotions you're dealing with. I understand what it is to be in love, to be in pain, to feel joy. I'm a singer. I'm able to interpret. That's what I do."

According to Simon, "Artie made a persuasive case that he could make it into a natural duo record." Added to that, as one observer noted, "People on the outside really started to put pressure on Paul to make it a Simon and Garfunkel record."

Paul was finally won over but demanded complete control of the recording. He contended, "I have to produce this because it's not like it was in the sixties. I know what I want to say musically. So if that's all right with you...we can try."

Paul's decision put him in the unenviable position of producing a Simon and Garfunkel album that could be expected to top the duo's last mega-hit album, *Bridge Over Troubled Water*. The relief he felt after the split in 1969 was due, in part, to his avoidance of that burden, and now he was faced with it after all.

Still feeling ambivalent about including Art on the new album, Simon rationalized that Simon and Garfunkel always did their best work in the studio rather than on the concert stage. Working together in the studio, he reasoned, they could easily top the success of the Central Park live album. He even mused that the reunion of Simon and Garfunkel might become an opportunity to "write that big ballad I wouldn't write for myself."

Meanwhile, Carrie had broken off her affair with Dan Aykroyd, explaining: "All of you are leading lives that are very fast. He's somewhere doing a film and you're not. I got back with Paul again. I was doing a play in New York." The play was the drama, *Agnes of God*. As a change of pace, she also did a guest shot as a *Playboy* bunny on her buddy Penny Marshall's television series, "Laverne and Shirley." Paul and Carrie, often with Art and Penny, again frequented the New York social scene.

But Carrie was still doing drugs. She listed acid, ecstasy, MDA, and Percodan as her current favorites. The troubled actress had to drop out of *Agnes of God* in April citing health reasons—problems with her vocal cords. Critics, however, speculated the real reason had to do with drugs. She and Paul continued their often difficult relationship while he and Art argued about music.

Signs of trouble had begun to surface. The enforced togetherness of touring was already getting to be oppressive. Tensions spilled over into the recording studio where they were magnified. Unlike all of their previous albums, this one had a fixed deadline—and nothing went smoothly. An observer noted "Everyone seemed to be taking forever. Art, too; it took him an awfully long time to work out those harmonies."

Paul as well as Warner Brothers saw the necessity for releasing the album in the wake of the popular interest created by the Central Park concert, the European tour, and the successful reunion album. He hoped to get the new album out by the spring of 1983 for the start of their U.S. tour. But Paul's ambivalence and Art's frustration at Paul's seizure of artistic control made for a combustible studio atmosphere. Paul also recognized that he had become more rigid in adhering to his artistic vision than ever before. Art balked. He refused to work in the studio together with Paul. Paul would lay down his tracks and vocals and then tell Art to do the same. Paul recalled Art's reply: "I'm not ready. I'd like to write my parts. I want to take my Walkman. I'm going to walk through Switzerland and write my harmony." Furthermore, Paul wanted to be in the studio when Art recorded his vocals in order to exert complete control by deciding which takes were acceptable and which ones should be done over again to his exacting specifications. Art was no longer a collaborator, as he and Halee had been in the old days. He was a singer and that was all. Moreover, he was a singer with a penchant for a style Paul had rejected years ago.

Art kept procrastinating. He said he wasn't pleased with his voice. He blamed the pressures of concert performances. He wanted to think some more about his vocals and harmonies. A year drifted by with no progress on the album. In July 1983, Art was still behind schedule. He commented: "The album is 85 percent complete when it should be 97 percent complete. The pressure is absolutely on to make a final 15 percent of the process happen in just 3 percent of the time."

Art later was more candid about the reasons for the delays: "With the idea of Paul as producer and me as helper, I denied my musical strengths. With me on the mike singing stuff and Paul going, 'No, I don't like that'... for Paul to sort of miss it, to shear off the whole level of creative possibility, that was bloody painful." In the past, Art had always thought of himself as "embedded in the songwriting process somewhere because I was nearby, and I was a good bounce." On the new album, "That was not the case. My input on writing the songs was next to nil."

Some said Art was still smoking marijuana and that Paul was furious, claiming Art was stoned most of the time. Certainly Carrie was using drugs, and Paul had to deal with them both. His patience was wearing thin. Every encounter became tension-filled. Paul later claimed the delay wasn't due to Art's indifference, saying cryptically, "He was fighting his demons. And he has a formidable array of demons."

The acrimony boiled over in a heated exchange that summoned up Art's long-buried feelings of betrayal and victimization. Paul angrily retorted that it had all happened when they were kids and Art should forget it. But Art said he couldn't forget because Paul was still the same person.

The album wasn't ready, but the U.S. tour dates had been set and couldn't be delayed. The tour was designed to replicate the magic of that evening in Central Park. Simon had again asserted his control by insisting on the exact format and arrangements used in the Central Park concert. He wanted the same band and the same arrangements on the road and, more important, he decided that the tour needed to play cavernous arenas in order to accommodate the anticipated crowds—something neither really enjoyed. Paul argued that the immense number of advance ticket requests justified the risky sound quality of large stadiums.

The fans across America who had shared their reunion on television and in the press were eagerly waiting to experience the reunion live. The tour opened in Akron on July 19, 1983.

They were booked into Dodger Stadium, Shea Stadium, the Meadowlands in New Jersey, the Astrodome—venues which could seat fifty or sixty thousand people. Art grew more frustrated at the impossible sound conditions. With very little argument, he had gone along with the original decision to tour with Paul's rock-flavored band because there seemed no other choice. But he remained convinced that the acoustics of such huge spaces would be impossible to master, and that their music would be sacrificed to spectacle.

Paul and the concert promoters had prevailed, but Art was not so quiet this time around. He relished saying "I told you so" when reviewers commented that the pure Simon and Garfunkel sound was lost amid the vast arenas and rock-band sounds.

Paul later could admit that the choice of large arenas had been a mistake, but he resented Art's pouting. Art continued to brood, his mood darkening as the huge caravan moved from city to city. Hundreds of thousands more bought tickets to retrieve their vanished youth. It didn't matter that intimacy, the essential ingredient of a Simon and Garfunkel concert, was gone. The tide of nostalgia rolled on, cresting each night with Art's soaring rendition of "Bridge Over Troubled Water." But for the duo, the euphoria of the original Central Park concert had worn off long ago. They weren't even speaking to one another. Art traveled alone while Paul was often joined by Carrie. They communicated by sending messages via their assistants. Art seemed generally unhappy with everything about the tour, but Paul ignored his tense mood; he was not about to yield his hard-won creative turf.

The concert tour rolled on while progress on the album slowed almost to a stop. Paul was growing more irritated with Art's reluctance to complete his part of the recording project. But Art hadn't given up on it. He argued, "Look, we're making an album, our first in thirteen years. Everything worth doing is hard. It's awkward and jerky and difficult. Soon the hard part will be over, and the good results will come in."

Artistic differences only grew wider as the struggle for control escalated. Paul said, "I was getting to feel that I didn't want him to paint on my painting. Finally, I said, 'This is not a good idea. I think what we have here is the partnership that wasn't.'" In spite of the mighty yearnings of millions of fans, the reconciliation had failed, and the divorce, when it came, would be final. At last, Paul had had enough of the waiting game. In mid-summer 1983, he called Art in New England and said, "I'm erasing all your harmonies from the tape, and I'm marrying Carrie Fisher next week."

Art's reaction: "I thought that was an interesting one-two punch."

15

After five years of their stormy love affair, Carrie and Paul had decided to make the relationship permanent. They had broken up several times and had dated other people, but they had always returned to each other.

Paul had charted the course of their rocky relationship in a song he called "Hearts and Bones:" "One and one-half wandering Jews / Returned to their natural coasts / To resume old acquaintances / Step out occasionally / And speculate who had been damaged the most."* He obliquely refers to marriage as "the last leg of the journey they started a long time ago." Some say the song convinced Carrie the time was ripe for marriage. She had suggested marriage earlier, but Paul had feared commitment. He later said, "It made me real nervous. I had been married and divorced and found it really painful."

Carrie threatened to leave him again. One night in August of 1983, Paul went alone to a doubleheader at Yankee Stadium. The soothing patterns of a baseball game often gave him refuge from his troubles as well as time to think. As he described it, toward the

*"Hearts and Bones" © 1982 by Paul Simon

228

seventh inning, while working on his second beer, he decided to
marry her after all. He said to himself, "Well, come on, Paul;
you're going to do it! I'd always loved Carrie, even when we were
most separated." After the games, he went home, proposed
marriage on the spot, and five days later they were wed.

Despite the short notice, the marriage ceremony became a gala
event—heralded as the show-biz wedding of the year. Celebrities
flew in from all over to attend the ceremony held at Paul's Central
Park West duplex.

The press feasted on the reunion of Carrie's parents. Debbie
Reynolds arrived from Los Angeles with her mother, Maxine
Reynolds, and Carrie's brother Todd. Eddie Fisher arrived an hour
later with his mother, Kate. It was the first time in more than two
years the one-time perfect Hollywood couple had seen each other.
Paul's parents also attended. Penny Marshall, Art's companion,
served as one of Carrie's bridesmaids. Standing up with Paul were
his brother Eddie and Lorne Michaels. In addition to Art, other
invited celebrities included Billy Joel and Christie Brinkley, Teri
Garr, Robin Williams, Randy Newman, Charles Grodin, George
Lucas, Kevin Kline, and, of course, Paul's son Harper.

Eddie Fisher gave the bride away in a traditional Jewish
ceremony. Immediately afterward, Carrie started the reception
with the comment, "Let's just say we've had a stormy romance
and the storms are finally over."

Between Paul and Art, things were not so calm. There were still
concert dates to fulfill, and, although their relations were at least
superficially cordial, one observer said Paul's abrupt decision to
eliminate Art from the album "strained their relationship" even
further. Paul was angry because many in his circle, including
Carrie, told him he was crazy to drop Art from the album. He was
fed up with hearing about "poor Artie."

Carrie and Paul flew to Houston where Simon and Garfunkel
were scheduled to perform at the Astrodome. But Hurricane Alicia
canceled the concert, and they went on to the Oakland Coliseum
where Carrie joined Paul onstage and joked to the thousands of
fans, "I'd like to thank you all for joining us on our honeymoon.
We couldn't have done it without you." Carrie was amused by
tabloid reports that they had finally married because she was three
months pregnant. It wasn't true.

Once again the newlyweds separated as Paul and Art traveled to a concert in Vancouver, and Carrie went back to Los Angeles to tape *Thumbelina* for their friend Shelley Duvall's "Faerie Tale Theater."

Even as the reunion tour was finally winding down, Paul and Art were still besieged with questions about a permanent reunion. In his interviews, Paul began to send signals that the reteaming of Simon and Garfunkel wouldn't last: "It does feel good onstage. But where would we continue? What would we do?...Release an album and go play the world again. Know what I mean? It's like we did it. We did it. What is there to prove? The only reason to continue is if we wanted to make a career out of Simon and Garfunkel. It's too hard to make a career out of Simon and Garfunkel. We are, after all, a group that broke up. And we broke up because it was hard. So we function together with some stress, you know? We perform, but it's stressful."

Relations between the two had deteriorated once again, and they exchanged salvos in the press. Art said, "This is a friendship to hold onto, but that also means it's someone who knows how to get under your skin, what buttons to push to make you a little crazy."

As the tour, like the reunion, was coming to an end, Paul noted, "On a certain level, not too far from the surface, he doesn't like me. I don't even know if Arthur admits that. The same goes for me." He continued, "Of course, you have to remember that there's something quite powerful between us. This is a friendship that is now thirty years old. And the feeling of understanding and love parallels the feeling of abuse. Artie's a very powerful and autonomous person until he comes into contact with me on a professional level. Then he loses a great degree of power, and it makes him very angry—at me."

They billed their appearance at the five-thousand-seat Ramat Gan stadium outside Tel Aviv, Israel, as "The Last Simon and Garfunkel Concert." The show, on September 26, 1983, was a fifty dollars-per-ticket benefit for the Variety Clubs of Israel.

Finally, it was over. Even the music had become a bore to Paul. He found himself struggling to find motivation for singing the old tunes, especially "Homeward Bound." But he prodded himself, "The mistake you're making is you act as if this is a representation of your work now, instead of a representation of you when you were twenty-three up in a railroad station in Liverpool. Then it's not so bad."

However, both Art and Paul knew the music wasn't the reason for this or any other Simon and Garfunkel split. "All of them were about personality conflicts," Paul later admitted.

When the tour ended, Paul and Carrie went on their honeymoon down the Nile, accompanied by Paul's best friend Lorne Michaels and Carrie's best pal Penny Marshall.

When he returned to New York, Paul had changed the working title of the new album from *Think Too Much* to *Hearts and Bones*, and he pushed himself to complete the tracks. Warner Brothers and Simon released a joint statement that explained that Art's departure from the album was made necessary by the "personal nature" of Paul's songs. Off the record, Paul admitted, "He makes the sound of my music more agreeable to many people. But I don't care."

An observer says there was another reason for making it a solo album: "Paul knew it was probably going to be as good as anything he'd ever done. So he didn't want Garfunkel on it. He's tired of falling back on 'Simon and Garfunkel' for a hit. He wanted this to be his record, his hit."

The only form of communication between the two came in bitter remarks to the press. Art told the *New York Times,* "Our Central Park reunion was a genuine event, but we strung it along until the juice ran out. Paul doesn't cherish our past work the way I do. Like many writers, he always on to the next thing. I have no problem in singing our old songs lovingly and nostalgically."

Although the bitter aftermath of the failed reunion and the aborted album may have silenced Simon and Garfunkel, it couldn't put an end to the relationship. Paul described the struggle: "As is always the case, because I essentially love him, I fall back in. Occasionally I think, 'I should sing one song with Artie'—that's how seductive it is.... But I'm never going back there." Phil Ramone, Paul's longtime friend and record producer, said, "If they ever do another album with each other, I'll shoot them both."

Paul and Art withdrew to their separate corners to sort out the residue of that euphoric September night in Central Park. Paul was eager to see the public reaction to *Hearts and Bones*. He had invested his heart and soul in the highly personal collection of songs and was certain its themes of love and loss would hit home.

On this album, as always, Paul charted the progress of his own emotional journey through life. In the past, his subject had often been women, but on *Hearts and Bones* he revealed more about the limits of love than ever before. And Carrie wasn't the only influence on *Hearts and Bones.*

About his first wife Peggy, Paul wrote the haunting "Train in the Distance," another sad tale. First, he assembled the details of how he pursued, finally won, and eventually lost Peggy, and then performed what he calls "the artist's job": he found a haunting, evocative image—the mournful sound of a train passing—which enabled him to instill simple facts with emotion and meaning.

The album included "The Late Great Johnny Ace," which Paul wrote while under the influence of his *One-Trick Pony* theme. On this song, Paul continued his habit of collaborating with some-times surprising talents. He asked avant-garde composer Philip Glass to write and orchestrate the song's haunting ending.

Most critics agreed with Paul's feeling that *Hearts and Bones* was his finest work to date. *Stereo Review* raved, "Paul Simon's new album...might easily have been called *Hearts and Minds,* for much of it deals with the conflict between emotion and intellect—the two edges along which Simon's music has always cut. Al-though his message is that the two are mutually exclusive, the album is, in fact, its own rebuttal, a nearly perfect collaboration between lyricism and logic....Musically, *Hearts and Bones* is characteristic rhymin' Simon—jazzy, but not jazz, folksy, but not folk, spry pop with gospel and doo-wop flourishes." The reviewer took note of the controversy surrounding the removal of Art's vocal tracks from the record: "They are not missed. In fact, Simon handles most of the backing vocals himself. After all, if he can refute himself, he can certainly back himself."

But the record-buying public had been primed for a Simon and Garfunkel album. They registered their disappointment with anemic sales. In addition, the album's rueful introspection (it contained not one but two versions of a song entitled "Think Too Much") and Paul's brooding examination of heartbreak may have been more heavy reflection than the audience could handle.

Hearts and Bones was rumored to have cost Warner Brothers almost two million dollars to produce, but the price to Paul Simon was inestimable. The album's best chart showing was a tepid number thirty-five, confirming Paul's worst fear—his audience wasn't listening to what he considered his best work. He confessed that he was totally unprepared to produce something less than a hit. He listened to the album over and over again in an attempt to discover its fatal flaw. Some preferred to speculate that Warner Brothers and others may have been right about Paul's need for Art after all.

Once again, Simon was devastated. The album's poor showing meant he had been unable to salvage anything from the doomed Simon and Garfunkel reunion. The massive wave of affection for the pair had been spent leaving little but bitter feelings and failure in its wake. After that tremendous high, Paul and Art were personally further apart than ever before. Paul revealed, "I didn't talk to him for a year. I really didn't talk to him. I was in a rage...I like to take chances. In this case, I lost."

Ironically, the album that was conceived as an account of his rocky love affair with Carrie Fisher, and even served as a touching proposal of marriage, failed at the same time their relationship was falling apart. They had tried marriage counseling, but "It was too much to work out," Fisher later admitted. "Marriage just couldn't save it, and I think that's what we did it for. You can't do that to a relationship. You can't get married to fix it. It was a relationship based on a great conversation. It probably should have stayed a great conversation." Less than a year after the hasty nuptials, Carrie moved out and filed for divorce.

The couple's friends said Carrie's drug addiction was also a significant problem. From her point of view, "I was doing drugs off to one side, and I was lying about it. I was not looking for a vote. If anyone cared about me, they knew it. There are two things to do with someone on drugs: take them, too, or object to it. Some of my friends did both."

But she claimed, "Drugs wasn't the variable that toppled [the marriage]. Bad timing did it. I was too young to have a relationship that wasn't 'Let's go to the Village and buy bright T-shirts.' I wanted to go to Disneyland, and Paul wanted to go to Sotheby's. I was 'How do you solve a problem like Maria?' and he was 'Edelweiss.' He was an artist, and I was an artist's buddy."

Drugs and bad timing aside, others believed the real issue between the two recalled Paul's earlier marital problem—who was going to compromise. According to Fisher, "There's a lot of stuff that goes with being with very successful men. If someone in the relationship is going to compromise, it's generally the chick. And I wasn't so good at adapting."

The end of the marriage was the last in a string of painful losses for Paul. With the fractious reunion tour and subsequent alienation from Art, the public's rejection of *Hearts and Bones,* and the final split from Carrie, Paul Simon suffered through the most difficult period of his life. Personally and professionally, he felt adrift.

Art was suffering, too. The aftermath of his tragic love affair with Laurie Bird still haunted him. He admitted that "the 1980s were largely a slow process of getting over that."

Art had been writing a little poetry, something he'd started as a hobby in the 1970s, and he briefly tried his hand at writing songs, picking out melodies on a guitar and playing with various word combinations, trying "to redirect a poem into a song—but in about an hour and a half all the inspiration dried up." He readily described the aborted attempt as writer's block: "Part of the obstacle may be my proximity to a great songwriter, Paul Simon...I would not enjoy the inevitable comparisons."

Art continued to date Penny Marshall, who accompanied him on a lengthy tour of Australia and New Zealand. His urge to travel increased, and every few months, he grew restless and took off for a new destination. From 1984 to 1986, he was totally estranged from Paul, revealing, "We're not talking. It's a shame. It gnaws at me, but I don't want to admit that. I'd like to say, 'No, it doesn't bother me,' but in all truth, it does."

What may also have bothered Art was Paul's twelve-city solo tour, in 1984, without a band and accompanying himself only with an acoustic guitar. It was exactly what Garfunkel had wanted to do when they reteamed.

After the tour Paul spent most of his time alone at his home on Long Island, "staring at the sea" and brooding about the painful series of events. He took long, solitary drives and struggled to sort out the chaos of his life. For the first time in his career, he had no new songs waiting to be written. He said, "I had no new ideas at all. I didn't know what to write."

Paul had decided to build a new house on Long Island and now had plenty of time to develop the plans with an old friend, architect Paul Krause. He had become interested in the building process and made frequent trips to the construction site.

Paul always kept a stack of music cassettes beside him as he drove. Among the tapes he listened to that summer was the work of the Talking Heads. He liked the sound of an African strain of music called "high-life" on their album, *Remain in Light*. He also listened again and again to the African-flavored *My Life in the Bush of Ghosts*, an album by the David Byrne and Brian Eno.

On one of his drives he played a new tape his friend guitarist Heidi Berg had given him earlier in the summer—an instrumental with the intriguing title, *Gumboots: Accordion Jive Hits, Volume II*. Ironically, the cassette was a bootleg, something Paul thoroughly disapproved of. He listened to the tape of African music for a month, gradually becoming spellbound by the upbeat rhythms and the strange, energetic pumping of an accordion. He found the music irresistible and sang his own melodies over it at the top of his lungs as he drove along. For the first time in weeks, he was able to take his mind off his obsessive, melancholy review of recent events and concentrate on music.

The sounds reminded him of his first musical love: "It sounded like very early rock 'n' roll to me, black, urban, mid-fifties rock 'n' roll, like the great Atlantic tracks from that period."

He could think of nothing but that music and spent all of his time researching its origins. The only thing Paul really knew about African music was that it formed the heart and soul of much of the best of American popular music. He had worked with South African singer Miriam Makeba and her husband Hugh Masakela during the sixties and learned about Nigerian "high-life" music on a vacation in Kenya with Carrie in 1981, but he knew very little about the real roots of the music which had inspired his whole career. He was determined to learn about it now because he loved the way it made him feel.

He finally found out the music on the bootleg tape was *mbaqanga,* commonly called "township jive." It came from the shanties and mean streets of Soweto in South Africa. The tape featured Tao Ea Matsekha and the ten-member, male a cappella singing group, Ladysmith Black Mambazo, a group he had heard in Australia during the 1982 Simon and Garfunkel tour.

Paul Simon had a new musical obsession, and it breathed life into his battered spirit. He contacted white South African record producer Hilton Rosenthal to enlist his aid in tracking down the musicians who made the infectious, hopeful sounds.

In January 1985 Paul and Roy Halee took off for Johannesburg to begin a momentous creative journey. There Paul met one of South Africa's biggest recording stars, Sipho Mabuse, who took him to visit Soweto, the squalid symbol of white South Africa's corrupt policy of apartheid. In Soweto Paul got his first taste of intense racial tension. They went to a speakeasy there, an illegal bar for blacks where people listened to music and danced. Initial mistrust melted away when Mabuse introduced Simon as the man who wrote "Bridge Over Troubled Water." Those words never failed to bring an instant smile of recognition wherever Paul went.

Paul trusted the language of music to communicate his sympathies, but there was dissension among the musicians over playing with a white American artist. The Reagan administration's policy toward South Africa was very unpopular among blacks and some felt cooperation with Simon would send the wrong message to the world and might even aid the South African economy. They wondered why Paul refused to work in neighboring Zimbabwe with exiled South African musicians there, and thus show his support for a U.N. cultural boycott instituted in 1980 to prohibit performances in South Africa until apartheid was abolished.

Paul stood firm on his decision to record in South Africa, so the black musicians there decided to put the issue to a secret vote. A majority eventually felt that Paul Simon could perhaps help them because he might have the power to popularize South African music in America as he had done with reggae.

In February 1985 Paul began a two-and-a-half-week series of recording sessions with several of South Africa's best groups. He paid them what the finest session musicians in America would get: triple union scale, or about four hundred dollars per person per day, in cash. Paul also guaranteed his collaborators royalties.

These sessions represented a complete reversal of Simon's lifelong composing and recording habits. Previously, he entered the studio with a batch of carefully crafted songs and then fleshed out the concepts, beginning with the words. The South African situation demanded a new approach, and Paul opened himself to a new method of making music. He simply let the musicians play, collected the tracks, and left the rest for later.

Paul returned to New York with six rhythm tracks and the goal of figuring out what to do with them. For days he tried to decode their structure. He found that the tracks suggested other styles of

American music with African roots and he decided to blend the new South African sounds with the let-the-good-times-roll, accordion-dominated feel of cajun zydeco, as well as with the Mexican-American rock sounds of an L.A. group called Los Lobos. In Lafayette, Louisiana, he recorded "That Was Your Mother" with Rockin' Dopsie, and in California he and Los Lobos recorded "All Around the World or the Myth of Fingerprints." Where previously his albums were woven around themes and concepts, now the connecting threads would be the accordion and saxophone, sound elements already present in the distinctive music he'd recorded in Africa.

He was finally discovering a way to integrate disparate musical styles with his own personal sensibility. The title track from the *Graceland* album set the tone, as well as the goal, of this new and exciting musical odyssey. The song conjured up the image of Paul's rock hero Elvis Presley, who first made black music accessible to large white audiences. But Paul stated that the song was really about "a state of peace." He claimed that he didn't name the album until all of the songs were finished, when he noticed several recurring themes—"a spiritual awakening, that for search tranquility or some kind of discovery of a greater idea than the self."

While writing one of the "Graceland" lines, "Losing love / Is like a window in your heart / Everybody sees you're blown apart,"* Paul said he experienced an important change: "Once the 'losing love' line came out, that was a catharsis. Everything began to flow. That's when the funny songs came out." Paul spent the rest of 1985 and several months of 1986 preparing *Graceland*. The technical demands of the complex album required using the most experienced and sophisticated engineers in the business.

Around the same time, Art Garfunkel was again working with his favorite composer, Jimmy Webb, on a new Christmas album. Webb had written a cantata called *The Animals' Christmas* which told the story of the birth of Jesus from the animals' point of view. In the early eighties, Art had performed the cantata in concert form and had always wanted to record it. He teamed with Christian pop singer Amy Grant, and the album was scheduled to be on the shelves in plenty of time for the Christmas season.

---

*"Graceland" © 1986 by Paul Simon

But Paul had asked Roy Halee, who had been working on Art's album, to join the *Graceland* team, and Halee had eagerly accepted. Art was angry over what he saw as Paul's talent raid, calling it an insensitive, selfish act. It would color Art's perception of the *Graceland* album forever. He later said, "I look at that record, and I think it has bad business underneath it."

16

Hearts and Bones was the only Paul Simon album that failed to achieve gold or platinum status, a fact which made both Paul and Warner Brothers feel a bit shaky about audience response to his new project. They all agreed the cheerful "You Can Call Me Al" might dispel the lingering, serious aftertaste of *Hearts and Bones,* and released it as a preliminary sample of the *Graceland* album. The popularity of MTV had made a music video an essential companion piece for the album, so Paul produced one that featured his old "Saturday Night Live" pal, Chevy Chase. Appearing in a bare-bones set, Chevy extravagantly lip syncs "You Can Call Me Al" as if he is Simon, while Paul himself dourly plays bass guitar accompaniment beside him.

It didn't take long for the single and the music video to become hits—and the album quickly followed suit. Paul promoted *Graceland* on "Saturday Night Live," appearing with Ladysmith Black Mambazo. Warner Brothers then released three other singles: "Boy in the Bubble," "Graceland," and "Under African Skies," all of which made the charts. The album would go on to sell more than five million copies and become Paul's biggest hit since *Bridge Over Troubled Water.*

The *Graceland* album owed its success to several factors. A recently released comprehensive set of Beatles CDs reminded the audience "It was twenty years ago today" that *Sgt. Pepper's Lonely Hearts Club Band* heralded the Summer of Love and focused new interest on the music of the sixties. The audience was again primed to hear what Paul Simon had to say.

Paul had never lost faith in his music's ability to speak to people about serious concerns. He said, "I believe in the power of rock 'n' roll to affect people, and I'd like to see it able to handle more mature subject matter." With *Graceland,* Paul followed his music back to its source and discovered a new reservoir of strength and creative possibility. He willingly opened himself up to it, and, "rather than bending the music to what I wanted to do... I said 'I'll just bend to whatever it does.'" With this album Paul Simon experienced a renaissance of his artistic powers.

To promote the album Paul invited twenty-five of his *Graceland* friends to join him on a triumphant, three-continent concert tour. Paul hired former Georgia state senator Julian Bond to promote a benefit tour of major American cities. A third of the proceeds would be donated to the Children of Apartheid Foundation, created by Simon and South African black leaders Allan Boesak and Archbishop Desmond Tutu. Another third would be given to the United Negro College Fund, and the remainder would go to local groups for the welfare and education of black children.

Paul had also made peace with the U.N. by writing a letter in which he promised to abide by its sanctions. In February 1987, he came as close as he could to performing in South Africa by taking the tour to a soccer stadium to Harare, Zimbabwe, just across the border. Before a black and white crowd of twenty thousand cheering, stomping, dancing fans, he paid homage to his musical roots and the unquenchable spirit of Soweto. It was the culmination of his own musical and spiritual odyssey.

The rave reviews for Paul's new musical direction kept coming. He had won back his old fans and gained a new generation of listeners as well. But it hadn't been easy. He had suffered through charges of cultural exploitation and risked the alienation of black audiences, especially in the United States. Paul was very sensitive to this criticism and took great pains to explain his motives. He accepted invitations to discuss the implications of *Graceland* at several universities, including NYU and UCLA—and to listen to "the black reaction." In February 1987, at predominantly-black Howard University in Washington, D.C., he ran into a hostile crowd. After a brief summary of the making of *Graceland,* he submitted to questions from the audience. One young man, barely controlling his rage, rose to speak. He asked, "How can you justify going there and taking all their music? For too long, artists have gone and stolen black music—you're taking it and bringing it back here and throwing it in my face! It's nothing but stealing."

Paul patiently explained his attempt to gain wider exposure for the music of South Africa, his payment agreement with his musicians, and his policy of giving full credit to individual musicians. Paul further argued, "This is a motion toward helping. It exposes a culture, a people....I'm trying to be in the dialogue....It's an experience to sit here and have people come to you and attack you. It's hard to know if you're being attacked as an artist or as a person."

At the heart of the heated exchange was a criticism Paul had heard since his days as a folksinger in the sixties: a middle-class Jewish man from Queens isn't qualified to explore other cultures. His motives must be exploitative and commercial. But the vast majority of Simon's global audience discounted the criticism and embraced his music as never before. He had proved both his resilience and continuing relevance.

One of the few who had a lukewarm reaction to the album was Art. He commented on the dominant African style of *Graceland* by saying it was "an interesting production element that may be worth a song, but he's made a whole album, a tour, and a season out of it. I wouldn't figure I had that much there to exploit so far."

Throughout much of the eighties, Art had lived the life of a semiretired millionaire. Home base was his East Side apartment in New York, but he traveled constantly. He liked to take long ocean voyages on freighters because he enjoyed the solitude and anonymity. On these seemingly aimless trips, he said, he "wrote, studied astronomy, or visited the chart room." He often took long auto trips cross-country with his brothers or friends.

But he was beginning to miss the thrill of making music. He said, "Years ago, I thought I could walk away from this business and leave it behind me. But that's hard to do. What happens is that

I take a rest and come back to it. I seem to need that." He also needed "the respect of my peers... and doing well in this business. That becomes more important as you get older."

Early in 1986, Art had once again tried his hand at acting in films. This time, it was a low-budget effort without a high-powered cast or a director like Mike Nichols. Much of *Good to Go* was shot in the ghettos of Washington, D.C. Art played a boozing journalist so desperate for a story he implicates himself in a racist police plot to close down the go-go clubs that feature powerful rap and rhythm-and-blues music as well as a plentiful supply of drugs. The film was released in July 1986, and quickly disappeared with barely a mention of Art's acting. His new album, *The Animals' Christmas*, was released in the fall of 1986 to tepid reviews and did not appear on its way to becoming a traditional seasonal favorite, selling only 110,000 copies.

Art suffered another, more personal loss in 1986 with the death of his father. Even though his relations with Paul had been strained, Art called him and asked him to attend the funeral: "He was there, of course. Paul's not a flaky guy. He and I know we'll be friends forever."

The death of Art's father and his own relationship with his son, Harper, prompted Paul to come to terms with his own father, who had wounded him years earlier by scorning his passion for rock 'n' roll. Paul finally found the courage to ask his father for a reevaluation of his music and his life. In a 1991 "60 Minutes" interview, Paul described his plea for his father's acceptance: "Dad, what do you think about me? It's pretty good, isn't it? Most people don't get this much stuff. Is it good? Was I a good son? What do you think?" Louis Simon finally acknowledged his son's achievements. Paul said he had known what his father would say, but he had to hear him say it.

In the late eighties, the outpouring of critical and popular acclaim for Paul's new musical effort was hard for Art to ignore, but Garfunkel gamely played along. In a "Saturday Night Live" skit in November 1986, Paul pretends to have the world's greatest memory but fails to recognize Art Garfunkel, who makes an unscheduled appearance. As they had been in the seventies, Paul and Art were once again comfortable poking fun at the Simon and Garfunkel legend. Simon was surprised Art agreed to do the bit, but attributed it to Art's offbeat sense of humor — which also prompted Art to privately comment to Paul: "I'm very happy about the success of *Graceland*. I'm so happy I don't even care that you can't find my record in the stores. That's how happy I am." Art wasn't afraid to laugh at himself, knowing that no matter what happened, as long as they lived, his name would always be linked with Paul's, and their fame was secure.

In light of Paul's strong comeback, people wondered what had happened to Art. His response was feisty: "I want people to know I'm out of my shell. I'm no dummy." He quickly let people know he was working again.

But Paul's success wasn't the only reason Art decided to return to singing. He was emerging at last from the shadows of Laurie Bird's suicide and had a new love interest, Kim Cermak, a singer with the rock band, Lime. He said of her influence, "She's awfully sweet. She always makes me feel real good, and so I've been rather happy the last year or two. She had something to do with the desire to record again. It would be easy to say, 'Who needs the difficulties?'"

Like Paul, Art sought to renew his career, but his method would stand in typically stark contrast to his former partner's adventurous route. Art surveyed the contemporary rock-music scene and found little to his taste. He had no interest in up-tempo, danceable tunes and rejected Paul's cross-cultural hybrid approach with its strong, political overtones. He especially disliked the electronic sounds that dominated much of the stuff he heard on the radio. Electronic gimmickry—which had, after all, created his phenomenal career in the sixties—held little appeal for Art Garfunkel now. He favored the simple pluck of a guitar string to the cacophony of electronic synthesizers.

For several years, he had been collecting song titles in the back of his address book, and it was now filled with old favorites he meant to record some time. He also had a list of songs he hummed aloud as he walked the streets. When he began to repeat a song, he said his subconscious was tellinghim it was finally time to record.

He selected several of his trademark romantic ballads and made arrangements to record in London with Geoff Emerick, who had engineered a number of Beatles' albums, including *Sergeant Pepper*. Not only were romantic ballads Art's natural preference, but his love affair with Kim had gotten serious; they talked of marriage and a family. Art felt he now had more to say about love than ever before. Half of the ten songs he originally chose had the word *love* in the title and he was eager to record them.

In London, Art worked hard on the tracks. He enjoyed working with other singers and invited Leah Kunkel, a member of the Coyote Sisters, to join him for a duet on "I Have a Love," from *West Side Story.* He finished his vocals in the summer of 1987 and returned to the States to give them to Columbia for packaging. Art was stunned by the reaction. Columbia had apparently lost patience with Garfunkel's poor-selling albums, and this one even lacked a promotable single. They demanded he add two sure-fire oldies, the Tymes' "So Much in Love" and David Foster's "This Is the Moment."

When Columbia decided to dress up some of the older tunes with new, electronic synthesizer arrangements, Art reacted strongly: "I delivered [the original tracks] to my record company, hoping they would put it out with love and enthusiasm. They made me feel absolutely rotten by telling me it's not exactly what they wanted. I was crushed."

He reluctantly went along with Columbia—he seemed to have little choice—but it took nearly a year before the revamped album was finally released in March 1988. Art called the album *Lefty* and chose a grainy snapshot of himself at age ten for the cover. The photograph, taken by his brother Jules outside the old family home in Queens, showed a left-handed boy tightly gripping a baseball bat and glaring straight ahead at the pitcher. The young Art looked deadly serious about hitting the next pitch out of the ballpark.

Art agreed to promote the album with the press but was leery of a follow-up tour. Columbia persisted, and he finally agreed to a trial tour of England in April that would culminate at London's Royal Albert Hall in an all-star benefit performance for the Prince's Trust. The gala was also scheduled to be aired as an ABC special later in the spring. A tour of the U.S. later in the summer would depend on how warmly *Lefty* was received.

In early spring 1988, Art prepared for the rigors of the interview circuit, and for the reaction of fans, by taking a skiing trip to Aspen with his old acting buddy, Jack Nicholson. He and Jack discussed potential film roles, and Art was especially intrigued by Jack's idea to do a sequel to *Carnal Knowledge.* He thought a modern update of the war between the sexes might be a challenging project. Though he hadn't given up his acting career entirely, it was certainly dormant. Studio executives were scarcely beating his door down with fascinating projects.

Art had mixed feelings about *Lefty*'s release and the attendant flurry of press interest. He said, "I don't like going public. But I have to. And being out there, I have to deal with the media. I have to let them take their shots at me. Hiding out was nice, but it's time to let the world in."

After being away from the spotlight for so long, Art braced for the worst, but to his delight, critics praised the new album. The *New York Times* called it "an impeccably crafted album of love songs" and another said, "Garfunkel proves himself a polished vocalist." And "Mr. Garfunkel has become an original and compelling song stylist and an understated but remarkably musical vocal technician." The reviewer concluded by calling it "a genuine triumph."

But the single release of the oldie "So Much in Love" didn't cause much of a stir. By May, *Lefty* peaked at only 134 on the charts and made virtually no impact in England. In May, Columbia made another attempt to revive interest in the album with a single release of the second oldie, "When a Man Loves a Woman," but it also failed to score.

Obviously disappointed by the cool audience reaction, Art was especially dismayed to find himself unable to carve out a distinctive musical niche for himself. Even when praising his solo work, several reviewers still couldn't resist mentioning Paul Simon's name and current stature in the music world. One found "Garfunkel singing with the intimacy and effortless clarity he brought to Paul Simon's gorgeous ballads." The reviewer for *People* was more blunt about Art's inability to escape Paul's shadow. He commented that while "Garfunkel is certainly more than just the guy who used to carry Paul Simon's spear," his "sweet, innocent-sounding voice has its limitations…the best tracks are collaborations."

Once again, Art had failed to convincingly capture the imagination of the record-buying public. He withdrew to ponder the implications, saying, "A lot of my enthusiasm to carry on and the kind of heat I can bring to recording really has to do with whether they're listening." He had even debated not renewing his contract with Columbia just before *Lefty* because he had lost confidence in his ability to make them listen to his solo efforts.

He had even for a time considered the possibility of becoming half of a newly-constituted team. He said, "For years, I resisted it, thinking it'd hurt the audience's feelings. And yet, Rodgers and Hart became Rodgers and Hammerstein. But I have an image in my head, and I don't know if I could wrap myself around another person as effectively as I did with Paul."

Art sent out signals through the press that he wouldn't mind getting together with Paul to do another reunion tour, but Paul ignored them. Art's frustration showed in his comments: "He's busy denying 'Simon and Garfunkel' and hating those songs and trying to be an artist who's outgrown the old stuff. But fans are always saying they love the old stuff and asking if there's a possibility of seeing us do it again...I'm with the fans."

Although he longed for a return to the glory days of unalloyed success, Art, like Paul, ultimately acknowledged the creative and emotional cul-de-sac a permanent reteaming would be. He said, "I hope I don't get seduced into another lap around Paul Simon's track."

In 1988, Art married Kim Cermak. He was finally free of the decade-long lawsuit instituted by his first wife, Linda Grossman. The court ruled the original divorce settlement was "valid and binding," and the case was closed, allowing Art to marry. Linda's lawyer finally admitted, "This is the end of the line for her. I guess we waited too long; there was just too much troubled water under the bridge."

Meanwhile, Paul continued the musical odyssey he began with *Graceland*. Now he became fascinated with a tape of Brazilian percussion music Rubén Blades had given him a few years before. So he traveled to Brazil at the suggestion of singer Milton Nascimento to look for Latin permutations of the sounds he had found in South Africa. As he explained, "Those rhythms were brought to Brazil by West Africans. They were the rhythms used in their religious ceremonies." Paul repeated his *Graceland* method of recording native musicians and bringing the tracks back to New York for further study and refinement. This time, he blended the dense, percussive tracks with African guitar and other related sounds.

Paul and Warner Brothers knew it would be some time before Simon had the new album ready, so in 1988 they released a compilation album, *Negotiations and Love Songs*, that peaked at a wan number 110. The audience that Paul had thrilled with the excitement of *Graceland* decided to take a pass and wait until Simon had something really new.

As Paul pursued his new musical odyssey, Art continued his own offbeat journeying. Beginning in 1985, he had almost reached the halfway mark to his goal of a five-thousand-mile east-west walk across the U.S. He had been walking in carefully plotted segments of approximately one hundred miles per week, sticking to small roads that connect the tiny towns of America, where he often saw no living thing but birds and cows during his long hours on the road.

The walk is still in progress and promises to consume several more years of Art's life. Every four months or so, from April to October, he flies to his last finish line, laces up his sneakers, and takes to the open road with little more than a map in hand.

Originally he walked with no help, but that arrangement wasn't very practical, so he hired an assistant to drive him to his starting point, pick him up in the evening, and deliver him to the local motel for the night. The next day, he'd begin again. He calls it traveling "rich-man style."

Occasionally he is joined by friends or his wife Kim and his younger brother Jerome, but, for the most part, he walks alone.

He keeps precise notes about the distances he covers and marks his progress with orange-headed pins stuck on a huge map in his study back home in New York. He has measured his stride and knows exactly how many steps he takes per mile. He usually wears a headset, and his Walkman spins out Ravel's Piano Concerto, some Peter Gabriel, or Richard Burton reading the poems of John Donne. He described his reason for the long walk: "The main thing I'm recording is the topography of the United States, the third dimension, the up and down of everything."

Art is also exploring his inner topography. He says one walks "to get off the main track of your life so as to look at that life, to sort out some things." The walk gives him the opportunity to think about singing, acting, and his latest artistic adventure, poetry.

In September 1989, Garfunkel had a slim volume of poems

published. Its title, *Still Waters,* suggests a contrast to the bygone days of troubled waters with Paul in the Simon and Garfunkel era. His poems represent another leg of his own journey toward self-realization. He has said he felt the same anxiety about public acceptance of his poems as he did with the release of his solo albums. Although he had amassed more than seven hundred poems by the time *Still Waters* was published, he remained unsure he would publish more. He said, "I'll keep on writing, but the whole process of offering them up has to do with taste....It depends on how much the process of going to the media and projecting my efforts is painless....If the answer is no, you won't be hearing about them anymore."

Art seems to regard the publication of his poetry in the same somewhat passive way he regards his acting and singing careers. If there is any audience, he'll respond. At present, his film career once again seems to be on hold, and as for his singing, the public seems relatively disinterested in him as a solo recording artist.

In January 1989, Columbia released a compilation of Art's biggest hits simply titled *Garfunkel.* One reviewer, who found nothing attractive about the package, scolded Columbia for trying to dupe the public into thinking the album was a new collection by neglecting to mention in the album title that it contained old material. The reviewer proceeded to comment on Garfunkel's strengths as a collaborator, finding his solo offerings "wan, like a bowl of matzo ball soup without any matzo balls in it."

No matter what the critics say, Art has achieved a special place in pop-music history. He and Paul are the only members of a duo to split up and make separate comebacks with gold record albums.

But as the eighties drew to a close, Art almost disappeared from the public eye. Aside from a concert tour of Scandinavia in 1989, he has lived the life of a retired millionaire, traveling frequently with his wife Kim. He remains very selective about his public engagements and has turned down several offers to perform, including a television situation comedy series.

Paul has been much more high-profile both personally and professionally. His fans, but not those people who are close to him, were surprised in the late eighties when Paul and Carrie began to see each other again. Rumors surfaced that the two would remarry, but there seems little chance they will make that journey again, at least together. Fisher discounts any possibility of remarriage: "He and I are very close. We really get along really well, but we have a hard time cohabitating. He's a very introverted person, and I'm very extroverted." Even though the marriage didn't work, Carrie has called their relationship "a genuine match." In 1991, Paul told an interviewer, "I took away from the experience that I could be really, deeply in love... On the negative side, I realized I could exhaust myself from emotional upheaval. That was a powerful love. And it still is."

After drug rehabilitation in the eighties, Fisher, reportedly a wealthy woman from her percentage of the *Star Wars* film trilogy, resumed her film career. She took on challenging supporting roles in films written or directed by old friends Woody Allen (*Hannah and Her Sisters*) and Rob Reiner and Nora Ephron (*When Harry Met Sally*). She also found a new career as a best-selling novelist. *Postcards From the Edge*, her first novel, published in 1987, tells a story strikingly similar to her own: The child of a movie queen and drug-taking crooner battles with drugs herself in the glare of the Hollywood spotlight. In 1990, it became a successful movie starring Meryl Streep and Shirley MacLaine. Paul read the book before publication and liked it, but thought the author was being too hard on herself. Simon was more reticent about commenting on her second novel, *Surrender the Pink*, which features a heroine who, divorced from a rock singer/songwriter, spies on him and his new lover. The ex-husband character, Rudy, bears more than a passing resemblance to Paul Simon, but Carrie insists he is a composite of all the strong men in her life, including Paul, Richard Dreyfuss, movie producer Dan Melnick, and the Eagles' Don Henley.

Fisher has been very open about her past drug use. She has admitted to snorting cocaine with her famous father and dropping LSD with her friend Penny Marshall, but has always been careful to avoid suggesting any connection between her drug use and Paul Simon.

Fisher maintains close friendships with Eddie Simon and Paul's son Harper, who often stays in her guest house when he visits Hollywood. Harper, a shade taller than Paul, attended the Professional Children's School in New York City and has talked of becoming a playwright. But he has spent a lot of time with his famous father and is well acquainted with the music world. He plays the guitar and, not surprisingly, hasn't ruled out a music career.

Paul took Harper along with him on a recent leg of the *Graceland* tour, and one night in Moscow during a sound check, Paul noticed his son playing guitar. During an encore, Paul called Harper out to play with the band. "It was a huge thrill," according to the younger Simon, and Paul made it a regular part of the show for the remainder of the tour.

As they approach their fiftieth birthdays, both Paul and Art seem at ease with the separate paths they have traveled. On December 15, 1990, Art became a father for the first time, and this seems to have added to a sense of contentment in both his personal and professional life.

Paul Simon has long since taken his rightful place among America's premier popular songwriters. His lyrics have become part of the vernacular; it would be difficult to find any member of the sixties generation who can't repeat at least four lines of a Paul Simon song.

At America's 1986 birthday celebration for its national symbol, the Statue of Liberty, Simon's "American Tune" set the tone as the nation paid homage.

Still eager to show fans the humorous side of his nature, Simon often does comic turns on "Saturday Night Live." He also appeared in Shelley Duvall's "Faerie Tale Theatre" production of an updated rock version of a Mother Goose nursery rhyme, playing a hip Simple Simon. (Art appeared as a jaded, older Georgie Porgie, working as a bartender.)

Simon has announced he is writing a children's book, *At the Zoo*, which will be published by Doubleday in late 1991. the proceeds will go to the Children's Health Fund, an organization he founded to provide pediatric care for homeless children in New York City.

Still, all of Simon's other interests remain secondary to his music career. In his continuing quest for the roots of rock 'n' roll and for other music with relevance for his audience, near the end of 1990 Paul Simon released another experiment in musical cross-pollination, *The Rhythm of the Saints*. Once again, his audience responded enthusiastically—the album quickly rose to number five on the charts. And four short weeks after its release, it had sold its first million copies.

The album is full of the compelling percussive sounds of Brazilian folk music, leavened with contemporary touches such as the sounds of composer Antonio Carlos Jobim and modern Latin rhythms. As with *Graceland*, he recorded the music tracks first, then found his lyrics hidden within the intriguing new rhythms and melodies.

To promote the *Rhythm of the Saints* album, Paul mounted another worldwide concert tour with a seventeen-piece band that included the Brazilian musicians as well as several of the band members featured on the *Graceland* album. The unique musical blend signifies another, important stage in Paul's search for musical kinship.

Some have charged Simon with cultural exploitation. But his supporters argue that his musical explorations are highly principled, bold adventures of the spirit that result in huge new worldwide audiences for his musical collaborators. In fact, audiences have finally stopped shouting "Where's Artie?" when Paul walks on the stage and have begun calling for Ladysmith Black Mombazo, one of the South African groups he featured on his *Graceland* album and tour.

The critical and public success of *Graceland* and *Rhythm* offers convincing evidence that Paul Simon's best work will always be in collaboration. But although he will share success, Simon seems determined not to share equal stardom with anyone.

His first collaborator, Art Garfunkel, decided several years ago to make a list of the relationships in his life that needed mending. He called Paul, and they met at Simon's summer home in Montauk where they aired their differences and came to an understanding. As Art has said, "You could say a lot about these guys, Paul and Art, about their competition, their love, and their hate. As one of Paul's songs says, our lives are intertwined."

On August 15, 1991, Paul returned to New York's Central Park as a solo act, matching the phenomenal success of the reunion concert a decade earlier. An estimated 750,000 fans heard him sing several Simon and Garfunkel classics, but he sang them alone.

There had been speculation about Garfunkel joining Simon.

Paul had invited Art, Kim, and their son, James, to his Long Island estate for a barbecue a few weeks earlier. But, as usual, communication between the two men was non-verbal.

Garfunkel, working on an album of his own, was bitter about being excluded. He sarcastically told the *New York Times*, "I'm not good enough to be invited." He felt used. HBO had run Simon and Garfunkel footage to promote the concert, and in a TV interview, Paul, too, had no qualms about using Simon and Garfunkel clips. Since he wasn't asked to perform, Art left the country saying, "I'd rather wish Paul well from afar." As to why Simon hadn't invited him, Garfunkel would only cryptically offer, "My guess is it would hurt his sense of stature." Invited or not, he would always be a part of Simon and Garfunkel. Their names will be forever linked.

In January 1990, Simon and Garfunkel were among a dozen inductees into the Rock and Roll Hall of Fame. They joined the ranks of rock 'n' roll greats like the Beatles, the Beach Boys, the Rolling Stones, nonperformers Alan Freed, Sam Phillips, and Phil Spector, as well as the "classic" heroes of their boyhood—Elvis Presley and the Everly Brothers.

At the induction, Garfunkel, appreciative of the honor, credited Paul "as the person who most enriched my life by putting those songs through me." Simon, as had become his habit, continued to kid about the Simon and Garfunkel partnership: "Arthur and I agree about almost nothing. But it's true, I have enriched his life quite a bit."

Paul also quipped: "Now we can join all the other happy couples: Ike and Tina Turner, the Everly Brothers, Mick and Keith, Paul and all the other Beatles." Like all the famous fractured groups he listed, Simon and Garfunkel would always be remembered as a team. Although one top rock critic dismissed Art with the comment, "Simon was the vision, Garfunkel was just the voice," it wasn't nearly that simple. Without Paul's songwriting talent and nerviness, the pair would never have succeeded, but without Art's angelic voice and harmonies, Paul's words and music would have lacked the full emotional range the audience found so appealing.

Despite the latest rift, there will always be questions about another reunion. As Art Garfunkel once said, "The real answer is who knows?"

Discography

Simon and Garfunkel Albums

1964

Wednesday Morning, 3 A.M.   Columbia PC 9049

"You Can Tell the World" / "Last Night I Had the Strangest Dream" / Bleecker Street" / "Sparrow" / "Benedictus" / "The Sounds of Silence" / "He Was My Brother" / "Peggy-O" / "Go Tell It on the Mountain" / "The Sun Is Burning" / "The Times They Are A-Changin'" / "Wednesday Morning, 3 A.M.

1966

Sounds of Silence   Columbia CS 9269

"The Sounds of Silence" / "Leaves That Are Green" / "Blessed" / "Kathy's Song" / "Somewhere They Can't Find Me" / "Anji" / "Richard Cory" / "A Most Peculiar Man" / "April Come She Will" / "We've Got a Groovy Thing Goin'" / "I Am a Rock"

1966

Simon and Garfunkel   Pickwick SPC 3059

(Rip Off Album): "Hey Schoolgirl" / "Dancin' Wild" / "Our Song" / "Teen Age Fool" / "True Or False" / "Tia-juana Blues" / "Simon Says" / "Don't Say Goodbye" / "Two Teen Agers" / "That's My Story"

966*

Parsley, Sage, Rosemary and Thyme   Columbia SC 9363

"Scarborough Fair / Canticle" / "Patterns" / "Cloudy" / "Homeward Bound" / "The Big Bright Green Pleasure Machine" / "The 59th Street Bridge Song (Feelin' Groovy)" / "The Dangling Conversation" / "Flowers Never Bend With the Rainfall" / "A Simple Desultory Philippic" / "For Emily, Whenever I May Find Her" / "A Poem on the Underground Wall" / "7 O'Clock News / Silent Night"

1968

Bookends   Columbia KCS 9529

"Bookends Theme (Instrumental)" / "Save the Life of My Child" / "America" / "Overs" / "Voices of Old People" / "Old Friends" / "Bookends Theme" / "Fakin' It" / "Punky's Dilemma" / "Mrs. Robinson" / "A Hazy Shade of Winter" / "At the Zoo"

1968

The Graduate   Columbia OS 3180

"The Sounds of Silence" / "The Singleman Party Foxtrot" / "Mrs. Robinson" / "Sunporch Cha-Cha-Cha" / "Scarborough Fair/Canticle" (Interlude) / "On The Strip" / "April Come She Will" / "The Folks" / "Scarborough Fair/Canticle" / "A Great Effect" / "The Big Bright Green Pleasure Machine" / "Whew" / "Mrs. Robinson" / "The Sounds of Silence"

1970

Bridge Over Troubled Water   Columbia KCS 9914

"Bridge Over Troubled Water" / "El Condor Pasa" / "Cecilia" / "Keep the Customer Satisfied" / "So Long, Frank Lloyd Wright" / "The Boxer" / "Baby Driver" / "The Only Living Boy in New York" / "Why Don't You Write Me" / "Bye Bye Love" / "Song for the Asking"

1972

Simon and Garfunkel's Greatest Hits   Columbia PC 31350

"Bridge Over Troubled Water" / "Mrs. Robinson" / "The Sound of Silence" / "The Boxer" / "The 59th Street Bridge Song" (Feelin' Groovy) / "Scarborough Fair/Canticle" / "I Am a Rock" / "Kathy's Song" /

"Cecilia" / "America" / "Bookends" / "Homeward Bound" / "El Condor Pasa" (If I Could) / "For Emily, Whenever I May Find Her"

1981

The Concert In Central Park   Warner Brothers 2 BSK 3654

Record 1: "Mrs. Robinson" / "Homeward Bound" / "America" / "Me and Julio Down by the Schoolyard" / "Scarborough Fair" / "April Come She Will" / "Wake Up, Little Susie" / "Still Crazy After All These Years" / "American Tune" / "Late in the Evening"
Record 2: "Slip Slidin' Away" / "A Heart in New York" / "Kodachrome/ Maybelline" / "Bridge Over Troubled Water" / "50 Ways to Leave Your Lover" / "The Boxer" / "Old Friends" / "The 59th Street Song (Feelin' Groovy)" / "The Sounds of Silence"

Paul Simon Solo Albums

1971

Paul Simon   Columbia KC 30750

"Mother and Child Reunion" / "Duncan" / "Everything Put Together Falls Apart" / "Run That Body Down" / "Armistice Day" / "Me and Julio Down by the Schoolyard" / "Peace Like a River" / "Papa Hobo" / "Hobo's Blues" / "Paranoia Blues" / "Congratulations"

1973

There Goes Rhymin' Simon   Columbia KC 32280

"Kodachrome" / "Tenderness" / "Take Me to the Mardi Gras" / "Something So Right" / "One Man's Ceiling Is Another Man's Floor" / "American Tune" / "Was a Sunny Day" / "Learn How to Fall" / "St. Judy's Comet" / "Loves Me Like a Rock"

1974

Live Rhymin'   Columbia PC 32855

"Me and Julio Down by the Schoolyard" / "Homeward Bound" / "American Tune" / "El Condor Pasa" / "Duncan" / "The Boxer" / "Mother and Child Reunion" / "The Sounds of Silence" / "Jesus Is the Answer" / "Bridge Over Troubled Water" / "Loves Me Like a Rock" / "America"

1975

Paul Simon: Still Crazy After All These Years   Columbia PC 33540

"Still Crazy After All These Years" / "My Little Town" / "I Do It for Your Love" / "50 Ways to Leave Your Lover" / "Night Game" / "Gone at Last" / "Some Folks' Lives Roll Easy" / "Have a Good Time" / "You're Kind" / "Silent Eyes"

1977

Paul Simon—Greatest Hits, Etc.   Columbia 35032

"Slip Slidin' Away" / "Stranded in a Limousine" / "Still Crazy After All These Years" / "Have a Good Time" / "Duncan" / "Me and Julio Down by the Schoolyard" / "Something So Right"

1980

One-Trick Pony   Warner Brothers HS 3472

"Late in the Evening" / "That's Why God Made the Movies" / "One-Trick Pony" / "How the Heart Approaches What It Yearns" / "Oh, Marion" / "Ace in the Hole" / "Nobody" / "Jonah" / "God Bless the Absentee" / "Long, Long Day"

1981

Hearts and Bones   Warner Brothers W1-23942

"Allergies" / "Hearts And Bones" / "When Numbers Get Serious" / "Think Too Much (b)" / "Song About the Moon" / "Think Too Much (a)" / "Train in the Distance" / "Rene and Georgette Magritte With Their Dog After the War" / "Cars Are Cars" / "The Late Great Johnny Ace"

1986

Graceland   Warner Brothers 25447-2

"The Boy in the Bubble" / "Graceland" / "I Know What I Know" / "Gumboots" / "Diamonds on the Soles of Her Shoes" / "You Can Call Me Al" / "Under African Skies" / "Homeless" / "Crazy Love: Vol. II" / "That Was Your Mother" / "All Around the World or the Myth of Fingerprints"

1988

Negotiations and Love Songs   Warner Brothers 25789

"Mother and Child Reunion" / "Me and Julio Down by the Schoolyard" / "Something So Right" / "St. Judy's Comet" / "Loves Me Like a Rock" / "Kodachrome" / "Have a Good Time" / "50 Ways to Leave Your Lover" / "Still Crazy After All These Years" / "Late in the Evening" / "Slip Slidin' Away" / "Hearts and Bones" / "Train in the Distance" / "Rene and Georgette Magritte With Their Dog After the War" / "Diamonds on the Soles of Her Shoes" / "You Can Call Me Al"

1990
Rhythm of the Saints   Warner Brothers 12 26098-2

"The Obvious Child" / "Can't Run But" / "The Coast" / "Proof" / "Further to Fly" / "She Moves On" / "Born at the Right Time" / "The Cool, Cool River" / "Spirit Voices" / "The Rhythm of the Saints"

Art Garfunkel Solo Albums

1973

Angel Clare   Columbia KC 31474

"Traveling Boy" / "Down in the Willow Garden" / "I Shall Sing" / "Old Man" / "Feuilles-Oh/Do Space Men Pass Dead Souls on Their Way to the Moon?" / "All I Know" / "Mary Was an Only Child" / "Woyaya" / "Barbara Allen" / "Another Lullaby"

1975

Breakaway   Columbia PC 33700

"I Believe (When I Fall in Love It Will Be Forever)" / "Rag Doll" / "Break Away" / "Disney Girls" / "Waters of March" / "My Little Town" / "I Only Have Eyes for You" / "Looking for the Right One" / "99 Miles From L.A." / "The Same Old Tears on a New Background"

1977

Watermark   Columbia AL 34975

"Crying in My Sleep" / "Marionette" / "Shine It on Me" / "Watermark" / "Saturday Suit" / "All My Love's Laughter" / "(What a) Wonderful World" / "Mr. Schuck 'n' Jive" / "Paper Chase" / "She Moved Through the Fair" / "Someone Else" / "Wooden Planes"

1979

Fate For Breakfast/Doubt For Dessert   Columbia BL 35780

"In a Little While (I'll Be on My Way)" / "Since I Don't Have You" / "And I Know" / "Sail on a Rainbow" / "Miss You Nights" / "Finally Found a Reason" / "Beyond the Tears" / "Oh How Happy" / "When Someone Doesn't Want You" / "Take Me Away"

1981

Scissors Cut   Columbia BL 37392

"A Heart in New York" / "Scissors Cut" / "Up in the World" / "Hang On In" / "So Easy to Begin" / "Bright Eyes" / "Can't Turn My Heart Away" / "The French Waltz" / "In Cars" / "That's All I've Got to Say"

1986

The Animal's Christmas   Columbia 40212

"Just a Simple Little Tune" / "Incredible Phat" / "Song of the Camels" / "Words From an Old Spanish Carol" / "Carol of the Birds" / "Herod" / "Wild Geese" / "Annunciation" / "The Creatures of the Field" / "Decree" / "The Friendly Beasts" / "The Frog"

Lefty   Columbia 40942

"This Is the Moment" / "I Have a Love" / "So Much in Love" / "Slow Breakup" / "Love Is the Only Chain" / "When a Man Loves a Woman" / "I Wonder Why" / "King of Tonga" / "If Love Takes You Away" / "The Promise"

1989

Garfunkel   Columbia 45008

"When a Man Loves a Woman" / "So Much in Love" / "Heart in New York" / "Scissors Cut" / "Second Avenue" / "All I Know" / "Bright Eyes" / "Break Away" / "98 Miles From L.A." / "I Have a Love" / "I Only Have Eyes For You" / "(What a) Wonderful World"

Simon and Garfunkel Singles

1966

"The Sounds of Silence" / "We've Got a Groovy Thing Goin'"
                                        Columbia 43396
"Homeward Bound" / "Leaves That Are Green"   Columbia 43511
"Flowers Never Bend With the Rainfall" / "I Am a Rock"
                                        Columbia 43617
"The Dangling Conversation" / "The Big Bright Green Pleasure Machine"   Columbia 43728

"A Hazy Shade of Winter" / "For Emily, Whenever I May Find Her"
                                        Columbia 43873

1967

"At the Zoo" / "The 59th Street Bridge Song"   Columbia 44046

1968

"Fakin' It" / "You Don't Know Where Your Interest Lies"
                                        Columbia 44232
"Scarborough Fair" / "April Come She Will"   Columbia 44465
"Mrs. Robinson" / "Old Friends / Bookends"   Columbia 44511

1969

"The Boxer" / "Baby Driver"   Columbia 44785

1970

"Bridge Over Troubled Water" / "Keep the Customer Satisfied"
                                        Columbia 45079
"Cecilia" / "The Only Living Boy in New York"   Columbia 45133
"El Condor Pasa" / "Why Don't You Write Me"   Columbia 45237

1972

"For Emily, Whenever I May Find Her" / "America" Columbia 45663
"My Little Town" / "Rag Doll / P.S. You're So Kind" Columbia 10230

Tom and Jerry Singles

1957

"Hey Schoolgirl" / "Dancin' Wild"	Big 613

1958

"Don't Say Goodbye" / "That's My Story"	Big 618
"Our Song" / "Two Teenagers"	Big 619
"Baby Talk" / "Two Teenagers"	Big 621

1959

"That's My Story" / "Don't Say Goodbye"	Hunt 319
"Baby Talk" (Tom and Jerry) / "I'm Going to Get Married" (Ronnie Lawrence)	Bell 120

1960

"Hey Schoolgirl" / "Dancin' Wild"	King 45-5167

1962

"Surrender, Please Surrender" / "Fightin' Mad"	ABC-Paramount 45-10363
"That's My Story" / "Tijuana Blues"	ABC-Paramount 45-10788

Singles Released Under Pseudonyms

Paul Simon as "True Taylor"
1958

"True or False" / "Teen Age Fool"	Big 614

Paul Simon as "Tico" of "Tico and the Triumphs."
1960

"Motorcycle" / "I Don't Believe Them"	Madison M-169
"Cry Little Boy Cry" / "Get Up and Do the Wobble"	Amy 860
"Express Train" / "Wildflower"	Amy 845
"Motorcycle" / "I Don't Believe Them"	Amy 835

Paul Simon as "Jerry Landis."
1961

"Cards of Love" / "Noise"	Amy 876
"The Lonely Teen Ranger" / "Lisa"	Amy 875
"Cards of Love" / "Noise"	Amy 861

1962

"The Lonely Teen Ranger" / "Lisa"	Jason Scott Records 22
"I'm Lonely" / "Wish I Weren't in Love"	Can-Am 130
"Swanee" / "Toot, Toot, Tootsie, Goodbye"	Warwick 522
"Just a Boy" / "Shy"	Warwick 552
"I Want to Be the Lipstick on Your Collar" / "Just a Boy"	Warwick 588
"Play Me a Sad Song" / "It Means a Lot"	Warwick 619
"Anna Belle" / "Loneliness"	MGM K-12822

Paul Simon as "Paul Kane"
1963

"Carlos Dominguez" / "He Was My Brother"	Tribute 1746

Art Garfunkel as "Artie Garr"
1961

"Private World" / "Forgive Me"	Octavia 8002
"Beat Love" / "Dream Alone"	Warwick 515

About the Authors

JOSEPH MORELLA is the author of twenty nonfiction books and coauthor of one novel. He has written eleven biographies including *Lana* and *Forever Lucy*, as well as books on nutrition and left-handedness. He is a former reporter for *Variety*, a free-lance magazine writer, a playwright, and a screenwriter.

PATRICIA BAREY has been an Emmy Award-winning producer, director, and writer for PBS stations. She owns a film and video production company.